Putting Class in Its Place

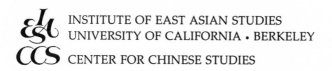

INSTITUTE OF EAST ASIAN STUDIES
UNIVERSITY OF CALIFORNIA • BERKELEY
CENTER FOR CHINESE STUDIES

Putting Class in Its Place

Worker Identities in East Asia

EDITED BY
Elizabeth J. Perry

A publication of the Institute of East Asian Studies, University of California, Berkeley. Although the Institute of East Asian Studies is responsible for the selection and acceptance of manuscripts in this series, responsibility for the opinions expressed and for the accuracy of statements rests with their authors.

Correspondence and manuscripts may be sent to:
Joanne Sandstrom, Managing Editor
Institute of East Asian Studies
University of California
Berkeley, California 94720-2318
E-mail: easia@uclink.berkeley.edu

The China Research Monograph series, whose first title appeared in 1967, is one of several publications series sponsored by the Institute of East Asian Studies in conjunction with its constituent units. The others include the Japan Research Monograph series, the Korea Research Monograph series, the Indochina Research Monograph series, and the Research Papers and Policy Studies series. A list of recent publications appears at the back of the book.

Library of Congress Cataloging-in-Publication Data

Putting class in its place : worker identies in East Asia / edited
   by Elizabeth J. Perry.
         p. cm. — (China research monograph ; 48)
      Includes bibliographical references and index.
      ISBN 1-55729-050-4 (trade paper)
         1. Working class—East Asia—Case studies.   I. Perry, Elizabeth
   J. II. University of California, Berkeley. Institute of East Asian
   Studies. III. Series.
   HD8720.5.P87 1996
   305.5′62′095—dc20   95-50860
                                                            CIP

Copyright © 1996 by The Regents of the University of California
ISBN 1-55729-050-4
Library of Congress Catalog Card Number 95-50860
Printed in the United States of America

Contents

Acknowledgments

This volume grew out of the conference "East Asian Labor in Comparative Perspective" held at Lake Tahoe in the fall of 1993. The conference was made possible by a grant from Taiwan's Ministry of Education to the Institute of East Asian Studies of the University of California at Berkeley. The editor is grateful to both the Ministry and the Institute for financial and administrative support. Above all, the tireless and expert efforts of IEAS Assistant Director Joan Kask were key to the smooth operations of the conference. Thanks go also to Martin Frazier for help in advance preparation and for serving as principal rapporteur.

Conference discussions were facilitated by the participation of several specialists on labor in other areas of the world: David Brody, David Collier, Ruth Collier, and Aihwa Ong. Editing was completed during a leave sponsored by the Guggenheim Foundation, National Endowment for the Humanities, and Chiang Ching-kuo Foundation. Credit for the index goes to Martin Beversdorf. Joanne Sandstrom did an outstanding job of shepherding the manuscript through production.

Contributors

Hill Gates is Senior Research Associate, Institute for International Studies, Stanford University.

Andrew Gordon is Professor of History, Department of History, Harvard University.

Gail Hershatter is Professor of History, University of California, Santa Cruz.

Emily Honig is Professor of Women's Studies, University of California, Santa Cruz.

Hsin-Huang Michael Hsiao is Research Fellow, Institute of Sociology, and Associate Director, Program for Southeast Asian Area Studies (PROSEA), Academia Sinica; and Professor of Sociology, National Taiwan University, Taipei, Taiwan.

Hagen Koo is Professor of Sociology, University of Hawai'i at Manoa.

Elizabeth J. Perry is Professor of Political Science, University of California, Berkeley.

Andrew G. Walder is Professor of Sociology, Stanford University.

Nai-teh Woo is Associate Research Fellow, Institute of Sociology, Academia Sinica, Taipei, Taiwan.

INTRODUCTION

Putting Class in Its Place: Bases of Worker Identity in East Asia

ELIZABETH J. PERRY

The stunning success of East Asia's industrialization drive over the past half century has prompted many a social science effort at explanation. Although scholars have generally stressed the role of activist state bureaucracies in promoting economic development,[1] an important subtheme in the literature spotlights the quiescence of labor as a key factor.[2] The combination of strong states and weak workers is often credited with the phenomenal growth rates enjoyed by East Asian newly industrializing countries (NICs) in recent decades.[3] Government regulation and repression, we are told, militated against unionization or collective protest on the part of workers and facilitated the exploitation of low-cost labor in producing goods for export.

Despite their acknowledged contribution to the seemingly miraculous expansion of their national economies, East Asian workers themselves were seen as politically excluded and impotent. Frederic Deyo notes of workers in East Asia that "nowhere—not in their workshops, firms, communities, or governments—have they been able to influence the political and economic decisions that have shaped their lives."[4] Whereas an

---

[1] See especially Chalmers A. Johnson, *MITI and the Japanese Miracle: The Growth of Industrial Policy, 1925–1975* (Stanford, Calif.: Stanford University Press, 1982); Alice H. Amsden, *Asia's Next Giant: South Korea and Late Industrialization* (New York: Oxford University Press, 1989); Robert Wade, *Governing the Market: Economic Theory and the Role of Government in East Asian Industrialization* (Princeton, N.J.: Princeton University Press, 1990).

[2] Frederic C. Deyo, *Beneath the Miracle: Labor Subordination in the New Asian Industrialism* (Berkeley: University of California Press, 1989).

[3] See Frederic C. Deyo, *The Political Economy of the New Asian Industrialism* (Ithaca, N.Y.: Cornell University Press, 1987), esp. chaps. 4, 5, and 6.

[4] Deyo, *Beneath the Miracle*, p. 1.

earlier generation was inclined to attribute this political weakness to a Confucian cultural heritage that demanded unquestioning obedience to higher authority, more recent approaches emphasize structural factors: political controls, relations of production, community organizations, and the like.[5] In either case, the mentalities and everyday practices of workers themselves have tended to escape serious examination; scholarly attention has centered instead upon those larger forces—whether cultural or structural —that allegedly compel workers to subordinate their own interests to the dictates of workplace authorities.

Taken as a whole, the essays in this volume mark a departure from the existing scholarship on East Asian labor. Much of the comparative work to date has been undertaken by generalists who lack facility in East Asian languages; in contrast, the contributors to this collection have all conducted extensive primary research in Chinese, Japanese, and/or Korean sources. The result, we hope, is a more in-depth and nuanced view of aspects of East Asian working-class life than available in other comparative volumes. Although many of the contributors are known for their previous analyses of labor relations from a political economy perspective, here they shift lenses somewhat to look more intensively at the concerns of workers themselves. Using a variety of fresh sources—ranging from short stories and novels to diaries, interviews, and attitude surveys—the authors reveal an East Asian workforce that is a good deal more feisty than commonly believed.

The substantive topics as well as the methodologies and approaches presented in the forthcoming chapters are heterogeneous, as one would naturally expect from a group of scholars trained in diverse disciplinary backgrounds (history, anthropology, sociology, and political science) who work on quite different societies (Japan, Korea, Taiwan, and China). Despite such variance, however, the contributions converge in highlighting the proactive dimensions of working-class practice. Whether focusing on conflicts surrounding unionization in the Japanese steel industry half a century ago (Gordon), the quest for humane treatment

---

[5] For an argument about the Confucian origins of management relations in Taiwan factories, see Robert H. Silin, *Leadership and Values: The Organization of Large-Scale Taiwanese Enterprises* (Cambridge: Harvard University Press, 1976). The most systematic structural arguments appear in Deyo, *Political Economy*, and idem, *Beneath the Miracle*.

among female factory workers in 1980s Korea (Koo), the growth of class identity among blue-collar workers in Taiwan as reflected in literary representations (Hsiao) or survey responses (Wu), the entrepreneurial spirit of petty-capitalist women in contemporary Taipei and Chengdu (Gates), the explosion of migration (Honig) and prostitution (Hershatter) as mobility strategies among Chinese workers in the post-Mao era, or their earlier factional struggles during the high tide of Maoism (Walder), these studies dispel the myth of the quiescent East Asian worker in favor of a more complicated and combative image.

Such activism, we discover in these chapters, is not fully explained by the familiar models of class consciousness inherited from the analysis of West European and North American capitalism.[6] Although the authors in this volume are engaged in a serious dialogue with that influential paradigm, applying certain of its features to their particular cases, they also emphasize the extent to which worker action in East Asia has been structured along other, nonclass axes of identity. We discover that educational aspirations, family pressures, gender roles, state directives, native-place origins, and clientelist networks have proven every bit as decisive as class consciousness in shaping the behavior—even the militant behavior—of East Asian workers. On the whole, workers in this part of the globe appear to have been more consumed with the politics of "place"—a quest for social and cultural status entailing a desire to elude, rather than to embrace, the ranks of the proletariat—than with a "class" struggle to further their interests qua workers.

The importance of "place" over "class" is evident in Andrew Gordon's insightful analysis of Japanese steelworkers. Gordon begins his paper with the observation that workers in Japan strive to escape from the working class; if they themselves are condemned to a life as laborers, they at least long for something better for their children. Citing scholar and social critic Kumazawa Makoto, he quotes two anonymous male workers in 1940: "One says 'I only hope my children don't become workers.... If possible, I'd like them to be bureaucrats.' Another agrees that

---

[6] Such models derive of course from the work of Karl Marx and Friedrich Engels. For a stimulating recent application of the model to the European and American contexts, see Ira Katznelson and Aristide R. Zolberg, eds., *Working-Class Formation: Nineteenth-Century Patterns in Western Europe and the United States* (Princeton, N.J.: Princeton University Press, 1986).

'after all, status is status and for my children at least, I'd like to send them to school and let them become technicians or something like that'" (p. 14). In part because of this lack of allegiance to a class identity, Gordon suggests, the Japanese working class has all but disappeared in recent decades. The militant strikes of the immediate postwar period gave way to the quiescent "enterprise society" of the late twentieth century in which, rather than promote working-class interests, unions emphasize workplace concerns. In tracing this process for the NKK steel mill, Gordon shows how white-collar staff were welcomed to the ranks of the unions, which were organized along factory (rather than trade or regional) lines. The result was that workers came to connect their personal fate with the survival of the mill: "the workplace was arguably [their] most important source of social identity" (p. 36).

Although other scholars have attributed Japan's relative lack of labor militancy to outside forces (management, the state, the American occupation), Gordon views it as a product of the labor movement itself. In Japan, even the most radical unionists "hardly ever viewed the workplace with the breezy detachment of their Anglo-American counterparts, as just a place to earn a wage; they rather saw it as a site for the creation of community and meaning in daily life" (p. 49). Emphasizing workplace concerns over strictly class interests, labor leaders established factory-based unions that quickly became embroiled in a wide range of managerial (as opposed to purely labor) issues.

Whereas Gordon tracks the disappearance of the Japanese working class, Hagen Koo traces the development of class in the Korean context. Moreover, while Gordon stresses the internal dynamics of the labor movement, Koo credits external political and cultural forces with altering the significance of class-based labor activism. Nevertheless, in both cases we find an initial reluctance on the part of workers to accept a working-class identity. Korean society, Koo notes, retains a status hierarchy rooted in the feudal past in which modern factory workers rank no higher than the slaves or domestic servants of a bygone era. Young workers, having embarked on industrial labor as a route to upward mobility, are stung by the social stigma attached to factory work. The discrimination is particularly painful for female workers, who suffer the additional burden of sexual innuendo. Pressed by feelings of obligation toward their natal families, such workers long for escape for their younger siblings, if not for themselves. Koo quotes the night school essay of one female worker,

"Why should I pass on this pain to my younger siblings and pound a nail into their hearts? No, I cannot do that. Yes, the sorrow of failing to become educated must stop with me" (p. 60). Consumed by a yearning for social dignity, workers deeply resent the inhumane treatment suffered at the hands of their employers. Critical in translating this resentment into collective resistance, according to Koo, has been the effect of outside political and cultural forces: progressive church organizations, student-run night schools for workers, and especially the *minjung* movement—a populist, nativist effort at cultural rejuvenation.

These external forces (along with changes in the industrial structure) worked to stimulate both a greater sense of pride and an increased militancy among Korean workers. Even so, according to Koo, "[f]or the majority of workers...concern about status seems to be no less strong than materialistic concerns, and class interest and status interest combined to form the basic contours of their struggles" (p. 72). The anxiety over social place, in other words, has not entirely evaporated in a newfound identity as members of a working class.

Family pressure, educational opportunity, and state intrusion also figure centrally in the chapters on Taiwan and China. Nai-teh Wu's methodologically rigorous investigation of worker attitudes in Taiwan finds, somewhat surprisingly, that "people in Taiwan are aware of class divisions and that they overwhelmingly define class in objective economic terms" (p. 86). Contrary to the situation in Western capitalist countries, however, in Taiwan second-generation workers are not more likely to consider themselves members of the working class than are first-generation entrants to the workforce. As we have seen in the cases of Japan and Korea, in Taiwan as well working-class families apparently do not socialize their progeny into accepting a working-class identity. Interestingly, Wu finds that a junior high school level of education (equivalent to workers' night schools in Korea, one wonders?) correlates most strongly with working-class identification.

Regardless of the causes of working-class identity, Wu's attitude survey reveals that in Taiwan self-definition as a member of the working class (or identity) is not related to anticapital views (or consciousness). To explain this paradox of "class identity" having no bearing on "class consciousness," a situation that runs counter to findings for other capitalist societies, Wu spotlights the role of the Taiwan state in elevating the status of the working class. Through the provision of welfare benefits (medical insurance, home loans, and so on), the Taiwan government has helped to construct a positive identity for workers at the same time that it dampens enthusiasm for a radical assault on the capitalist system.

In stark contrast to Wu's reliance on quantitative data from attitude surveys, Michael Hsiao turns to fictional representations in novels and short stories to explore the changing bases of worker identity in contemporary Taiwan. Much as has the *minjung* movement in Korea described by Koo, in Taiwan as well an indigenization movement has stimulated newfound interest on the part of intellectuals in rescuing the voices and feelings of ordinary workers from obscurity. The result has been an outpouring of literary representations of lower-class life in recent decades. Surveying the trends in this literature over its thirty-year existence, Hsiao detects a major shift from workers as passive victims in the 1960s to the emergence of collective action in the 1970s and 1980s. Over the course of this momentous period in the history of Taiwan's industrialization, workers are depicted as shedding their atomization in favor first of a group and then of a class identity.

One of the more poignant themes in Hsiao's sympathetic presentation is the marked variation within the Taiwan labor force. Temporary laborers form a kind of underclass, whose only hope for attaining the status and security of a permanent job lies not in their skill or diligence at work but rather in their cultivation of personal connections with higher authorities. Female workers, whether temporary or permanent, suffer a host of additional abuses at the hands of managers and male co-workers alike. While earlier writers represent these downtrodden workers as passive and compliant, the picture changes over time—in step with the startling increase in labor disputes in Taiwan during the 1970s and 1980s. Hsiao cautions, however, that, despite the growth in labor militance, worker ambitions remain modest. Far from advocating a class struggle aimed at the capitalist system itself, labor leaders are content to seek a better place in the existing social hierarchy: "the intention is to improve the working-class position within the social class structure rather than to reject it" (p. 126).

Not surprisingly, procapitalist sentiments are even more pronounced among the female entrepreneurs studied by Hill Gates. Gates emphasizes striking parallels between the forms of "petty capitalism" being practiced in Taiwan and the People's Republic of China. Operating under an extraordinary degree of state involvement in the economy (which Gates dubs a "tributary" mode of production) and absent the legal protections available to Western capitalists, Chinese petty producers turn to personalistic networks—especially kinship ties—to carve out a profitable niche for themselves and their families. Although much of their activity involves a defensive effort to keep the avaricious state at bay, female entrepreneurs evince an impressive resourcefulness in developing successful business ventures. In the process, according to Gates, many of them also acquire a positive self-identity based upon the satisfaction derived from work itself as well as from the money it generates. These women enjoy substantial discretionary power over their earnings, thereby laying the groundwork for a relatively egalitarian relationship with their husbands.

Even so, Gates detects among her informants "regret that they had not achieved success via education and promotion through a socially sanctioned hierarchy" (p. 150). In both Taiwan and China, "[p]eople who can afford to have their children try to climb the educational ladder in the heights of government service continue to do so, showing where their strongest aspirations lie and how they disvalue their own class and its opportunities" (p. 151). Even to these prosperous beneficiaries of economic growth, social place still exerts a stronger attraction than class.

As Nai-teh Wu has suggested for Taiwan, state intervention is credited with attenuating class-based expressions of labor activism in China, too. Andrew Walder's analysis of worker unrest during the Cultural Revolution emphasizes the Communist state's role in having developed a new system of industrial relations "that anchored workers to their workplaces" (p. 167). Paternalistic arrangements and preferential opportunities centered on the work unit created the foundation for Party-sponsored networks that divided the workforce along nonclass lines. Although such divisions served ordinarily to defuse collective labor protest,[7] during the Cultural Revolution these official networks heavily shaped the patterns of collective action that emerged among factory workers.

Whereas previous discussions of workers' activism during the Cultural Revolution have centered on their economic interests and demands, Walder stresses the political divisions separating "rebel" critics of the factory leadership from their "loyalist" opponents.

---

[7] This is a central theme in Walder's earlier book, *Communist Neo-Traditionalism: Work and Authority in Chinese Industry* (Berkeley: University of California Press, 1986).

That these struggles revolved around state-sponsored political networks, rather than being played out along strictly class lines, did not prevent their often developing into very bloody affairs. Moreover, the terror unleashed upon Chinese factories in the subsequent persecution campaigns of 1968–71 demonstrated the continuing effort of the Chinese state to impose its will in draconian fashion.

Much has changed since the Cultural Revolution, of course. Yet the Chinese state continues to wield a major influence on worker identities. As Gail Hershatter shows in her essay on prostitution in post-Mao China, state efforts to categorize and regulate the sex trade exert a decisive effect both on public understanding of the phenomenon and on the daily lives of those classified as prostitutes.

Relying on a mobilization campaign (*yundong*) style of policy implementation—a state orchestration of mass political participation that reached its apogee in the Cultural Revolution—the post-Mao authorities launched an attack on prostitution as a social vice attributable to foreign bourgeois influence. As Hershatter points out, this official assault on prostitution is not unlike the campaign against petty capitalism during the Cultural Revolution. If state-imposed obstacles played a major role in structuring the entrepreneurial behavior of petty capitalists (as shown by Gates), the same is even more true for prostitutes. In part as a reaction against state sanctions, Chinese sex workers—like petty businesswomen—have (ironically enough) become shrewd economic operators. The official unwillingness to consider their activity as a form of remunerative labor, Hershatter suggests, actually undermines the state's attempt to curb the phenomenon.

Along with prostitution, migrant labor has emerged as a prominent feature of China's post-Mao socioeconomic landscape. And like prostitutes, migrant laborers are also widely blamed for the disturbing escalation in urban crime and disorder of recent years. Honig raises the intriguing question of whether the growing popular resentment against outsiders may be contributing to the construction of a native-place "ethnic identity" among migrant workers. As she explains, migratory labor is often structured—both occupationally and residentially—along lines of native-place origin, a phenomenon that has been well documented for imperial China as well as for Taiwan, Japan, and Korea.

In an earlier study, Honig argued that an ethnic identity did develop for immigrants from northern Jiangsu to Shanghai after the midnineteenth century.[8] Here she raises, but does not resolve, the applicability of the concept of ethnicity to contemporary patterns of labor migration. Although ethnographic evidence from the Pearl River Delta points to the increasing salience of native-place networks, Honig cautions that the phenomenon is still too new and the data too fragmentary to permit a clear judgment about the construction of ethnic identity among recent migrants. Honig's reluctance to draw firm conclusions about the directions of identity formation among contemporary Chinese migrants sets an appropriately cautious tone on which to end this volume. As she observes, ethnicity needs to be analyzed in "more symbolic and complex ways, attending to the...processes through which ...meanings are created and transformed" (p. 243).

This volume is truly a pioneering effort. To the extent that it succeeds in generating a greater appreciation for the diversity and dynamism of East Asian workers, we hope it will also stimulate further comparative research into both the processes and the substance of labor identity formation. Is the concern for "place" a distinctively East Asian phenomenon? Can its origins be traced to a Confucian obsession with social hierarchy and "face," or is this orientation the product of a newly emergent labor force still reluctant to embrace a class-based definition of itself? What role have states played in diluting class consciousness and fostering workplace identity? And how and why does the expression of such identity vary from one East Asian setting to the next?

The chapters of this volume offer a more variegated and unruly portrait of East Asian workers than the dominant image conveyed in the general literature. Although state intervention did indeed figure prominently in the industrialization effort, East Asian labor was not rendered politically inconsequential in the process. State agents (not only through macroeconomic policy, but also by setting the parameters of moral discourse and welfare distribution) have admittedly exercised a powerful influence on worker identity. But workers in turn have exhibited a remarkable degree of initiative, ingenuity, and imagination in resisting and recasting official directives. In this process, they have been both aided and inhibited by an attachment to "place" that assigns a higher priority to bettering their social status than to furthering their interests as members of a working "class." Just as the intrusive modern

---

[8] Emily Honig, *Creating Chinese Ethnicity: Subei People in Shanghai, 1850–1980* (New Haven, Conn.: Yale University Press, 1992).

East Asian state has important precedents in its Confucian forerunner,[9] so the politics of "place" (whether defined in terms of regional origin or work unit) can claim a respectable pedigree in the history of East Asian labor movements.[10] But even if we accept the importance of "place" over "class" in East Asian constructions of worker identity, the actual meanings of this orientation remain largely unexplored. That critical task remains for another volume to accomplish.

---

[9] On the important, albeit limited, role that the bureaucratic state and its officials played in Qing socioeconomic development, see, for example, Peter C. Perdue, *Exhausting the Earth: State and Peasant in Hunan, 1500–1850* (Cambridge: Harvard University Press, 1987).

[10] For the earlier Chinese labor movement, see Gail Hershatter, *The Workers of Tianjin, 1900–1945* (Stanford, Calif.: Stanford University Press, 1986); Emily Honig, *Sisters and Strangers: Women in the Shanghai Cotton Mills, 1911–1949* (Stanford, Calif.: Stanford University Press, 1986); and Elizabeth J. Perry, *Shanghai on Strike: The Politics of Chinese Labor* (Stanford, Calif.: Stanford University Press, 1992); A discussion of the salience of place-based politics in contemporary Chinese labor relations can be found in Elizabeth J. Perry, "From Native Place to Workplace: Labor Origins and Outcomes of China's *Danwei* System" (paper prepared for the conference "China's Midcentury Transitions," Fairbank Center for East Asian Research, Harvard University, September 1994).

ONE

Conditions for the Disappearance of the Japanese Working-Class Movement

ANDREW GORDON

Some Japanologists will question the premise of this essay. Why discuss the disappearance of something that could never have existed in the first place? These commentators deny that "working-class" movements, consciousness, or culture are relevant concepts for the study of Japan. A classic of this genre is the 1970 book *Japanese Society*, by the well-known anthropologist Nakane Chie. She presents Japan as a "vertical" and "homogeneous" society, both historically and at the time of her writing. She also denies the possibility for significant social action on the basis of horizontal classes:

> Even if social classes like those in Europe can be detected in Japan, and even if something vaguely resembling those classes that are illustrated in the textbooks of western sociology can also be found in Japan, the point is that in actual society this stratification is unlikely to function and that it does not really reflect the social structure. In Japanese society it is really not a matter of workers struggling against capitalists or managers but of Company A ranged against Company B.[1]

A decade later, Murakami Yasusuke and his colleagues presented a grand argument in a similar vein. They stressed that vertical, hierarchical social structures modeled on the Japanese household (*ie*) have been central and durable across centuries of history, and they explicitly connected these underlying structures to a contemporary (1980s) "Japanese management system" that relied on

---

[1] Nakane Chie, *Japanese Society* (Berkeley: University of California Press, 1970). This is a modified version of *Tate shakai no ningen kankei* (Tokyo: Kōdansha, 1967). Quotation at p. 87.

"community-like practices" in contrast to the "individualistic West."[2]

Such arguments have deep roots and powerful effect. They create and sustain on both sides of the Pacific a common wisdom about Japan that is further disseminated in best-selling works such as *The Japan That Can Say No* (this book sold more than a million copies in its Japanese edition). One of the book's two authors, Morita Akio, differs from Nakane Chie by at least nodding in the direction of history and the salience of class: "I think prewar Japanese corporations resembled those in the United States. If the company president said 'you're fired,' you were fired. So there were various labor movements." He then claims that under the impact of "MacArthur's" reforms, Japanese managers in the postwar era "invented a new form and way of thinking, the enterprise as a community of fate."[3]

I am tempted to dismiss these works out of hand. Contra Nakane and Morita, it is possible to uncover rich evidence of the importance of class, in either its objective or subjective sense, in prewar *and* postwar Japanese history. Using Katznelson and Zolberg's concepts of four "levels" of class, we can certainly identify level one, an objective or structural class of men and women who worked for wages in a capitalist, industrial Japan (although there is likely to be debate as to who belongs in this class). We can also find and describe class on the second level of their analysis, the realm of working-class "experience" or ways of life, both at the workplace and in the community.[4]

---

[2] Murakami Yasusuke "Ie Society As a Pattern of Civilization," *Journal of Japanese Studies* 10, 2 (Summer 1984): 356–57. This is an abbreviated version of Murakami Yasusuke, Kumon Shunpei, and Sato Seizaburo, *Bunmei to shite no ie shakai* (Tokyo: Chūō kōronsha, 1979).

[3] Morita Akio and Ishihara Shintarō, *"No" to ieru Nihon* [The Japan that can say 'no'] (Tokyo: Kobunsha, 1989), pp. 96–97.

[4] Ira Katznelson and Aristide R. Zolberg, eds., *Working-Class Formation: Nineteenth-Century Patterns in Western Europe and the United States* (Princeton, N.J.: Princeton University Press, 1986), pp. 14–17. At this level, however, much work remains to be done for Japan. Many abundant sources have yet to be fully exploited. These include turn-of-the century classics such as Yokoyama Gennosuke's *Nihon no kasō shakai* [Japanese lower-class society] (1898; reprint Tokyo: Iwanami shoten, 1949. Translated by Eiji Yutani in "*Nihon no kasō shakai* of Yokoyama Gennosuke," Ph.D. dissertation, University of California, Berkeley, 1985); and Nōshōmushō, shōmu kyoku, ed., *Shokkō jijō* [Conditions of workers] (1903; reprint, Tokyo: Shinkigensha, 1976; 3 vols.), as well as post–World War I accounts such as the Tsukishima report (Naimushō eisei kyoku, *Tokyo shi, Kyōbashi-ku, Tsukishima ni ōkeru jitchi chōsa hōkoku* [Field survey report for Tsukishima, Kyōbashi Ward, Tokyo], 1921, reprinted as *Tsukishima chōsa* [Tokyo: Koseikan, 1970]); and Hosoi Wak-

But when we turn to the third and fourth of Katznelson and Zolberg's levels of class, those that reflect the spirit of E. P. Thompson's understanding of the concept, the story turns more complex, and the views quoted at the outset cannot be dismissed simply. Level three is that of classes as "formed groups, sharing dispositions." The fourth level refers to collective action or working-class movements.[5] Thompson's formulation, encompassing both of these, is the one that has influenced me the most, the idea that class "happens" when working people "feel an identity of interests as between themselves and as against their rulers and employers" and act collectively on that feeling.[6]

Even scholars who believe that the "working class" or the "working-class culture" is a relevant concept for the study of events in Japan recognize that moments when class "happened" in Japanese history are elusive and that working-class "dispositions" or consciousness as well as social actions are ambiguous. One example is Kumazawa Makoto, among the most insightful critical voices writing today on the topic of work and workers in Japan (as distinct from the celebratory voices of Murakami or Morita). He describes the social world of wage workers in prewar and postwar Japan with great sensitivity. It is a world far removed from Nakane's vision of workers comfortably integrated into vertical organizations. But when he describes the consciousness of these workers, he writes of their intense desire to escape "lower-class" or working-class society, or failing that, at least to let their children do so. He quotes two anonymous male workers from a

izo, *Jokō aishi* [Sad story of factory girls, 1925; reprint Tokyo: Iwanami shoten, 1982]. The former offers a comprehensive picture of the working-class community on the island of Tsukishima at the mouth of the Sumida River in Tokyo; the original data used in compiling the report, including hundreds of worker family budgets, are available to researchers at the Ohara Institute for Social Research. The latter chronicles the "pitiful" story of women textile workers in the mid-1920s. One rare scholarly effort to put together a picture at these levels, analyzing the material experience of working-class life, with attention to Korean laborers and outcastes as well as native Japanese, is Sugihara Kaoru and Tamai Kingo, eds., *Taishō/Osaka/Suramu: Mō hitotsu no Nihon kindai shi* [Taishō, Osaka, Slum: Another modern Japanese history] (Tokyo: Shinhyoron, 1986). Another, which goes beyond these levels to those of consciousness and collective action discussed below, is Nimura Kazuo, *Ashio bōdō no shiteki bunseki: Dōzan rōdōsha no shakai shi* [Historical analysis at the Ashio riot: A social history of copper mine workers] (Tokyo: Tokyo University Press, 1988).

[5] Katznelson and Zolberg, *Working-Class Formation*, pp. 17–19.

[6] E. P. Thompson, *The Making of the English Working Class* (New York: Vintage, 1966) pp. 9, 11.

discussion published in 1940. One says, "I only hope my children don't become workers....If possible, I'd like them to be bureaucrats." Another agrees that "after all, status is status and for my children at least, I'd like to send them to school and let them become technicians or something like that."[7]

The problem for Japan, then, is that although it is possible to delineate the distinct social world—the life experience, the "disposition," *and* the collective actions—of workers who made such statements and who opposed their superiors, this disposition is often expressed as the denial of the status of "worker" or the desire to escape it. Of course, this "problem" is interesting only if Japanese workers differ in this regard from those elsewhere. Implicit in the discussion so far is a contrast to a Western, especially a British, mode of worker consciousness and action. Certainly the desire to escape the status of "working class" or allow one's children to do so through education is not unknown in the West. But with Ronald Dore, I am convinced that Japanese workers' resentment "is less likely than in Britain to be shared, echoed, magnified and crystallized into category [i.e., class] antagonism."[8] This essay explores some reasons why this is the case, and perhaps this volume can suggest whether workers elsewhere in Asia share important characteristics with those in Japan.

Thus, here I will identify aspects of thought and behavior of Japanese steelworkers in the early postwar years, at a high point of labor union power and prestige, that arguably constituted the conditions for the subsequent "disappearance" of the working class in Thompson's sense of the term. I will not analyze the process of "disappearance" itself in this essay but will describe the situation in a particular steel mill at a prior point, when few expected the following decades would witness the withering away of organizations whose members in part acted upon an identity of interests "between themselves and against their employers."

---

[7] Kumazawa Makoto, *Nihon no rōdōsha zō* [Portraits of Japanese workers] (Tokyo: Chikuma shobo, 1981,) p. 59.

[8] Ronald Dore, *British Factory–Japanese Factory* (Berkeley: University of California Press, 1973), p. 260.

Remembering the Labor Movement at NKK

The following 1973 remembrance of an early postwar Japanese workplace offers a concrete view of my concerns in this paper:

> In May, 1949 I was assigned to head the labor section [of Nippon Kōkan (NKK)]. To be honest, I approached the new position with great trepidation, for the labor-management relationship at the time was one continuous, intense confrontation....
>
> [During negotiations] large crowds of union members were present, in addition to the union and management committee representatives who sat at the bargaining table. It was a sort of mass bargaining, probably a strategy to intimidate management with the force of the crowd. But on the other hand, the union leaders at the time had not yet built sufficient authority, and the mass of union members would not necessarily accept the results of bargaining carried out [privately] by union and management representatives, so it was common practice for a mass of onlookers to join the negotiations.
>
> Negotiations at our company were typical. The union would even use a PA system to make periodic progress reports to the members, crowded outside, who could not fit into the conference room. On numerous occasions the union leaders would come to understand the management position, but then, influenced by the response of onlookers or union members who heard the report over the PA, they would come back with an even stronger position. In such bargaining, union members would shout at the top of their voices: "Take a look at the workers' dining hall. We haven't seen a grain of rice in days. Do you think we can do heavy labor to rebuild the nation's industry drinking soup that doesn't even taste of *miso*, with maybe 4 or 5 dumplings in it? Prices are going up. Even rationed goods have doubled or tripled in price. We want a cup of rice a day! We want the money to buy it!"[9]

The author of this recollection was Orii Hyūga, graduate of Tokyo University, a self-described "enlightened" personnel manager at Japan's second-largest steel maker. If he had read E. P. Thompson, he might have added to his memoir "Yes, class was 'happening' at NKK in those days, and my job was to make it stop happening." He eventually succeeded.

The turning point came a decade after the scene just described. Orii's subordinate in the labor section at NKK was Konda

---

[9] Orii Hyūga, *Rōmu kanri 20 nen* [Twenty years of labor management], pp. 4–5, for this quote. See pp. i–ii for Orii's succinct presentation of a modern, scientific philosophy of labor management.

Masaharu, laughingly described in 1992 by his wife as "the last soldier of the Imperial Japanese Army." Konda himself remarked that for two weeks at the height of the forty-nine-day strike at NKK in 1959 he had slept on a cot at the company. On the day before a mass bargaining session of the sort described by Orii, the union threatened to bring 120 people, but agreed to limit the delegation to 20. Yet at daybreak, 120 union members showed up after all, and Konda's superiors had not yet arrived. "I stood and faced them, resigned to a beating. Besides the fourteenth of August, 1945, when I was stationed at Atsugi Base awaiting the American arrival, these were the tensest days of my life."[10]

The 1959 strike was the final confrontation between company and union at NKK to partake of the full flavor of Orii's remembrance. Orii published his thoughtful memoir in 1973. This was just fourteen years after the 1959 strike, yet at the outset of his account he wrote that "negotiations back then were menacing to an extent impossible to imagine today." This claim restates my central problem: how do we explain the transformation, in little more than a decade, of what is "imaginable" to people in a society? Was Orii simply exaggerating the "bad old days"? Or is it possible that a working class in some meaningful sense of the term once existed, but then disappeared?

In a larger study to which this essay is prelude, I will argue the latter: in the postwar decades, a hegemonic system emerged that marginalized, if it did not eliminate, the early postwar mode of working-class consciousness and behavior. Such a view is not totally at odds with Morita's claim that the enterprise-as-community was a new creation of postwar Japan, although I differ concerning the timing and dynamics of the process (an exquisitely managed "coercive consensus") and the assessment of the result.[11] I am much closer to critics who call the system that resulted "the enterprise society." As with any system of hegemony, it came to limit and prescribe for its inhabitants that which seemed possible, natural, or imaginable. Thus, not only are foreign observers who know only the quiescent unions of late-twentieth-century Japan likely to be surprised by Orii's account; as early as the 1970s, most Japanese together with Orii would have had trouble imagining such an "unnatural" scene. They would have agreed that early

---

10 Interview with Konda Masaharu, Feb. 28, 1992.
11 The term "coercive consensus" is from Norma Field, *In the Realm of a Dying Emperor: Japan at Century's End* (New York: Random House, 1991), p. 29.

postwar society was part of "another world" and that militant actions of employees against employers were at best relics appropriate to a bygone day, if not a foolish stance in any era.

My view of this transformation also differs some from those who describe postwar history as primarily the suppression from without (by management, the state, the Americans, and colluding elements of the workforce) of the working-class movement.[12] I recognize this aspect to the story, but I argue on balance that the seeds that produced Orii's mental world of the 1970s, in which early postwar confrontations were "unimaginable" (at least in large, private-sector unions), can be found *within* the labor movement of the prior era, the time when the working class was most arguably present. Here I will describe those seeds, some key features of steelworkers' consciousness in early postwar Japan.

Overview: The Transformation of the Labor Movement

Immediately after the war, Japanese unions, backed by U.S. occupation policy and fueled by the deprivation and anger of masses of workers, achieved unprecedented power in the workplace. From the late 1940s through the 1950s, an intense contest unfolded for control of workplaces, enterprises, and unions.

The intensity of the contest varied by industry, but the steel case was relatively typical in that two peak eras of confrontation occurred, with successively diminished intensity—the first between 1946 and 1949, the second in the mid-to-late 1950s. In 1946, the Tsurumi mill of NKK was one of the sites of a so-called production control dispute. Through June of 1946, some 157,000 newly organized men and women engaged in 255 instances of this tactic, locking out managers and running factories on their own when demands for higher wages and the "democratization" of the workplace were denied.[13] This same year, thousands more unions, including the giant NKK mill at Kawasaki, won contracts giving them a substantial voice in "managerial" decisions, and most of these unions protected their new prerogatives for several years.[14]

---

[12] Yamamoto Kiyoshi's many studies of postwar labor disputes, labor markets, and labor-management relations offer a strong statement of this claim. See, for example, *Tōshiba sōgi: 1949* [The Tōshiba debate] (Tokyo: Ochanomizu shobo, 1983).

[13] Joe Moore, *Japanese Workers and the Struggle for Power, 1945–1947* (Madison: University of Wisconsin Press, 1983).

[14] The broad outline of the surge of strikes and union organizing that took place just after the war is well known. Union membership rose from about five thousand in October 1945 to nearly five million by December 1946, more than 40

A brief period of stagnation followed the Red Purge of 1950, when about twelve thousand (accused) Communist Party members were fired from their jobs and union posts, but unions gradually rebuilt toward a second peak of confrontation that stretched from about 1952 through the great Miike coal strike of 1960. The newly founded national union federation (Sōhyō) surprised Japanese critics and dismayed occupation officials with its so-called transformation "from chicken to duck," as it came to support the left-wing Socialist Party in national politics, aggressive wage bargaining at the industrial level, and militant day-to-day struggles in the workplace. With NKK at the forefront, Sōhyō's industrial union of steelworkers (Tekkō Rōren) led strikes throughout the decade, most notably in 1957 and 1959.

With extraordinary regularity, militant unions were defeated in these confrontations: in electric power in 1952, auto plants in 1953, steel mills in 1957 and 1959, paper mills in 1958, coal mines in 1960, and shipyards in the mid-1960s. In the wake of such disputes, new leaders calling for cooperation with management either wrested control from militants in existing unions or formed "second unions" that quickly came to enroll the vast majority of a firm's employees.

The spring wage offensives that began during the 1950s continued through the 1960s and beyond, but unions increasingly began to call off strikes at the last moment. In steel mills and throughout the society, the annual sequence of demands, replies, threatened strikes, last-minute negotiations, more demands, further responses, and ultimate union concessions became a predictable springtime ritual. The outlook of the nation's dominant private-sector unions (especially in export-oriented industries) converged toward that of management even before the 1973 oil crisis rocked the economy and put unions on the defensive. In the 1970s, the remaining militant and radical unions in the public sector underwent a transformation similar to that of private-sector unions before them, and the hegemony of the enterprise society was entrenched in workplaces and, more broadly, throughout Japanese society.

---

percent of the nation's adult wage earners. Workers who engaged in production control were challenging fundamental notions of private property and managerial authority, and given the extraordinary disarray of the old guard of business and political leaders in early 1946, a case can be made that a revolutionary situation existed *within Japan*.

These decades of transformation were marked by a battle of ideas that produced a contesting swirl of union and managerial visions of how society, economy, and company ought to be organized. In the 1940s and 1950s, the dominant position among workers active in labor unions can be called a "radical" unionism. Adherents to the radical vision sought a socialist revolution, and they saw unions, allied to either the Socialist or the Communist party, as the most important building blocks of a new society. Through activism and bargaining, unions sought veto power over personnel decisions and a voice in (sometimes control over) day-to-day operation of firm and factory. Radical unions sought to undermine the legitimacy of the managerial chain of command. They resisted massive investments in "rationalization," which they claimed would lead to a more intense work pace, lower wages, and less secure jobs. At the industrial level, they demanded large annual pay increases indexed to the cost of living and reflecting employee needs rather than the firm's purported "ability to pay."

A second important position was an early postwar "cooperative" vision articulated most forcefully by the venerable Sōdōmei federation (founded in 1919). Although never radical, these unions could be militant. This distinction is important. Sōdōmei unions accepted the basic framework of a capitalist society and saw their role as the defense of workers within it, but locals such as NKK's Kawasaki mill union on occasion fought vigorously with managers seen to be uncooperative.

The third important position on the union side was a revision of the Sōdōmei stance, what we may call "ultra-cooperative" unionism. This came into its own in the 1960s and 1970s and remains ascendant in the 1990s. It was the unionism of the steel federation in the 1960s and of the Japan Council of the International Metalworkers Federation. Such unionism was particularly strong in private firms competing fiercely for shares of domestic and export markets. It has been controversial, to say the least. Critics condemn it as the ultimate perversion of anything resembling "true" unionism; advocates laud it as the perfection of pragmatic Japanese industrial relations and a model for the world. It was (and is) distinguished ideologically by an extraordinary emphasis on the almost organic compatibility of management and worker interests. This is the ideology of labor unions in a world in which class, in Thompson's sense, has disappeared. It is the ideology of Nakane Chie's "vertical society" where struggle between workers and managers is preempted by struggle to improve a company's productivity and profits.

Among managers, some hardliners never came to terms with the occupation reforms; they continued to treat unions as a threat to be suppressed.[15] Others, particularly in firms with relatively unchallenged monopolies in an industry, for a time made their peace with radical unions.[16] But the mainstream of Japanese managers, typified at NKK by Orii Hyūga and his subordinates, came to the "enlightened" view that they should both attack the radicals and nurture cooperative unionists who could ultimately help manage and motivate the workforce, although they differed among themselves significantly as they groped toward this objective. As cooperative unionism won out over the radical vision, and as it shifted from the relatively militant Sōdōmei brand to a new, ultra-cooperative spirit, managers became ever more comfortable with unions. By the late 1970s they were so confident of the wisdom of their policies that they began proselytizing on behalf of "Japanese-style management" to Westerners and other Asians. Firmly consolidated at home, the hegemony of Japan's enterprise society now had a global reach.

Managerial views thus differed from those of some unions, while unions and managers were divided among themselves. But it is important not to lose sight of the significant ideological overlap both within and across the boundaries of union and management. First, workers in unions across the political spectrum (as well as managers) saw the workplace as the site of a community that gave meaning as well as economic sustenance to their lives. Second, all sorts of unions sought a voice in an unusually broad range of decisions about corporate operations and planning. At least implicitly, they agreed with management that corporate survival, then prosperity, were crucial priorities. Third, despite

---

[15] For a dramatic 1946 example, see Theodore Cohen, *Remaking Japan: The American Occupation As New Deal* (New York: Macmillan, 1987), pp. 271–72.

[16] See Takeda Makoto, "Kindaishugiteki rōmu seisaku no zasetsu to gendai Nihon-gata keieisha no tōjō" [The failure of modern management policies and the advent of contemporary Japanese-style management], *Ōhara shakai mondai kenkyūjo zasshi*, no. 366 (May 1989): 21–23, on the Ōji paper mill case; and Ueda Osamu, "Kigyōkan kyōsō to 'shokuba shakai': M Zōsen M Zōsenjo (1)" [Interfirm competition and 'workplace society': M shipbuilding, M shipyard], *Ōhara shakai mondai kenkyūjo zasshi*, no. 350 (January 1988): 1–16, on Mitsubishi Shipbuilding's Nagasaki shipyard. Both writers argue that the company's loss of its monopoly position in the industry forced managers to change this tolerant or passive stance toward the union.

intense antagonism between blue- and white-collar workers, unions and managers tended to seek to erase or deny this opposition, rather than institutionalize and mediate it. The case of NKK reveals that these areas of overlap were present even in the earliest postwar days of union militance and radicalism. They provided conditions for the subsequent disappearance of the working-class movement.

The Steel Industry and NKK

The rest of this essay will focus on the Kawasaki and Tsurumi mills of Nippon Kōkan. I choose steel in general, and NKK in particular, first because they are representative in two ways. What happened in steel mills was remarkably similar to what happened in most major manufacturing industries. And the story at NKK was more or less identical to that at the rest of the big five (Yawata, Fuji, NKK, Sumitomo, Kōbe).[17] This holds true whether we speak of the ideology of the contestants, the outcome of disputes, or the innovations in technology and labor management.

Second, I choose these cases because they are strategic. The steel industry has been economically and politically dominant in

---

[17] This choice of cases is also nonrepresentative in that it excludes many workers. I am focusing here on what one might call the "3M" segment of Japanese society: men working in mammoth manufacturing companies. Such stories account for only a small proportion of the experience of Japanese at work, yet a truly disproportionate volume of Japanological musing. This "3M" story is not objectively more important than any other. But what happened to male employees as regular workers in big factories mattered to many other Japanese people in at least two ways. First, because popular pundits and intellectuals, for better or worse, offered unbalanced attention to life in the factories and offices of big companies, the practices of this world became models to which many others, owners and employees alike, aspired and against which they measured themselves. Second, the work life of men in big companies depended on a division of labor among men and women derived from a particular view of gender roles.

In a separate work I plan to address directly this issue of the link between the rationalization of male and female spheres in postwar Japanese society. What I find fascinating is that the men in management (and the union) at NKK anxiously sought to rationalize the role of the housewife just as they rationalized the workplace; they saw the proper behavior of women at home as critical to the proper behavior of men at work. The success of such efforts not only influenced homebound housewives; it also affected the lives of millions of women who worked both at home and in factories. This later inquiry will explore how patterns of family life, gender, and consumption shaped and reflected the workplace and enterprise society as it evolved in the 1950s and 1960s.

postwar Japan. Throughout the postwar era, steel industry managers were fond of quoting the maxim "whither steel, so goes the nation."[18] For decades, wage settlements in the steel industry served as benchmarks for other industries, as did innovations in quality control and work organization. Likewise, steel unions led the way toward the political coalition that promulgated cooperative unionism nationwide and led to the Rengō federation.

In addition, NKK itself occupied a strategic niche in two ways. Its proximity to the academic and journalistic capital of Tokyo (and to the U.S. occupation headquarters) encouraged close scrutiny of whatever went on at the mill, leaving to us a rich documentary record of observers' reports from the 1940s through the present. Second, it was the failure of the forty-nine-day strike at NKK and Fuji steel in 1959 that opened the way to the ascendance of cooperative unionism in the steel industry. Yawata's union had turned this corner several years before, and resentment of Yawata's overbearing power prompted NKK and Fuji unions to take a stand alone in 1959 to, as their leaders put it, "escape from Yawata-dependence." If NKK's and Fuji's unions had prevailed, Yawata would have stood isolated, and the dominoes might have fallen the other way.

Creation Stories

Nippon Kōkan was founded in the city of Kawasaki, along the coast between Tokyo and Yokohama, in 1912 by two university classmates. Imaizumi Kiichirō, until then an engineer at the Yawata Ironworks, provided the technology, and Shiraishi Genjirō provided the money, drawing on the resources of his father-in-law, Asano Sōichirō, founder of the Asano financial empire. By the end of World War I, the Kawasaki mill employed several thousand steelworkers. In 1936 NKK fired its first blast furnace, making the Kawasaki mill an integrated facility producing a complete sequence of iron, steel, and rolled metal products. By the end of World War II, the mill boasted five blast furnaces and eighteen thousand workers. Along the way, NKK in 1940 gained a captive customer and strengthened its rolling and plate making capacity by absorbing the Asano empire's nearby Tsurumi steel mill and shipyard.

---

18 *Tetsu wa kokka nari.*

In the 1920s and early 1930s, workers in Kawasaki conducted a number of substantial industrial actions, including several strikes by the NKK local of the Sōdōmei federation in the mid-1920s. But the company managed to crush this union within several years. By the eve of World War II, even before all Japan's unions were dissolved by state order, unions in Kawasaki were nearly extinct. But within two months of surrender, in October 1945, union organizing began in Kawasaki once more, first at several nearby plants, then at the NKK mills.

Communist Party members led some of these efforts; prewar Sōdōmei unionists led others. At Tsurumi, a CP activist organized a movement demanding the company rehire several dismissed workers, and this drive led to formation of a union. At Kawasaki, men in several work sites separately began to discuss forming a union, and Sōdōmei veterans played a role in pulling these impulses together into a union by January 1946. Quite independently of each other, famous strikes then took place in each mill in October 1946.

The work sites of Nippon Kōkan at this time could hardly be called "steel mills." Managers had no operable strategy for the future of the firm. They were paralyzed by uncertainty over the occupation purge of executives for wartime collaboration, the U.S. trust-busting plan to divide NKK into several independent companies, and the ceiling placed on Japanese steel-making capacity by the war reparations plan. Further, government (and U.S.) control over access to materials and capital inhibited operation, and even if managers had wanted to refire the blast furnaces, they needed approval from both the occupation authority (Supreme Commander, Allied Powers [SCAP]) and from the Japanese government.

Thus, in late 1945 the company's twenty open hearth furnaces and five blast furnaces all stood idle. A few rolling machines processed those ingots in stock, and workers produced tertiary products such as buckets, pots, and pans.[19] Managers had fired most of the workers. By early fall, attrition and dismissals had reduced the force at Tsurumi from a wartime peak of six thousand to two thousand and at Kawasaki from eighteen thousand to under four thousand. Even so, there was precious little to do.

---

[19] Nippon kōkan kabushiki kaisha, ed., *Nippon kōkan kabushiki kaisha 40 nen shi* [Nippon Kōkan forty-year history] (Tokyo, 1952), pp. 285–87.

The first head of the Tsurumi union, Hayashi Takeo, was a
Communist Party member who had been a student, then union,
activist in the 1920s. Hayashi recalled:

In September 1945, burnt-out enemy shells lay scattered around the
Tsurumi mill. The scorched fields of the town had not been
touched. The blast furnace was shut down. Work commenced with
a trickle from the steel section. With the first round of dismissals,
the work force was cut by two-thirds. With prices going up daily,
those of us left could not eat on our wages. Some of the workers
would bake sweet potatoes they had bartered for in the countryside
in the mill's electric furnace, sell these, and supplement their pay.
Others made eating utensils from the company's stock of plate iron
and sold them. People who went by the rules [i.e., did not trade on
the black market] could not live. If things continued this way the
company would lose [money] as well. If we did not start up production so the workers could work and eat, the company and
Japan's economy would collapse. This is why I set out to build a
union.[20]

As at many firms in late 1945, the company tried to create a
captive union in advance of independent worker efforts, in this
case by urging sympathetic assistant section managers (kakari-chō)
to form a union. Hayashi's group got wind of this plan and
quickly proclaimed itself a "Union Preparation Committee."
Caught off guard, the mill director recognized Hayashi's group,
lamely telling him, "We were just thinking Tsurumi ought to have
a union, and after all, it's better that this be done by the workers
on their own."[21] Hayashi recalls that in their haste, the organizers
drew in people with influence from as many different workshops
as possible, even if they were bosslike foremen. The union held
an inauguration ceremony on December 12, 1945, and immediately
presented demands for a pay raise, recognition of the union, and
control of company welfare facilities.

Hayashi's statement neatly presents a view, held even on the
left wing of the union movement, that the fates of workers, nation,
and company were inseparably linked. The Tsurumi union was
also typical in building on workshops as the "local" unit of organizing and in giving a prominent role to foremen as union leaders.
All these features of union building were even more pronounced
at the founding of the Kawasaki mill (Kawatetsu) union several

---

[20] Nippon kōkan Tsurumi seitetsujo rōdō kumiai, ed., *Tsurutetsu rōdō undō shi*
[Tsurumi steel mill labor movement history] (Tokyo: Shundaisha, 1955), p. 51.

[21] Ibid., p. 53.

weeks later. In addition, the Kawatetsu creation story sheds light on a crucial social issue, the extraordinary antagonism of production workers toward staff.

The drive for a union at Kawatetsu began with blue-collar production workers. In mid-September, one Iijima Kiyoshi, a worker in the battery-charging room of the transport section, started talking up the idea of a union as a means to get the mill going again and protect worker livelihoods.[22] This was several weeks before SCAP gave official blessing to union organizing, and Iijima met a cool, worried response from those he talked to. To allay these fears, he first secured a promise of noninterference from staff members in the labor section (*kinrōka*), who were apparently aware that SCAP was likely to legalize unions, but this private permission was not enough. Iijima decided he needed a public display of the company's approval before employees would give him a hearing, so he insisted that someone from the labor section walk around with him as he promoted the union in various workshops, as proof that the company would tolerate a union.

With help from a few workers with prewar experience in Sōdōmei unions at NKK and other companies, Iijima gradually drew together a corps of organizers from around the mill. By late October, they were meeting each day in the battery room. Early discussions were conducted in fearful whispers, but as reports surfaced of unions formed elsewhere, workers' anxiety gradually subsided.[23]

One young man drawn into the preparatory committee who needed little prompting was Kamimura Hideji.[24] He vividly testifies to the depth of the status divide and the animosity of blue- toward white-collar men. Kamimura was born in 1915 to a tenant farming family. His formal education ended in sixth grade. Childhood memories of his father's humiliation as a tenant farmer powerfully shaped his social conscience. In December each year, his father would take a day off from work in the fields to take the rent rice to the landlord. Handing it over, he would bow low and

---

[22] This workplace recharged batteries used to power forklifts.

[23] Nihon kōkan Kawasaki seitetsujo rōdō kumiai, *Jū nen no ayumi* [Tsurumi steel mill labor movement history] (Kawasaki: Privately published, 1956), pp. 3–5, for information in this and previous paragraph, and p. 33 for timetable of organizing activities. This is an extremely valuable source. It provides an accurate chronology of union actions together with numerous essays written by various activists in 1956.

[24] Interview with Kamimura Hideji, Oct. 14, 1992.

thank the landlord. In a 1992 interview, Kamimura remembered watching this little ceremony sixty-five years earlier and "thinking as a child 'What the hell is going on? Why thank the landlord?' This seemed to me such a contradiction."

Kamimura's first and only industrial employer was NKK. He entered the mill in 1935 and worked as a crane operator unloading shipments of coal and iron ore. A skinny youth, he was overwhelmed at first by the twelve-hour shifts and the "heavy work, heat, oil." He was also stubborn and proud. In 1941, he and about fifty others in his section, including his foreman and assistant foreman, carried out a wildcat strike for higher output rates.

Kamimura's sense of grievance remained with him after the war. "I was truly discontented with my place in the company's hierarchy. If we ever complained we were put down. I deeply desired to change this." His discontents were dual. He was unhappy with the domineering foremen, assistant foremen, and crew bosses within the category of "production worker" (*kōin*), and he detested the high status of "white-collar staff" (*shokuin*) compared to all production workers. "There was so much discrimination. I felt extraordinary animosity toward the white-collar staff."

Thus it is no surprise that Kamimura, as a representative of the transport section, joined the workers-only Committee to Form a Union. This group, originally intending to create a union for blue-collar workers only, consisted of representatives from all the workshops in the mill. One of the most powerful, Suzuki Sōichirō, was an old foreman, respected and skilled, who fiercely opposed the idea of including white-collar staff, calling them the chief exploiters of workers and arguing that a union with staff in it would be worse than no union.[25] By mid-December, the committee was ready to hold a public meeting and announce plans to found a union.

The steel mill's staff of managers, engineers, and technicians consisted of graduates of universities and vocational high schools. Until the end of the war their positions had indeed been far more secure, their social status far higher, than the positions and status of lowly production workers. Their social status survived the war intact to some degree, but their economic status did not. In the fall of 1945, a prestigious white-collar position at NKK staff no

---

[25] Ibid. for the information and the quotations in this and preceding three paragraphs.

longer offered a livable wage or a secure job. According to Nakajima Hideo, the key activist on the staff side, "In September and
October the company had been aggressively cutting back by firing
assistant section chiefs and even section chiefs, so the emotions of
the white-collar men were very stirred up."[26]

The story of Nakajima's organizing drive was told to me by
Matsuda Takezō.[27] Matsuda grew up in northern Japan, graduat-
ing from the Morioka Industrial High School with training as a
machinist. In 1939 he entered NKK as a white-collar employee.
He recalls that with this status, at the tender age of seventeen he
could wear a yellow stripe on the arm of his uniform and give
orders to skilled foremen three times his age. He was given the
title of "machine supervisor" and assigned to the maintenance
shop of one of the mill's blast furnaces. Nakajima Hideo was
from the same town, had gone to the same school, and studied
construction. He entered NKK one year after Matsuda, in the
same job and position.

Matsuda recalls Nakajima as a man who "really worked well
with people." He was a "boss with a sense of righteousness" who
looked after his employees.[28] In the face of the awful postwar
deprivation, Nakajima felt he "had to do something." He came
into contact with a prewar activist and founder of the postwar
Sōdōmei federation. According to Matsuda, Nakajima came to
believe that economic recovery depended on improving the lives
of workers, "that one couldn't just go to work and follow company orders as in the past, but that workers themselves had to join
together to act, somehow." The Kanagawa headquarters of the
Sōdōmei union federation was just outside NKK's main gate, and
Nakajima developed close ties with the federation's prefectural
leaders. Matsuda recalls that Nakajima stayed up past midnight
most nights, engaged in discussions with his Sōdōmei friends.[29]

The date of Nakajima's first public step is unclear, but it was
probably early December. With permission from the labor section,
he made a broadcast over the company's public address system
calling on white-collar staff to form a union. In the union's 1956
history, Nakajima recalled his feeling at the time: "We had to do
something to start production and protect our livelihoods." The

---

26 *Jū nen no ayumi*, pp. 6–7.
27 Interview, Oct. 23, 1992.
28 Matsuda's expression was "mendo mi no ii, seigi-ha no oyabun taipu."
29 Interview, Oct. 23, 1992.

gist of his broadcast was that "workers at companies all around
the area are forming unions. We should form a union, join all our
strength to break out of this uncertain situation."[30] A group of
staff members formed around Nakajima, identified in the union
history by their work site: "Uno of transport, Kawagoshi of
machine shop."

Like the blue-collar men, by mid-December Nakajima's group
had formed a "preparatory committee." The white-collar group
considered forming a separate union, but its leaders decided their
group could be more effective by joining the blue-collar men in a
single union. On December 25, they approached the latter group
and proposed a meeting to discuss this. An week of intense
debate ensued.

The timing of this overture is important. Believing themselves
ready to publicly announce plans for their union, in mid-
December the men in Iijima's blue-collar group had called an open
"discussion meeting" in the workers' dining hall to test their support. Fewer than thirty people attended a desultory meeting.
Afterward, a few workers told Iijima, "We can't talk freely with
workers and staff together. Please hold a meeting for workers
only." Iijima was reluctant, for his motive in organizing a union
was to promote recovery of mill operations, and he had
envisioned a common organization of production workers and
staff. But, as the *Ten-Year History* of the Kawasaki union recorded,
"At Kawatetsu up until then, the status discrimination of staff and
worker was awful. Staff wore yellow stripes on their arms as
signs of their supervisory status, and workers were not even
allowed to wear the NKK mark on their uniforms. Dining halls
were separate. Even utensils were different. The position of
worker (*kōin*) was humiliating. They hated the staff." So, on
December 23, a meeting was held for workers only. It was a huge
success, lively, with a packed room. Iijima spoke on behalf of
unity, but the overwhelming sentiment of the meeting was for a
union of workers, only.[31]

Thus, when the staff group two days later proposed a union
embracing white and blue collar, a tense debate was inevitable. A
group of three staffers and four workers held the first round of
negotiations. An interesting sign of the extent of social distance
between worker and staff is that these meetings were the first

---

[30] *Jū nen no ayumi,* p. 6.
[31] Ibid.

occasion for Nakajima to meet the four worker leaders. In the *Ten-Year History* he frankly describes his anxious first impression of "the huge Nikaidō and fierce Arai, the latter standing guard at the entrance to the conference room, shouting at others to 'keep out!' "[32] The meeting produced no decision.

Among blue-collar leaders, the opponents of a unified body argued that (1) with 75 percent of employees being production workers, they could form a union on their own, (2) the tremendous animosity toward staff over "status discrimination" ruled out common action, and (3) letting in staff would allow the company to capture the union. One older worker "feared that if the staff were included, it would be a yellow union. I was impressed by Nakajima's logic, but could not overcome my feelings from the Yūaikai era."[33]

Despite their own reservations and in the face of the strong opposition expressed by those at the December 23 meeting, Iijima and his closest allies nonetheless supported the idea of a joint union. One important young activist, Takeda Ryūsuke, recalled that he felt animosity toward the staff, but believed there was need to work together with staff to overcome it. Iijima had looked into the situation at neighboring Sanki Industry, where there were separate staff and worker unions, and had concluded the two-union structure was a failure. He felt that staff brains and worker brawn would be a powerful combination. Yet he also recalls that when he "first went around the yard promoting a union [in September], the staff was cool to the idea. Then [in December] they suddenly got excited about it, and soon they were in control of the union. This probably reflected the social situation of those days, but the union was completely dominated by the staff after its founding, and I did feel somewhat burned by this."[34]

On the other side, the motives and reasoning of Nakajima and his white-collar allies were complex. They seem to have been moved by an intense belief that a union was necessary to ensure both personal survival and the survival of the company. Despite their relatively high status, they suspected the motives of top management and feared that if they did not take initiative, the company would form a useless captive union. Thus, in their view, men up to the level of section chief (*kachō*) were to be union

---

[32] Ibid., p. 8.
[33] Ibid.
[34] Ibid., p. 10.

members, since even the section chiefs were as economically
desperate as their subordinates.[35] Matsuda claims that Nakajima
never preferred a separate staff union, but initially felt the workers' animosity toward staff would almost certainly rule out a single union. By Matsuda's recollection, in the late fall Nakajima
learned of a management plan to form a union amenable to its
guidance, under the leadership of a section chief in the labor section. Convinced of the need to head off such a yellow union,
Nakajima and his staff buddies suddenly approached the workers
in late December.[36]

For roughly two days, an intense argument took place. On the
second day, the blue-collar leaders met separately and decided to
accept a joint union on the condition that it make "unity of worker
and staff statuses" and abolition of status discrimination top priorities. The staff group agreed to this. For the blue-collar men, one
key aspect of this discrimination was the ceiling that made foreman (kumichō) the highest supervisory position open to a man
hired as a "worker."[37]

Despite this agreement, detailed preparations remained conten-
tious. Debates carried over into the new year concerning the ratio
of staff to workers among delegates to the union assembly.
Should this be regulated (i.e., separate elections for delegates from
the two groups), or should candidacy be open to all? Finally a
decision was taken that delegates would be elected in a ratio of
one for each twenty employees, by work group, with no restriction
on the status of candidates, but this issue cast a long shadow. In
the words of the union's *Ten-Year History* it "left a sort of tumor"
that was not eliminated for years. Finally, on January 15, 1946, a
section chief and union official, Aoki Fujio, presided over a grand
founding ceremony in the workers' dining hall attended by fifteen
hundred union members.[38] Eight of the twelve members of the
union's first executive committee were white-collar staff.

---

[35] Section chiefs in fact were union members until October 1946, when a contract
was concluded that set the ceiling at assistant section chief (kakari-chō).

[36] Fujiwara Kenzō, the labor section chief accused of this by Matsuda, denied he
was involved in such a plot (interview, Dec. 1, 1992). He said he only wanted to
see a non-Communist union and felt the best way to ensure this was to have
white-collar people on it, so that he welcomed Nakajima's effort.

[37] Matsuda interview (Oct. 23, 1992), Kamimura interview (Oct. 14, 1992), and *Jū
nen no ayumi*, p. 8, all mention the imposition of this condition.

[38] *Jū nen no ayumi*, pp. 10, 11.

Two summary points can be made concerning this extended story of the Kawasaki mill union's founding. First, although the attitudes of men such as Kamimura dramatically reveal an antagonistic class "disposition" or "consciousness" rooted in common experiences of discrimination and difficult, dangerous work conditions, this consciousness did not lead NKK employees to draw a clear organizational line between "worker" and "manager." While they debated at length the divisive issue of admitting white-collar staff to the union, they opted for an inclusive organization.[39] And they hardly discussed problems that might arise from having the union embrace supervisors and supervisees from within the worker category.

Kamimura recalls that the preparatory committee members were overwhelmingly ranked men: foremen, subforemen, crew bosses. Although they had little formal management power, these men had considerable informal day-to-day authority concerning work assignments and discipline, and they advised staff on performance of subordinates and candidates for promotion or pay raises. On the other hand, most of these man had in common with unranked workers a rural upbringing and limited (elementary) education. They had typically spent ten to fifteen years as unranked workers before promotion. Their humble origins seem to have combined with seniority and skill to give them legitimacy among their subordinates as both fellow workers and leaders. This perception allowed the ranked men to mobilize collective action on the basis of a sort of working-class consciousness.

While these workplace bosses (and their subordinates) deeply resented the privileges of white-collar staff, their supervisory role also seems to have given them an ambiguous sense of who was on the other side. In the face of intensive and evidently sincere appeals by the white-collar group, they accepted the proposal for a "joint" union of white and blue collar, so long as the union committed itself to seeking a less discriminatory workplace order. Rather than organize a union that would crystallize a division

---

[39] Debate on the matter of separate or united blue- and white-collar unions was widespread at this time, and in some cases, such as at the nation's largest steel mill, at Yawata, separate unions were formed. But almost without exception, such separate unions began to work closely together in short order and eventually merged. On the Yawata case, see Michael H. Gibbs, "The Labor Movement at the Yawata Steel Works, 1945–1957" (Ph.d. dissertation, University of California, Berkeley, 1990).

between positions of "worker" and "manager," they agreed to use the union to seek to erase this division.

Second, in the process of creating their unions, NKK workers made clear the importance of the workplace as the focus of their community. Workers in other societies have often organized unions on the basis of categories or units other than the workplace, such as the trade, but I found no trace of debate among NKK workers of the appropriate organizing unit. It struck union founders at both Tsurumi and Kawasaki as so "natural" to create factory unions comprised of workshop locals that they never discussed the relative merits of other organizing principles, such as craft or regional organization.

It is important to distinguish these factory-based unions from the enterprise-based unions that later emerged. The organization of workers by factory did not signal effective integration of the hopes of workers and the goals of executives at corporate headquarters, although it did not rule out such integration in the future. The key points are that workshop and factory were seen by union organizers as the significant social and economic foci of the members' lives and that this view led unions to concern themselves with a wide range of managerial issues.[40]

Equality and the Status System

Following up on the commitment made when blue-collar men accepted the white-collar staff into the union, both the Tsurumi and Kawasaki unions addressed the "status discrimination" issue concretely and aggressively beginning in mid-1946. But this divisive problem was not easily or quickly resolved.

The heart of the matter was the NKK wage structure. As before and during the war, the manner of calculating wages for worker and staff remained fundamentally different in 1946. The former received a combination of a "daily wage" and an output premium, the latter a monthly base salary plus allowances. This difference was amplified by the fact that bonuses and retirement pay were both calculated as a multiple of the base wage. Also, although both staff (such as section managers) and workers in supervisory positions (foreman and crew bosses) received "rank

---

[40] Nimura Kazuo, "Nihon rōshi kankei no rekishiteki tokushitsu" [Special historical features of Japanese labor-management relations], in Shakai seisaku gakkai, ed., *Nihon no rōshi kankei no tokushitsu* [Special features of Japan's labor-management relations] (Tokyo: Ochanomizu shobō, 1987), p. 91.

allowances," the staff allowances were far higher.

Some in the union favored the more radical step of abolishing the separate categories of "worker" and "staff" themselves, placing everybody in a single new category such as "employee," with a uniform wage structure. Others would keep the two categories but make the structure and the level of wages the same for workers and staff. Although the dynamics of decision making within the union and negotiating between union and company on this issue are murky, it appears that some combination of company resistance to the more radical former step and continued antagonism and social distance between workers and staff within the union kept negotiations focused on the latter course.

At the time of the union's founding, the head of the planning division (a white-collar employee) began working on a proposal to reform the status system. The union history notes that the issue's "complexity" slowed completion of this proposal.[41] We should certainly read "complexity" to mean sharp division inside the union between staff and worker over what "equality" or "abolition of the status system" meant in practice.

Thus, when the Kawasaki union presented its first wage demands, in February 1946, it did not mention the status system. Wage negotiations proceeded within the framework of separate wage structures for staff and operatives.[42] Not until a little more than a year later did the union raise the wage and status issues together. Negotiations were conducted on the union side by a newly formed "NKK union federation" (*rengōkai*) bargaining on behalf of all the company's plant or mill unions. In April 1947 this federation demanded an increase in the average worker's monthly income from 1,500 to 2,700 yen, a new wage structure that would eliminate almost all supplementary allowances and fold that money into the base wage, and an end to the "status system." Three concrete demands were made concerning this last issue: eliminate the statuses of *shokuin* and *kōin*, create a unified wage structure, and adopt a monthly salary system for both staff and worker. That the first and third demands potentially contradict one another suggests the union had not reached a consensus on the matter. In addition, the federation demanded that blue-collar workers be allowed to elect their foremen and crew bosses.[43]

---

[41] *Jū nen no ayumi*, p. 71.

[42] Ibid., p. 236.

[43] Ibid., p. 239.

Despite these demands, the major issue by far in spring 1947 was the amount of the pay raise. NKK's initial offer was for a 2,000-yen average wage, but the union effectively threatened a strike and won a 2,300-yen average wage by the end of May. But the status issue was not resolved, and the union accepted continued separate wage structures for staff and worker.[44]

In these years of intense inflation, basic wage levels were negotiated at least twice a year by most unions. At NKK the fall 1947 negotiations began just four months after the spring round ended. The bargaining was a repeat of the spring round in that the union demanded both a pay raise and a "unified wage structure" that would eliminate separate worker and staff statuses. But the situation differed in that a group of radical young workers in the Kawasaki mill pushed the mill union leadership to change tactics considerably. Bargaining was carried out by the Kawasaki mill union, not the NKK federation, and to better reflect rank-and-file sentiment, a "struggle committee" of fifteen workplace representatives, including six Communist Party members, was elected to lead the dispute. The committee organized a vigorous drive from below in support of the demands. To bring union leaders physically closer to the rank and file, negotiations were held at the mill, not at NKK's corporate headquarters. The mill's electric workers rigged up microphones to broadcast progress of negotiations to workers outside the meeting room, a scene that probably provided the model for Orii's recollection of the "unimaginable" tension of early postwar labor-management relations.[45]

The Kawasaki union ended up compromising weakly on the wage demand, in late November finally accepting an offer that it had earlier rejected as grossly inadequate. This left the young left-wing leaders of the union's struggle committee furious with the cautious senior leadership. But negotiations continued over the status and wage structures, and in the settlement reached in March 1948, union and company agreed on a common wage structure for *shokuin* and *kōin*. In it, the base wage would be paid to all employees as a monthly wage. At the same time, the workforce would continue to be divided into categories of "worker" and "staff," and the level of the base wage as well as various allowances still reflected this difference.[46] This was basically the

---

[44] Ibid., pp. 49, 239.
[45] Ibid., p. 53.
[46] Ibid., pp. 54–56, 241.

system that remained in place until the 1960s.

That the status issue had been and remained deeply controversial is illustrated best in a strange brouhaha over status designation for a small group of workers that surfaced in the summer of 1948, six months after this settlement. In March 1946, soon after its founding, the Kawasaki union, as part of its strategy to abolish the status system, had demanded that all new hires for positions where blue- and white-collar workers were engaged in identical tasks at the same work site be enrolled as blue-collar workers and paid blue-collar wages, no matter what their education levels. Probably because it was hiring almost no one in any case, the company had agreed.[47] For more than two years resentment at this policy had simmered among a small group of newly hired men who were placed in the "worker" category even though they were graduates of technical schools and universities. They submitted petitions asking the union's executive committee to push the company to redesignate them as white-collar staff.

For reference, the executive committee looked into policy at other mills. At Yawata, the company had abolished the old categories and made everyone an "employee" (*shain*), but then divided workers into "day-wage employees" and "monthly-wage employees," a transparent sleight-of-hand that reportedly had lowered morale among blue-collar men. At Kawasaki, the issue was formally raised in July 1948 at a tumultuous union assembly dominated by angry denunciations of the executive committee: "Have you forgotten our founding slogan: abolish the status system?" Those who agreed with the petition for a status upgrade argued for something like the Yawata solution: "What's wrong with designating people as 'staff'? If it's a problem, let's make everyone staff, with subdivision of office staff, operative staff, technical staff." Or "the designation 'staff' no longer connotes superiority" and "those who do staff work should get staff pay." Opponents argued that this step contradicted the overall goal of eliminating the status system and discrimination. The matter was put to a vote in mid-August, at a second union assembly, with a bare majority of 164 to 152 in favor of requesting the upgrade. The company eventually accepted this demand. The *Ten-Year History* called this the "end" of the status issue.[48] I rather read it as a clear sign that differential treatment and status designations

---

[47] This is the reason Matsuda Takezo offers. Interview, Nov. 17, 1992.

[48] *Jū nen no ayumi*, pp. 71–72.

remained attractive to those with higher education and repugnant to the blue-collar men. For years thereafter, addressing this emotional issue would remain crucial to efforts of both union and company to win the contest for the workplace.

The union thus moved in fits and starts to bring equality to the workplace by reforming the status system. We can see in the contention between blue and white collar a horizontally structured sentiment of "us versus them" that contradicts Nakane's presentation of Japan as a vertically organized society. Yet the solution toward which the union seems to be moving is to reconstitute all regular male workers into a new community that would almost inevitably erase the class "disposition" of these early postwar days.[49]

Survival, Salt-making, and Weddings

The union's founders viewed the workplace and factory as the natural units for organizing. In addition, the workplace was a site for numerous activities to enable employees to survive these desperate years. Although hundreds of NKK workers simply left the mill to fend for themselves on the black market or return to a rural home where food was available, the workplace was arguably the most important source of social identity for those who remained and became the core of the NKK workforce when recovery began.

The nation's food crisis reached its peak between May 1946 and the following April. Deliveries of rations to the cities were chronically late, and workers were taking unauthorized leaves to barter for food in the countryside. Like the union at Tsurumi and others throughout the city, the Kawasaki mill union set up a Committee to Overcome the Food Crisis, headed by its president, Matsumoto Sakae, and vice-president, Suzuki Sōichirō. In cooperation with the company's Welfare Section, this committee began the risky enterprise of trading on the black market. The committee also secured permission from the mill director to

---

[49] At the same time, the union was relatively passive about bringing workers ranked below the "regular" level into this community. Temporary workers were not admitted as members of the union, and at both Kawasaki and Tsurumi the temporary workers organized their own separate unions. When the numbers of temporary workers climbed sharply in the early 1950s, the "regular" union worked with these groups to demand the "upgrade" of temporaries to regular status, with some success. *Jū nen no ayumi*, p. 211. *Tsurutetsu rōdō undō shi*, pp. 479–81.

manufacture salt on the premises. Workers formed teams to raise seawater and boil it down in the mill's gigantic kettles. In an incentive system devised by the union (suggesting that workers were not opposed to incentive wages in all circumstances), workers were given salt rations in proportion to team output, and they traded these for food on the black market.[50]

The committee also negotiated with the company for paid "food supply" holidays, which workers used for travel to the countryside to barter for food. Cooperation between company and union was no doubt facilitated by the fact that an assistant section chief in the personnel section was head of the union's personnel section local. He arranged for the planting of crops on unused company land, and he distributed coked coal and other company supplies to union locals, to be given to workers as bartering material. Suzuki Sōichirō contacted farmers' cooperatives along the nearby Tama River in 1946 and arranged for the union to exchange pumping equipment for food. He recalls shedding tears of gratitude when these co-ops donated cartloads of potatoes during the strike later that year. Union president Matsumoto recalled that local gossips called Kawatetsu "not a steel mill but the Kawasaki Salt Mine."[51]

Virtually all steel mills in Japan produced salt in 1946 and 1947, and the economics of bartering could be complex. At Tsurumi, except for two shops making buckets, pots, and pans, the entire workforce was engaged in salt making in mid-1946. Some of the product was given to the electric company to pay for power, some was sold to the Japan Salt Monopoly (by law, *all* salt was to be sold through this monopoly), and the rest was distributed to the workers. The union even paid visiting lecturers in salt![52]

In addition to a Food Crisis Committee, the Tsurumi union had its own Welfare Section. This body supervised the gathering of shellfish and seaweed from the bay. It negotiated salt-for-sweet-potato "exchange rates" with farmers, begged Kanagawa authorities for permission to import food from another prefecture, and (illegally) traded steel barrels for rice with a village agricultural cooperative in Niigata. In this last instance, a rival agricultural association leaked information on the deal to the press. Headlines

---

[50] *Jū nen no ayumi*, pp. 17–18.

[51] Ibid., pp. 18, 24.

[52] *Tsurutetsu rōdō undō shi*, pp. 87–88.

screamed of "NKK Black Marketeering," and a union member was jailed briefly for violating the economic control laws.[53]

These episodes are signs of the nation's general regression from a money toward a barter economy between 1945 and 1947. They also point to links between farmers and workers with interesting political implications. Sometimes these developed in the radical direction of union-controlled circuits of production and exchange, as in a case involving exchanges among workers at chemical plants in Niigata and in Tokyo; farmer associations in Niigata, Tohoku, and Hokkaido; and coal miners.[54] In Kawasaki, the labor-farmer connections were as yet limited to serving the cause of survival, with occasional gestures of solidarity, but the union role in setting up bartering networks was nonetheless unprecedented.

Another sign that NKK steelmakers saw the mill as their community was that the union pressed the company for a "ceremony fund" to provide marriage, birth, and funeral allowances. As at virtually all unions, Kawatetsu (which employed a small number of female office workers) had formed a "women and youth division" at the time of the union's founding. In August 1947 this group took the lead in drawing up its own proposal for a "marriage allowance." The NKK union federation then began negotiating in earnest for a more comprehensive schedule of marriage, childbirth, and funeral allowances, as well as paid leave on such occasions. A first agreement was reached in November 1947, but inflation soon rendered the allowances nominal. The levels were renegotiated the following summer, and the group of eligible workers was expanded to those with at least one year, instead of two years, of employment.[55]

All these activities suggest how strongly the NKK workers connected their personal fate with the survival of the mill. It is thus no surprise that a rhetoric of cooperation and common interest surfaced even at moments of harsh conflict. One is struck at such times by effective pleas from union leaders as well as managers for cooperation, mutual sacrifice, and sincerity. Although to some extent these were no doubt calculated appeals to emotionally resonant themes, it is hard to dismiss them as nothing more than

---

[53] Ibid., pp. 82–87.

[54] Moore, *Japanese Workers*, pp. 156–60.

[55] *Jū nen no ayumi*, pp. 72–73. Also, important account of youth and women's activities on pp. 219–34.

this. Even Communist Party activists at the Tsurumi mill responded to convincing displays of proper "attitude" and "sincerity" by management negotiators. In bargaining over the 1946 year-end bonus, the Tsurumi union broke off talks in fury at the haughty attitude of one executive, while in simultaneous negotiations over a pay raise, it agreed to a compromise when leaders were convinced that mill director Tanaka had indeed "endeavored to the ultimate degree" to offer as much as the mill could afford.[56]

Thus, the NKK steel mills at Kawasaki and Tsurumi, with their separate plant unions, and the workshops within them, constituted as union locals, were sites of far more than bargaining over the exchange of labor for wages. They were home to intense struggle over terms of membership in a community. Blue-collar men vented fury at the arrogance, domination, and privileged status of white-collar staff and sought to remake the workplace hierarchy. Staff officials were drawn to the union out of their economic insecurity as well as distrust of the motives and ability of top management. In this context, union organizers sought to improve work conditions and reform personnel practices. They also wanted the union to act as at least an equal partner with management in implementing a strategy for the survival of the steel mill and the recovery of the economy.

The Contract Dispute at Kawasaki

The platform of the Kawasaki union, adopted in January 1946, exemplified the Sōdōmei view of such a partnership. It proclaimed the "principle of the mutual prosperity of labor and capital" as the guiding spirit of the contract the union hoped to conclude. The platform then spoke of "raising our skill, increasing our efficiency" to "dramatically increase steel production, the motor of national reconstruction," and went on to faithfully echo a union rhetoric reaching back to the eve of World War I: "We hope to build a healthy workers' culture by raising our social status and forging our character (*jinkaku*) in a spirit of freedom, equality, fraternal love, and by enlightening ourselves and perfecting our skills."[57]

The first wage demands raised by this group reflected a similar, carefully calibrated moderation. On February 8, 1946, the

---

[56] *Tsurutetsu rōdō undō shi*, pp. 142–45.
[57] *Jū nen no ayumi*, p. 13.

Kawasaki union presented and "won" a demand for a 200 percent average pay raise, just two weeks after the Tsurumi mill union's production control tactic had forced NKK managers to grant a 300 percent wage hike. The Kawasaki union reportedly accepted the company's contention that the Tsurumi settlement had been so costly that NKK could afford no more than this for Kawasaki mill workers. In negotiating sessions, union representatives spoke of "our burning love of company which is the true reason for presenting these demands for improved pay to protect our livelihoods" and claimed, in a neat reversal of paternal rhetoric where the company was usually the loving father, "We love the company as we love our wives and our children. Please [grant this raise] so we can revive Japan from this tragic condition."[58] As one might expect, Tsurumi and other radical unions denounced NKK Kawasaki as a co-opted "company union."[59]

Given this reputation, the Kawasaki union's successful week-long strike in October 1946 drew national attention and surprise. The strike serves first as an important example of a Sōdōmei union's potential for nonradical militance. The willingness of the Kawasaki workers to risk this strike cautions us to read the above proclamations of loyalty at least in part as instrumental, conditional statements, rhetorical strategies to elicit material support and win social respect. Second, the issue of the strike was not wages but the terms of the union contract with management, and the union's stance confirms that workers across the ideological spectrum were seeking at least an equal voice with management in planning for economic recovery.

In spring 1946 the Kawasaki union formed a committee to plan its contract demands in line with Sōdōmei guidelines. A union assembly ratified these demands on August 19, and they were presented to management, but the negotiations stalled. The company objected adamantly to two of the most important clauses in the union's proposed contract: article one, stipulating a closed shop, and article three, giving the union a veto over any company decisions to fire, hire, transfer, reward, or punish workers. Company negotiators objected that such a contract signed away their

---

[58] Ibid.

[59] Nihon rōdō sōdōmei, *Sōdōmei go jū nen shi* [Fifty-year history of Sōdōmei] (Tokyo: Taiyō, 1962), pp. 129–30; and Rōdō sōgi chōsa kai, ed., *Sengo rōdō sōgi jittai chōsa: Tekkō sōgi* [Field surveys of postwar labor disputes: Steel industry] (Tokyo: Chūō kōronsha, 1958), 7:107–112, for information in this paragraph.

fundamental "personnel authority." They promised instead to "consult" on such decisions and take disputed cases to an in-house "management council" composed of company and union representatives.[60] With no sign of movement, the union prepared for a strike. A final company offer conceded a veto on the transfer and firing decisions, except for section chiefs, but the union refused this "because section chiefs are also union members."[61]

The strike began on October 4. The two sides immediately quarreled over who bore responsibility for protecting the furnaces and blame for impeding "recovery," but the strikers managed to shut the furnace down without damage. The key sticking point remained the position of section chiefs. The union issued a "Declaration by Section Chiefs" to the effect that "we recognize the need to be on the union side." Union negotiators claimed that because the union stood for "mutual prosperity of company and union," there was nothing to fear in having section chiefs in the union. The company insisted it had given away too much already in its desire to avoid a strike. On October 9 a mediator from the newly created Regional Labor Mediation Committee (Chirōi) proposed (1) that disagreements on closed-shop issues be brought to an outside "labor committee" and (2) that the company accept a union veto on firing and transfer cases, but not in hiring, rewards, or punishments. Both sides agreed to the first proposal, but the union held to its original demand on the second point. Sometime past midnight, management agreed that the union would have a veto on general policy concerning hiring, rewards, and punishments, but not in individual cases. The union accepted this.[62]

Justifiably enough, the Kawasaki mill union leaders presented this settlement to the union members as a great victory, and the union assembly happily ratified the agreement. The *Ten-Year History* boasts of the members' pride in having repudiated the label of "yellow union." One worker in the research section grandly proclaimed that "harmony without struggle is the road to death. Harmony backed by struggle is the great ideal." The statement neatly captures the militant tone that lay under the surface of the "cooperative" unionism of this era.[63]

---

[60] *Jū nen no ayumi*, pp. 25–27. The account of the strike relies mainly on this source. Other accounts, which are essentially identical (and usually derived from this source, with or without acknowledgment), can be found in *Sōdōmei go jū nen shi*, pp. 133–34, and *Tekkō sōgi*, 107–12.

[61] *Jū nen no ayumi*, p. 28.

[62] *Sōdōmei go jū nen shi*, p. 134; *Jū nen no ayumi*, p. 29.

[63] *Jū nen no ayumi*, p. 30.

Recovery Councils and Labor-Management Councils

Together with such contracts, entities called Recovery Councils at the national level and Management Discussion Councils at the company and plant levels were forums in which unions articulated their wish to share in the management of the economy and the enterprise. In the spring of 1946, the Sōdōmei called for a Movement for Industrial Recovery to Overcome the Production Crisis, in which unions would participate in corporate and national economic planning to the ends of "democratizing industry" and realizing a "planned economy." Over the next six months, Sōdōmei and the new business federation of Japan's young, so-called Reform Capitalists (Keizai Dōyūkai) worked out an agreement on plans for an Economic Recovery Council. For Sōdōmei, the council was a step toward union participation in economic planning. For the Keizai Dōyūkai, it was a means to build a "reformed capitalism" of a high-wage, high-productivity economy, avoiding strikes through cooperative labor-management relations.[64]

The leaders of the much larger Sanbetsu Federation, on the left wing of the early postwar labor movement, warily observed these negotiations. Sanbetsu's vision of "recovery" was far more radical: workers would participate in a recovery controlled by "laborers, scientists, and technicians." With considerable misgivings, Sanbetsu made a strategic, temporary peace with capitalists, joining the council as a means to strengthen the hegemony of labor unions, building toward ultimate victory in a class struggle. Its premise was utterly at odds with the cooperative program of the Sōdōmei, not to mention the Keizai Dōyūkai.[65]

Three strange bedfellows thus came together on February 6, 1947, to found the Economic Recovery Council. At the apex of a complex structure stood a national council with a central committee of delegates from member organizations, an executive committee, and various specialized planning and policy committees, carefully balanced between union and industry representatives. Below this stood prefectural and industrial recovery councils. By October 1947, twenty-one prefectural and twenty-two industrial

---

[64] Hayakawa Seiichirō and Yoshida Kenji, "Keizai fukkō kaigi no soshiki to undō, 1" [The organization and movement of the Economic Recovery Council, part 1], *Hōsei daigaku Ōhara shakai mondai kenkyū jo kenkyū shiryō geppō*, no. 283 (February 1982): 3, 6.

[65] Ibid., p. 14.

bodies had been established. Twenty-nine industrial federations and twelve union federations joined the council, as did seventy-six individual corporations and a handful of factory-based unions. In theory at least, Management Discussion Councils at the company or plant level were to be the basic building blocks of the edifice, or, to switch metaphors, the motors pushing recovery ahead. The organizational pyramid was remarkably similar to that of the wartime Industrial Patriotic Association, with the important exception that almost no bureaucrats sat on the national or local committees. The council sought to influence state policy via discussions with government ministers and vice-ministers and presentation of formal policy proposals.

Despite this activity, the council had accomplished little at the time of its dissolution in April 1948.[66] This "recovery movement" is important to us not for its achievements, but as a sign of the immediate postwar aspiration of national union leaders for a voice in economic policy making. An important sign of similar aspirations at the local level, which probably left a more significant legacy, is the ubiquity of company- and factory-based Management Discussion Councils. Almost all labor contracts negotiated in the immediate postwar era, including those concluded by NKK's Kawasaki and Tsurumi mill unions, provided for creation of these councils, typically composed of equal numbers of worker and company representatives, the former chosen by the union.[67] These bodies were authorized to discuss wages and other work conditions, production, company finances, and management planning. In most cases, issues brought before the councils required majority approval, giving unions huge formal power. The impulse to participate that we see in the demand for such bodies has remained a central part of Japanese labor-management relations, however transmuted, for decades.

A striking attempt to use such a council to set up a virtual shadow management structure took place at the Tsurumi mill in 1948. A hint of the union's ambition appeared when the company refused any bonus during year-end negotiations in 1947 that dragged on into January 1948. The Tsurumi union eventually

---

[66] "Keizai fukkō kaigi, 2," no. 284 (March 1982): 3–12, on organizational structure; pp. 19–20 on activities. "Keizai fukkō kaigi, 3," no. 292 (December 1982): 1–9, on dissolution.

[67] Nishinarita Yutaka, "Senryōki Nihon no rōshi kankei" [Labor-capital relations in Japan under occupation], in *Nihon no kindai to shihonshugi* [Japan's modernity and capitalism], ed. Nakamura Masanori (Tokyo: Tokyo University Press, 1992), p. 209.

broke off talks and announced it would find the money itself. The union announced it would investigate the company's relations to its suppliers to expose unnecessary entertainment expenses, and it ordered workplace locals to survey material use to expose waste and hidden goods. As these investigations proceeded through the month of February, managers apparently panicked, and on March 6 they agreed to pay a bonus.[68]

Building on this momentum, on March 15 the union announced a "Draft for a Movement to Revive Production." Movement goals were reviving production "by and for workers"; protecting jobs in the process of recovery; and ensuring a "fair" division of profits among labor, management, and capital, while strengthening discipline at work. To this end, the movement was to involve three types of activity: (1) business decisions on product mix, production volume, marketing, purchasing, quality; (2) personnel management initiatives to raise morale and increase efficiency (improved discipline, awards for efficient use of materials); (3) "rationalized" operations and improved work conditions (wages) to remove "obstacles to production."

The structure in which the union hoped to take these actions is shown in figure 1. In essence, to be able to make effective use of the Management Discussion Council, the union was setting up its own managerial structure, in political terms an opposition party's shadow cabinet: production council, management council, and labor-management subcouncil, as well as workplace councils.[69] The draft was adopted as union policy in April and remained in effect through August. But in the apt words of the union history, "In fact, amidst continuous struggles, the union could not implement this program. Rather [the episode] tells us how aggressive the union's attitude was, at that time, to revive production to improve work conditions."[70]

The long-run implications of this abortive endeavor were important. The core concept of this movement, that the union should act to raise, even rationalize, production and fairly distribute the fruits to labor, management, and capital, is virtually identical to that of the management-led "productivity movement" of the 1950s, a drive that unions such as NKK's would resist fiercely. For union leaders, the issue was not "rationalization" as such, but

---

[68] *Tsurutetsu rōdō undō shi,* pp. 150–51.

[69] Ibid., pp. 151–53.

[70] Ibid., p. 154.

Figure 1: Union plan for the organization of the Production Recovery Movement at Nippon Kōkan, Tsurumi Steel Mill, 1948

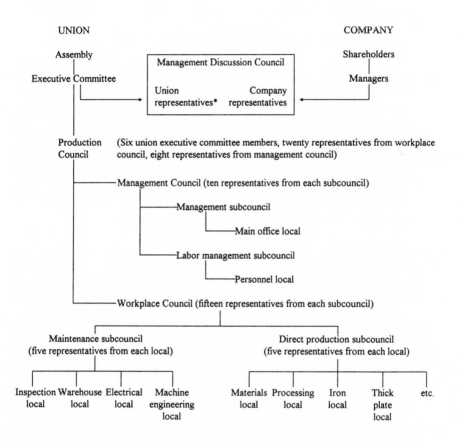

* Union representatives to this body organized into a "policy committee" of sixteen members (seven executive committee members, nine production council members) with specialized subcommittees.

Source: Adapted from Nippon kōkan tsurumi seitetsujo rōdō kumiai, ed., *Tsurutetsu rōdō undō shi* (Tokyo 1956), p. 153.

control of the process. For many rank-and-file members, the opportunity to share in the fruits of recovery or increased production might have been attractive whether proposed by this union in 1948 or a management federation in 1955.

At Kawasaki, the union's position on economic recovery was less grand, but nonetheless significant. The focus of Kawatetsu's Economic Recovery Movement was the brand-new, undamaged Number 5 Blast Furnace, completed in 1944 but never fired. In February 1947, just days after the union's parent Sōdōmei federation had inaugurated the Economic Recovery Council, union locals in four workshops petitioned the union executive committee: the furnace was in perfect condition, needing only the go-ahead from authorities to start up, so the union should push to start it.

In the ensuing weeks, the union convened rallies to build public support, and for about a year it worked with NKK management and the Kawasaki city council to lobby the Ministries of Commerce and Labor, the Economic Stablization Board, and other authorities. Permission was finally granted in early 1948, and seven hundred guests from the Japanese government, SCAP, and the local community attended a grand firing ceremony on April 1. Although it is not clear how much credit the movement deserves for the decision to start the furnace, the relevant point is that the union placed great importance on such activity.[71]

From the outset of the recovery movement, the leaders of the Sanbetsu federation cautioned that giving excessive priority to recovery played into management hands by constraining demands for better conditions. In the drive to start the Kawasaki furnace, the union indeed called not only for cooperation but for sacrifice for the sake of recovery.[72] But at a time when NKK's union leaders could realistically imagine they might hold the upper hand in reviving the firm and the industry, or at least have a voice equal to management's, such cautions apparently were unconvincing. A speech by the blue-collar leader Takeda Ryusuke on the eve of the drive to start the blast furnace nicely conveys the spirit that moved the Kawasaki union:

> Industrial recovery and increased production are the only ways to save the Japanese race (*minzoku*) from destruction. We are proud that steel is Japan's star industry (*hanagata*), and NKK is a cham-

---

[71] *Jū nen no ayumi*, pp. 40–43.

[72] Ibid., p. 43, for one example of union willingness to "make considerable demands on its members" to speed up the timetable for firing the furnace.

pion of steel. We have already created a management discussion council and made it into a decision-making, not advisory, body. *We are not merely hired hands as in the past. With an awareness of ourselves as participants in management, we are determined to bring about recovery by the hands of the workers themselves.*[73]

Conclusion: The Disappearance of the Working Class in Comparative Perspective

The postwar history of labor in Japan has at least three important general features in common with the postwar histories of "enterprise societies" across the advanced capitalist world. First, early postwar Japanese were tremendously uncertain about the prospects for capitalist survival, not to mention hegemony. In this respect, the Japanese case has much in common with European postwar history. Visions of apocalypse (or deliverance) were common in Japan not only in the immediate postsurrender turbulence, but well into the 1950s. NKK's union publications of these years occasionally advertised the collected works of Stalin and published surveys of international steel production showing the Soviet Union running neck and neck with Japan.[74]

The ads for Stalin disappeared in the mid-1950s, and in the 1960s new production graphs began to appear, showing the Japanese line first catching, then surpassing, the lines of Britain, West Germany, and then the United States. Thus, a second common feature is that in all these nations, but especially in Japan and the United States, expectations of capitalist demise and uncertainty about the viability or desirability of a capitalist future gave way to a hegemony of the values and goals of the corporation and the penetration of these into the body politic, the system of education, and the mass media. In both these ways, then, Japan's postwar history is a particularly "postwar capitalist" story more than a peculiarly "Japanese" one.

Third, Japan's postwar experience is part of a global history in that workplaces in Japan, as elsewhere, were sites of distinct social worlds where the workers' customary expectations and practices (in other words, experience and disposition) differed from, and sometimes opposed, those of corporate managers. During the decade of the 1950s, a time of intensive technological innovation

---

[73] Ibid., p. 39. Emphasis added.
[74] *Kawatetsu shinbun*, January 1, 1955, p. 1; July 18, 1955, pp. 3–4.

in Japan's steel industry, this parallel experience continued. Tensions abounded between managers pushing to control the workplace in new ways and employees hoping to protect customary work routines, resenting or fearing new forms of evaluation, complaining about some divisions among workers (staff vs. blue-collar) while accepting others (regular vs. temporary).

To recognize these common experiences is important, especially in the face of the contemporary onslaught of exceptionalist portrayals of Japanese uniqueness, given legitimacy by the academic work of Nakane, Murakami, and others. But it is not enough to dismiss such portrayals and end with a banal conclusion that life was and is essentially the same across the industrial or postindustrial world. Early postwar uncertainty was surely greater in Japan and Europe than in North America. In their own way, both the United States and Japan then came to harbor extreme versions of the enterprise society, in contrast to Europe, where social democracy sank deeper roots, or the third world, including much of Asia, where capitalism was far more profoundly challenged.

And even in contrast to the U.S. version, postwar Japan's enterprise society came to be structured and viewed distinctively. Over the course of the postwar decades, despite tensions similar to those found elsewhere, Japanese came to integrate the social worlds of male employee and enterprise in a remarkably total fashion. In Japan, that is, although we do find evidence of a working-class "disposition" in which an informal sense of "us" and "them" (sometimes worker vs. staff, sometimes union vs. company) shaped an employee's behavior and view of the boss, this attitude was not durably linked to a radical or even a militant unionism in the private sector. Rather, the "us" of the workplace world came to be tightly integrated with the "us" of our company (and our company's union), against a "them" of other companies (or other unions).

This claim to some extent affirms the view of Nakane Chie cited at the outset: over the postwar decades, male workers in large private companies became unusually committed to corporate success. In comparison to other nations, they participated in corporate activities outside day-to-day work routines to an unusual extent. Unions participated in labor-management "consultation" (as opposed to bargaining) over a wide range of managerial issues. In addition, in later years millions of workers were drawn into small-group activities, such as quality circles, to increase productivity. In such activities, Japanese managers did not merely remove workers' "brains" through industrial engineering to simplify work.[75] Managers also maintained hegemony in the workplace by mobilizing worker brains toward corporate goals; they drew them into the analysis of work even as they imposed expert analysis upon them. How and why did this distinctive version of the enterprise society evolve? Put differently, why did class disappear?

In this essay, I have described three aspects of the thought and behavior of steelworkers that help explain the disappearance of class and the ascendance of the enterprise society. First, I have suggested that NKK's radical and militant unionists as much as loyal company men (and certainly the many who saw themselves as both militant and loyal) hardly ever viewed the workplace with the breezy detachment of their Anglo-American counterparts, as just a place to earn a wage; they rather saw it as a site for the creation of community and meaning in daily life.[76] As opposed to European or Chinese cases, where workers focused on trade association, neighborhood, church, or native place, Japan's unionists focused on the workplace as the center of their community. That all parties to the contest for control of the workplace gave priority to the need for the company to survive, if not prosper, helps explain how cooperative unions won the day; they could effectively point to a contradiction between this priority and the confrontational tactics of radical or militant unions.[77]

Second, the NKK story shows that unions of all stripes sought to be involved in a truly broad range of decisions, not only about wages or hours, but about operational matters and long-range planning. From the moment of their creation, unions sought "total involvement" in various initiatives that cut across the spectrum of ideology and the categories of "labor" and "management," a stance that created grounds for cooperation between managers

---

[75] Contrary to some simplistic views of Japan's quality control and production management, such rationalizing endeavors *were* part of the story, especially in the 1950s and 1960s.

[76] This is a contrast that has been made eloquently by Ronald Dore in *British Factory–Japanese Factory*, pp. 156, 201–21. But Dore looks only at the cooperative Hitachi union of the 1960s. The additional point of this paper is that even radical unions of the 1940s shared this "difference" vis-à-vis Dore's "British factory."

[77] It also helps explain why cooperative unions developed into something quite distinct from any U.S. model, even as they claimed to be drawing on an American pattern of postwar business unionism.

and union leaders. All participants thought they and their organizations should have responsibility for, and a voice concerning, the task of "reconstruction." Unions tried to shoulder or share managerial tasks, by taking over production in early labor disputes and later by joining "economic recovery councils" and "labor-management councils." Further, unions voiced their broadly conceived sense of mission by demanding control over personnel decisions in both contract bargaining and day-to-day activities. Although unions on the left and right differed about how strong a voice they demanded, they agreed that unions (and employees) ought to be concerned with such matters.

Third, we have seen dramatic evidence that steelworkers were deeply divided along the fault line of "worker" and "staff" employment categories but desired to bridge this gap more than to reinforce it. Workers struggled to decide where to set the boundaries of membership: Did white-collar staff (*shokuin*) need unions? Should they and production workers (*kōin*) have separate organizations or be united? If the latter, how high into white-collar ranks should the ceiling for union membership go? It is particularly significant that regardless of partisan affiliation, workers at NKK and all over Japan usually opted for unity and chose an extremely high ceiling for union membership. It is also important to recognize that such decisions were relatively autonomous ones, for this was a moment of minimal state or corporate power to constrain the workers and a time when the Americans would have accepted, indeed expected, a narrower, blue-collar unionism. The process by which the NKK union made this choice reveals both a sharp divide in practice along lines of white- and blue-collar status and a powerful belief that ideally all employees shared a common interest.

To explain the disappearance of class in postwar Japan as the result of such self-denying working-class dispositions of course begs a further, perilous question. Where did these dispositions come from in the first place? To some extent, they may have roots in social structures and ideas of the Tokugawa era. For example, intense concern with status and terms of membership in the enterprise motivated nineteenth-century disputes led by men who grew up in pre-Meiji days, and we have seen evidence of the ongoing centrality of these concerns in the postwar era. But I believe that two characteristics of Japan's modern historical experience are keys to answering this question. One cluster of causes of working-class self-denial falls under the rubric of the "late development effect" identified by Ronald Dore, the idea that the timing of a nation's industrialization and integration into the global economy influences a wide range of matters: the economic role of the state, the role and structure of corporations, characteristics of the labor market and labor movement, even social ideas and social policies. Of particular concern here is that the nation's "late developing" industry came of age when few Japanese possessed the technical or managerial skills demanded by the high-tech industries of the day. Beginning in the nineteenth century, this late development effect shaped the attitude of employers and employees, managers and unions, toward job switching, wages, skills, training, and retraining. It led managers to introduce programs of annual wage increments to induce scarce skilled workers to stay with a firm. It led workers to organize factory-based unions rather than community-based trade unions because relevant crafts were not widely spread in the community.

The legacy of World War II is the second relevant historical factor. Bombs demolished factories and cities, extraordinary inflation leveled differentials of wealth, and the occupation authorities initially planned to demand stiff war reparations. These circumstances fostered a widely felt belief that "we are all in this together," and this sense of common fate helps explain the distinctive decision of so many postwar unions, despite misgivings and opposition, to include white-collar workers as members.

Wartime devastation and postwar uncertainty also fostered an intense concern first with economic survival, then with recovery, causing unions of all stripes to worry about far more than wages and work conditions. Leaders and members of unions felt it "natural" to concern themselves with what managers were doing to revive production, to find new materials to replace colonial resources and new markets to replace military demand. Thus, a distinctive result of early postwar collective bargaining was the formation at the firm level of Management Discussion Councils in which unions claimed decision-making power, and at the industrial, regional, and national levels of various joint Recovery Councils. Union power on such bodies was never secure. Some councils quickly collapsed, while the mandate of others shrank drastically under management pressure. But the practice of labor-management consultation on a broad range of issues and the idea that such matters are the business of unions (an idea that was only weakly developed in prewar or wartime Japan) cut across the political spectrum and has persisted to this day.

All this said, we must quickly add that the persistently confrontational stance of a wide array of unions in Korea from the 1960s through the 1990s, described by Hagen Koo later in this book, immediately suggests that we proceed cautiously with this causal analysis. Korea, after all, is a late developer as well, and it too suffered a devastating midcentury war. These common factors leave us several choices. We can argue that they will eventually lead Korea further in a Japanese direction. We can deny that either late development or wartime and postwar devastation had much effect in either case. We can identify relevant differences in the Japanese and Korean experiences of either late development or midcentury devastation. Or we can identify other differences between the two cases that "overrode" these common factors, perhaps in the areas of managerial strategy or state policy.

This chapter and this volume may provide a point of departure for such a comparative inquiry. Any such investigation must recognize that the profound antagonism between "labor" and "management" in the early postwar era did not produce an enduring, oppositional working-class consciousness or movement. Rather, it provided categories that most parties to the contest for the workplace, for diverse reasons, sought to deny or erase.

TWO

Work, Culture, and Consciousness of the Korean Working Class

HAGEN KOO

The dominant theme in the writings on East Asian labor is its docility, its organizational weakness, and its exclusion from politics. Indeed, nowhere in capitalist East Asia can we find strong organized labor or a strong labor party. In these countries, as Deyo observes, "organized labor plays a politically marginal and insignificant role in national affairs. Labor organizations confront employers from a position of weakness in collective bargaining, industrial work stoppages are few and generally easily suppressed, and there is rarely more than symbolic labor participation in economic policy-making." This docility of labor, most scholars agree, has played a critical role in bringing rapid economic development in Taiwan, South Korea, Singapore, and Hong Kong. Yet rapid industrial growth in this region, as Deyo continues to note, "has not altered the weak political position of labor," and "labor movements in general remain controlled and inconsequential."[1]

Furthermore, when and where labor actions occur, they seldom express class conflicts or class interest. In her critical review of the ethnographic literature on factory women in Asian industrializing societies, Aihwa Ong concludes that these workers "rarely construct their identities or organize themselves in terms of collective or global interests." She further argues that "workers' struggles and resistances are often not based upon class interests or class solidarity, but comprise individual and even covert acts against various forms of control. The interest defended, or the

---

[1] Frederic Deyo, *Beneath the Miracle: Labor Subordination in the New Asian Industrialism* (Berkeley: University of California Press, 1989), pp. 3–5.

solidarity built, through such acts are [*sic*] more often linked to kinship and gender than to class."[2]

Given this generic East Asian model of weak labor movements and the insignificance of class, the South Korean labor situation clearly stands out as an anomaly. As both Deyo and Ong recognize, the pattern of the South Korean labor movement in recent decades clearly diverges from those of its neighboring countries. Although the overall level of industrial conflict in South Korea had been relatively low until the late 1980s, and although Korea's organized labor has been politically weak as in other East Asian societies, Korean workers have demonstrated a substantially higher level of mobilization and combativeness in confronting capital. Like Taiwan and Singapore, the South Korean state also sought to impose a corporatist industrial system with severe restrictions on labor organizations, but it could not be maintained as smoothly as in those places, largely because of virulent challenges from independent grassroots labor unions. Violent labor conflicts erupted whenever the government's grip on labor loosened a little, often causing unexpected political changes and modifications in the labor regime.

Class is also far from being inconsequential in South Korean society. In fact, South Korea is one of a few societies in the present world where class seems to be alive and well, screaming and kicking to become a major social force. Here we do not need to focus primarily on covert, "everyday forms of resistance" to uncover class actions, because there exists more obvious evidence that class is becoming a major category in interpreting and organizing people's lives and their relationships with others and with society.

The purpose of this essay is to describe how and why Korean industrial workers reacted to their experiences of proletarianization differently from their counterparts in other East Asian countries. To that end I describe the ways in which South Korean workers have adapted to, and reacted against, the world of the industrial proletariat, the ways in which they have forged a new sense of identity as "workers" (*nodongja*), and the ways in which they have recognized common class interest and struggled to defend this interest. I seek to demonstrate the important role played by culture and politics in the formation of the South

---

[2] Aihwa Ong, "The Gender and Labor Politics of Postmodernity," *Annual Review of Anthropology* 20 (1991): 269, 280.

Korean working class. One of the most interesting aspects of class formation in South Korea is the way in which culture has functioned simultaneously to inhibit and facilitate the development of working-class identity and solidarity. Politics and social movements played a critical role in determining exactly how culture would be appropriated for worker mobilization and consciousness raising. The exceptional quality of the South Korean working-class movement comes only partly from sources internal to the industrial system; political and cultural movements outside the industrial arena also exerted tremendous influence on the labor movement by providing necessary organizational, ideological, and personnel resources.

Work and Authority

The transition from a preindustrial to an industrial work setting requires more than a change of work site. As Thompson writes, it "entails a severe restructuring of working habits—new disciplines, new incentives, and a new human nature upon which these incentives could bite effectively."[3] This restructuring of working habits proved extremely frustrating to early industrialists in Europe and America.[4] The same was true for Japanese and Chinese capitalists at the early stage of industrialization.[5] Workers typically brought with them preindustrial work habits and cultural patterns that clashed with the imperatives of factory work. How to harness the irregular and undisciplined workers to the factory system was a main concern for manufacturers.

Equally troubling to early industrialists was the persistence of a powerful artisan culture, which demanded autonomy and dignity of work and refused to be subjugated to the regimented work routines in the factory. Artisans, as many historical studies have abundantly documented, provided the most potent source of protests against the factory system of production in Europe and

---

[3] E. P. Thompson, "Time, Work-Discipline, and Industrial Capitalism," *Past and Present* 38 (1967): 57.

[4] Herbert G. Gutman, *Work, Culture, and Society in Industrializing America* (New York: Vintage, 1977); an excellent review of other relevant references is provided in pp. 3–78 of this book.

[5] Andrew Gordon, *The Evolution of Labor Relations in Japan: Heavy Industry, 1853–1955* (Cambridge: Council on East Asian Studies, Harvard University, 1985); Gail Hershatter, *The Workers of Tianjin, 1900–1949* (Stanford, Calif.: Stanford University Press, 1986).

America.[6] The artisan culture also exerted a strong influence on
the evolution of industrial relations in Japan and China.[7]

In contrast, first-generation Korean industrial workers made a
relatively smooth transition to factory work.[8] Although the majority of them came from rural areas and had no prior experience of
industrial employment, a relatively high level of literacy and the
urban exposure helped them quickly to acquire new skills and
adjust to the rhythm of factory work. Unlike early manufacturers
in Europe and America, Korean employers did not have to fight
against the traditional customs, rituals, and beliefs the workers
brought with them from the countryside. On the contrary, Korean
capitalists used workers' traditional attitudes and personal relationships to their own advantage, exploiting these traits to develop
a despotic, patriarchal workplace.

The absence of a strong artisan culture in Korea facilitated
Korea's smooth transition to the factory system. Although artisans
did, of course, exist in nineteenth-century Korea, they neither
enjoyed a respectable status in society nor developed any strong
organizations or a distinct occupational culture. Korean workers
thus entered the new era of mass factory production without any
proud craft tradition or cohesive working-class community.
Largely as atomized individuals, with a fresh memory of economic
hardship in the countryside and a strong desire for a better life,
new Korean factory workers made a swift and smooth transition
to industrial labor.

[6] E. P. Thompson, *The Making of the English Working Class* (New York: Vintage
Books, 1963); William Sewell, Jr., *Work and Revolution in France: The Language of La-
bor from the Old Regime to 1848* (Cambridge: Cambridge University Press, 1980);
Ronald Aminzade, *Class, Politics, and Early Industrial Capitalism: A Study of Mid-
Nineteenth-Century Toulouse, France* (Albany, N.Y.: State University of New York
Press, 1981); Craig Calhoun, *The Question of Class Struggle: The Social Foundations of
Popular Radicalism during the Industrial Revolution* (Chicago: University of Chicago
Press, 1981).

[7] Gordon, *Labor Relations*; Elizabeth Perry, *Shanghai on Strike: The Politics of
Chinese Labor* (Stanford, Calif.: Stanford University Press, 1993).

[8] Strictly speaking, it may be incorrect to call them the first generation of factory
workers because their predecessors appeared in large numbers in the 1930s to meet
the demands of the Japanese war industry. But with the end of colonialism and
the demolition of war-related industries, this early generation of wage workers
more or less dissipated without a succeeding generation of industrial workers. Not
until the early 1960s did there emerge in South Korea a large group of factory
workers that was to be reproduced with a distinct occupational status and identity.

If these historical and demographic factors helped to create a productive and docile industrial labor force, it was the harsh working conditions and despotic work relations in Korean industry that began to trigger workers' protests from the mid-1960s. Though hard work was nothing new, the long hours and the intensity of factory work were more than the workers could endure, causing widespread health problems among even the young and agile. The early phase of industrialization has meant extremely poor working conditions for workers everywhere, but laborers in South Korean industry seem to have suffered an extra dose of bloody Taylorism in the 1960s and the 1970s. For instance, South Korea enjoys the dubious distinction of enforcing the world's longest workweek[9] and having one of its highest rates of industrial accidents. Even in the late 1970s, the most pressing problem for the majority of Korean factory workers was how to keep up with intense work schedules while maintaining their health.

Hard and wrenching as factory work was, there was an even more acute source of pain and resentment in the form of despotic and patriarchal authority. Korean work organizations are a product of both old Japanese colonial practices and contemporary military regimes. Both patterns of control are hierarchical, authoritarian, and violence prone.[10] Workers are constantly subjected to physical and verbal abuse by employers and managers, and women are especially vulnerable to patriarchal control and sexual harassment. Although the rhetoric of familism and family enterprise is often used in Korean factories, neither the industrialists nor the workers seem to take such rhetoric as seriously as seems to be the case in Japan.

Despotic authority in Korean firms respects no equality of relations between buyers and sellers of labor power, no contractual relationships, and no privacy or freedom over personal space. In most Korean firms, there is of course a fixed time to start but no definite time to finish. In small factories, work hours are typically

---

[9] According to labor statistics calculated by the International Labor Organization (ILO), an average workweek for Korean workers in 1980 was 53.1 hours, compared with 39.7 hours in the United States, 38.8 hours in Japan, 48.6 hours in Singapore, and 50.9 hours in Taiwan.

[10] Choong Soon Kim, *The Culture of Korean Industry: An Ethnography of Poongsan Corporation* (Tucson: University of Arizona Press, 1992); Roger Janelli with Dawnhee Yim Janelli, *Making Capitalism: The Social and Cultural Construction of a South Korean Conglomerate* (Stanford, Calif.: Stanford University Press, 1993).

determined by the amount and the urgency of orders to be met on a given day. Workers cannot even claim a right to ask, let alone demand, when their workday will end.

Workers' frustration regarding their work hours and other workplace indignities are frequently described in their personal essays written in small-circle activities or at workers' night schools.[11] A worker wonders, "Can we finish work today a little early? I keep looking at my watch. Time passes by but there is no sign that our work will end. I guess we have to do overtime work today again." As the end of the day approaches, the worker hears the boss repeating the same tune: "I am making you work tonight both for you and for the company, so even if you may have some complaints toward the company please work hard. You can live well at your old age by working hard when you are young."[12] No consent is asked. No special incentive or remuneration needs to be offered. The employer simply assumes he has a right to put workers to work any time he needs them. He exercises his authority as a patriarch does over his household, but without assuming the reciprocal moral obligations expected of a traditional patriarch.

Despotism is more characteristic of the authority exercised in small-scale workshops where young women are predominantly employed. The regular workday in a garment shop is from 8:30 A.M. to 8:30 P.M., yet workers living in the dormitory can rarely get off at that time. A worker describes how the manager reacted when she requested permission to leave at 8:30 P.M. to take care of some personal business: "Hey, you, do you think you are the only

---

[11] Unlike workers in the early industrialized countries, contemporary Korean factory workers left a large number of writings, such as diaries, personal essays on daily experiences and personal histories, casual poems, and reports on their union activities. Most of them were written by workers who attended worker night schools, as part of their writing assignments, or by workers who participated in church-sponsored educational and cultural activities. From the late 1970s, their writings attracted attention from intellectuals sympathetic toward labor issues, and several collections of workers' essays were published by small publication houses run mostly by progressive intellectuals. Given the political context in which much of the workers' writings were produced, one must exercise due caution in interpreting these materials. Presumably, workers' descriptions of their work, family, social life, and other daily concerns, which are the focus of my analysis here, are not much affected by the political atmosphere.

[12] Dolbegae, *Kŭrŏna ijenŭn ŏjeui urika anita: 80 nyŏndae nodongja saenghwal kŭl moŭm* (But we are not yesterdays' we: A collection of workers' life story essays in the 1980s) (Seoul: Dolbegae, 1986), p. 144.

one who has personal business to do? They [other workers] must all have something to do. You see? So go back and finish your work, and then go do your own thing or go to bed as it pleases you. You understand?"

In addition to facing despotism on the job, the factory women who live in company dormitories are subjected to close surveillance and restriction of their personal freedom. Workers often require permission from the chamberlain to leave the compound, even to go out to a neighborhood store late at night. Workers at a garment factory were told by the assistant director at their morning gathering, "You girls won't be allowed to take telephone calls from now on. You can receive letters, but only after you first open and read them in front of me. You must understand why I do this." The reason, the women presume, is to shield them from anything that might reduce their concentration and thereby slow down their work. When the young women grumble here and there, the assistant manager shouts, "Hey, you girls; why doesn't anyone stand up and say something as a representative?" But nobody dares to stand up.[13]

Despotism in the workplace prompts Korean workers to constantly demand more "humane" treatment. To be treated as a human being in the Korean workplace means not to be treated like a machine always at someone's disposal, not to be shouted at, not to be ridiculed as "ignorant and uneducated," and not to be the object of physical and sexual assault. How to be freed from constant symbolic and physical violence is thus an overriding concern among Korean factory workers and the source of their deep-seated resentment and anger.

Family as a Source of Hard Work and Discipline

Suffering from enormous physical hardship and crying out for humane treatment, Korean workers nevertheless submitted relatively peacefully to the harsh factory regime during the early period of export-led industrialization. What facilitated such submission and discipline? The answer lies only partially in the authority pattern within the workshop; it must also be sought in the societal mechanisms of control exercised on workers.

---

[13] Ibid., p. 238.

The most important societal mechanism of control is the family. Status within the patriarchal family is reproduced within the workplace, subjecting the workers to the exercise of patriarchal authority by their managers. This is particularly the case for young female workers, who have been aptly dubbed "working daughters" or "factory daughters" by some scholars.[14]

Patriarchal authority is only one link between family and factory. Probably a more powerful mechanism restraining workers' lives and aspirations is the thick emotional bonds and ethic of self-sacrifice deeply ingrained in their minds.[15] If patriarchal authority is relatively easy to debunk and resist, family obligation is not. Nowhere can we see the power of the family ethic of self-sacrifice more clearly than in the diaries of female factory workers. The most common and deepest agony among these young women is that they could not attend high school because they had to support their impoverished families; often, their wages paid for their brothers' education. Sad and frustrated when they reflect on it, most of these women reach the same conclusion: "It's bad enough that I myself have to suffer. Why should I pass on this pain to my younger siblings and pound a nail into their hearts? No, I cannot do that. Yes, the sorrow of failing to become educated must stop with me."[16]

Family is also an important source of strength and perseverance in their work life. Laboring twelve hours or more, the workers have to constantly fight fatigue and sleepiness; but the thought of their family members sustains them: "When I get sleepy I think of my father who is sick in bed, and when my body gets too tired and my hands become numb, I crunch my hands thinking of my younger brothers and sisters. [Then] my eyes begin to sparkle."[17] Family obligation is also the chief reason why workers willingly undertake overtime work even after laboring ten to twelve hours. As one workers writes, "Because overnight work is so hard and

[14] Janet Salaff, *Working Daughters of Hong Kong* (Cambridge: Cambridge University Press, 1981); Diane L. Wolf, *Factory Daughters: Gender, Household Dynamics, and Rural Industrialization in Java* (Berkeley: University of California Press, 1992).

[15] Hyun-Baek Chung, "Yosŭng nodongjaui uisikwa nodong sege" (Consciousness and the world of work among women workers: Focus on the analysis of workers' essays), *Yosung* (Women) 1 (1985): 116–62.

[16] Chum-suk Chun, ed., *Ingan tapge salja: Pusanchiyŏk yahak nodongja kŭl moŭm* (Let's live like human beings: A collection of Pusan-area night school workers' essays) (Seoul: Noktu, 1985), pp. 136–37.

[17] Dolbegae, *Kŭrŏna urinŭn*, p. 97.

painful I hesitate to take it, but thinking of my mother and younger siblings in our rural hometown, I realize I must endure it no matter how hard it is on me."[18] Here we find the real secret of Korean workers' hard work: not a work ethic or a strong commitment to one's job, certainly not to the company, but a deeply ingrained ethic of self-sacrifice for the family.

"Dirty Workers"

If it is family poverty and family obligation that forced these workers into the hard life of factory labor, it is the contemptuous attitude of society toward them that causes severe psychological pain in their daily lives. From the 1960s through the mid-1970s, factory workers were often called *kongsuni* (for female workers) or *kongdoli* (for male workers). Both terms carry the image of a housemaid or a servant, only working in a different setting (*kong*, meaning factory or industry). Although the factory worker is a modern phenomenon, and although the traditional Korean status system was by and large dismantled by the time of the postwar period, the negative societal attitude toward physical labor remains strong, and society has been slow to accord any significant difference between factory work and the menial labor performed by the slave-servants of bygone days. Despite drastic economic and social changes in modern times, the status image rooted in the feudalistic past seems to have remained intact, serving as a framework of status ranking and social identity today.

The label *kongsuni*, in particular, troubled sensitive young women who left their rural homes with high aspirations for upward social mobility. Their stories are replete with despair at the negative social image thrust upon them as factory workers.

> Women working in factories are *kongsuni*; men working in factories are *kongdoli*. *Kongsuni* and *kongdoli* are lowly, disreputable people, not worth counting, just loose folks. They call us this as a whole group. We have to be *kongsuni* even if we hate it, simply because we are working in factories. If someone asks us where we are working, we simply say, "I work at a small company." But *kongsuni* cannot really hide their identity. They show it no matter how hard they try to hide it through makeup and dressing well. To hide their status they pay more attention to clothes, hairdos, and cosmetics.

---

[18] Hyo-soon Song, *Sŏulo kanŭn kil* (Road to Seoul) (Seoul: Hyungsungsa, 1982), p. 46.

People blame us for spending so much money on appearances despite our meager income, but the reason is to shed the label of *kongsuni* they pin on us.[19]

Female workers confess that they are so afraid of being seen in factory uniform that they change clothes whenever they venture outside the factory gate, even to make a quick telephone call during a break. The negative societal evaluation of the factory worker is apt to be internalized by the workers themselves. "When I started factory work," one worker recollects, "I did not understand the meaning of the term 'worker' (*nodongja*), but after a while I came to realize that I am the dirty worker that society often talks about."[20] The phrase "dirty worker" (*chonhan nodongja* —meaning a low-status, contemptible laborer) was part of the workers' vocabulary in the 1960s through the 1970s. When a female factory worker met a college-graduate teacher at some worker night school, she wondered, "Why does a man with a college education spend [his] time dealing with dirty workers...? Perhaps he couldn't find a decent job, just like us."[21]

Apart from this status degradation of the factory worker in general, female factory workers experience more acute and pernicious attacks on their sense of femininity. To be employed as a factory hand and do hard manual work in a rough factory environment is considered tantamount to losing one's feminine virtues, becoming unwomanly. Young women are constantly plagued by this thought of becoming unfeminine: "They say that a woman's voice must not be heard over the fence of the house and that women must be polite, talk in a refined manner, and behave quietly...but what about us? We must be at the zero mark by this measuring yardstick. We cannot be heard unless we shout at each other, and our behavior naturally becomes rough as we rush between machines in our work uniforms."[22]

As is reported in many ethnographic studies of factory women in other societies, Korean factory women also are widely stigmatized as sexually wanton.[23] Vicious rumors spread around factory

[19] Dolbegae, *Kŭrŏna urinŭn*, p. 111.

[20] Ibid., p. 117.

[21] Jung-nam Suk, *Kongjangui pulpit* (Lights of the factory) (Seoul: Ilwol Sukak, 1984), p. 22.

[22] Nam-soo Chang, *Bbaeatkkin iltŏ* (Stolen workplace) (Seoul: Ch'angchakkwa Pipyong, 1984), pp. 42–43.

[23] See Ong's review of this subject in her "Gender and Labor Politics"; Maria Patricia Fernandez-Kelly, *For We Are Sold, I and My People: Women and Industry in Mexico's Frontier* (Albany: State University of New York Press, 1983); Hershatter,

towns that "there is no virgin inside the industrial complex." This sexual stigmatization is one important reason why female factory workers detest being labeled *kongsuni* and try to pass as students or white-collar workers and desire to get out of factory work as soon as possible.

Workers' Responses

How did first-generation Korean factory workers react to their world of work and to the societal attitude toward them? As is very common in the early stage of industrialization, Korean workers' initial responses were individualistic and defensive, their protests at best a demand for minimal subsistence. In the 1960s and 1970s, the majority of workers did not fight but looked instead for a way to escape the working world as soon as possible. Korean workers revealed a remarkable concern for upward mobility, an orientation that was reflected in their strong aspiration for education. A large number of young workers attended schools run by companies, commercial institutions, religious organizations, or college students. "It would be rare," one worker remarked, "to find a worker who has not attended at least some *hakwon* [commercially run institutes offering evening classes]."[24] It must have been hard for these workers to go to school after a long day of grueling labor, but workers seem to have found great joy and satisfaction in attending school after work. As one worker wrote, "It was difficult to study after work, but I could not stand the fact of just working in the factory. I had a firm belief that by studying as hard as I could, I would be able to escape this world."[25]

It did not take long, however, for workers to realize that opportunities for upward mobility were limited. Even those who obtain high-school diplomas by examination find that the door to white-collar office jobs is likely to be shut to them. Moreover, the highly centralized industrial structure of South Korea, with financial and trade structures heavily skewed in favor of big capital, allows little room for most workers to go into business for themselves. In this regard, South Korea is quite different from Taiwan or China, where (as we see in the chapter by Hill Gates) a petty-

---

Mexico's Frontier (Albany: State University of New York Press, 1983); Hershatter, *Workers.*

[24] Hyo-soon Song, *Sŏulo kanŭn kil,* p. 99.
[25] Nam-soo Chang, *Bbaeatkkin iltŏ,* p. 27.

bourgeois route to mobility is relatively open to working people. In South Korea the industrial structure forces workers eventually to come to grips with the fact that they must fight out in the world of proletarians, that factory work cannot be taken as a stepping-stone to a viable "entrepreneurial strategy."[26] The "part-time proletariat" orientation noted among Taiwanese workers is much weaker, if not absent, among Koreans.[27]

With exiting from factory work unlikely, a more realistic strategy is to search for a better job within industrial employment. Not surprisingly, the job turnover rate among Korean manufacturing workers has been very high. In 1980, for instance, the monthly job turnover rate in the Korean manufacturing sector was 5.6, compared with 1.4 in Japan, 3.4 in Taiwan, and 4.0 in the United States.[28] Wages are a major motivation for job change, but not the only concern. A 1977 survey of a nationwide sample of female factory workers revealed that among those who changed jobs, nearly half (46 percent) did so because of low wages; other reasons included lack of "humane" treatment (12 percent), factory closures (10 percent), and excessively strenuous work (9 percent). When asked to describe their ideal workplace, however, respondents stressed noneconomic factors above economic ones: 48 percent depicted a place where they would receive "humane" treatment and 15 percent a place where they could continue their education (14 percent identified a place where pay was high and 11 percent a place that offered a better career opportunity).[29]

These data and the writings of the workers themselves demonstrate that the overriding concern of Korean workers in the 1970s and, to a certain extent, in the 1980s, was with "human dignity": a desire to be treated "like a human being, not like an animal grabbed by the nape of the neck."[30]

---

[26] Richard Stites, "Industrial Work As an Entrepreneurial Strategy," *Modern China* 11 (1985): 227–46; Gwo-shyong Shieh, *"Boss" Island: The Subcontracting Network and Micro-Entrepreneurship in Taiwan's Development* (New York: Peter Lang, 1992).

[27] See Hill Gates, "Dependency and the Part-time Proletariat in Taiwan," *Modern China* 5 (1979): 381–408.

[28] ILO labor statistics, each year.

[29] Federation of Korean Trade Unions, *Chochik yŏsung nodongjaui kŭnrosiltaee kwanhan chosayŏnku pokosŏ I* (Research report on the working conditions of the organized women factory workers, part 1) (Seoul: FKTU, 1978), pp. 162, 167.

[30] A strong status concern among early Japanese workers was noted in Gordon, *Labor Relations*; Thomas C. Smith, *Native Sources of Japanese Industrialization, 1750–1920* (Berkeley: University of California Press, 1988).

Development of a Grassroots Labor Movement

After a relatively smooth and peaceful adaptation to industrial labor, Korean workers began to react to their situation with active resistance from the late 1960s. But labor unrest in this period was largely unorganized and individualistic protest against wretched working conditions in the many small sweatshops of the garment and textile industries. Organized spontaneously in protest against intolerable working conditions, these small-scale demonstrations had little effect on developing a new labor movement until 1970, when a momentous event provided the Korean labor movement with a galvanizing shock.

In that year, a young worker named Chun Tai-il immolated himself in a desperate attempt to publicize the inhumane working conditions in garment factories. Chun was a tailor working in a small garment factory at Pyungwha Market in the eastern section of Seoul, where a large number of small garment factories were concentrated. The majority of workers in this area were teenage women from the countryside who worked thirteen to fourteen hours a day with only two days off per month. The physical conditions of the workshops were extremely poor: minimal ventilation, no sunshine in the daytime, and barely enough space to move around or even to stand upright because the ceilings were so low. Most of these young workers suffered from chronic stomach problems and other job-related illnesses. In protest against such inhumane conditions, Chun wrote many letters to the Bureau of Labor Affairs and other agencies. His pleas for government intervention were ignored, however, so Chun decided to resort to the ultimate form of protest. On November 13, 1970, during a demonstration in Pyunghwa Market that he and a few fellow workers organized, Chun poured gasoline over his body and set himself on fire. As his body was engulfed in flames, he gripped a booklet describing the labor standard laws in his hand as a reminder of the employers' blatant violations of these laws. People heard him shouting from the flames, "We are not machines!" "Let us rest on Sunday!" "Abide by the labor standard laws!" He died in a hospital emergency room, where he uttered his last words to his mother and fellow workers: "Please don't let my life be wasted."[31]

---

[31] Tae-il Chun, *Nae chukŭmŭl hŏttoei malla* (Don't waste my life: A collection of Chun's writings) (Seoul: Dolbegae, 1988).

Chun's self-immolation became a powerful symbol for the working-class struggles that followed. His death was a dramatic announcement that factory workers had appeared on the stage as a new actor, as a potentially powerful political force in a rapidly industrializing society. This tragic incident portended the coming of a new era in the Korean labor movement. In many ways, this event marks the beginning of working-class formation in South Korea.

One important consequence of Chun's suicide was its effect on intellectuals, students, and church leaders. It awakened them to where society's most serious problems lay and to how strategic the labor movement could be for their struggles against the authoritarian regime. Student-labor linkages began to develop, as did links between labor and activist church groups. Thus economics and politics became closely intertwined to shape the character of the working-class struggles to come.

The Korean labor movement in the 1970s was led by female workers employed in the labor-intensive export industries: garments, textiles, food processing, and other light-manufacturing concerns. This situation presents an interesting contrast to the experiences of other Asian industrializing countries, where, as Deyo suggests, the female-dominant light-manufacturing sectors contributed to the dampening, rather than the heightening, of labor conflict.[32] On the other hand, female textile workers spearheading early labor protests finds many historical precedents elsewhere, East and West. For example, Perry's study demonstrates that in China, female workers were at the forefront of the early, pre-Communist labor movement in Shanghai.[33]

One can think of many reasons why Korean women played such an active role at the early stage of the labor movement. They were more exploited than male workers (female workers' average wage was half that of male workers throughout the 1970s and 1980s); they were objects of widespread physical, sexual, and symbolic abuse; and they were more homogeneous than male workers in terms of age, marital status, and family background. Another important factor is that almost all of these factory women were unmarried and were expected to leave their jobs upon getting

---

[32] Frederic Deyo, "Export-Manufacturing and Labor: The Asian Case," in *Labor in the Capitalist World-Economy*, ed. Charles Bergquist (Beverly Hills, Calif.: Sage, 1984); see also idem, *Beneath the Miracle*.

[33] Perry, *Shanghai on Strike*.

married (as all were expected to do); as "short-timers" in the system, they could "rock the boat" with more impunity than could male workers. But these same factors have not led women in other Asian societies to become active in the labor movement; the most important reason for Korean women's involvement must lie elsewhere.

The active assisting role played by progressive church organizations and students was a critical factor in mobilizing Korean female workers to spearhead labor struggles in the 1970s. Both humanitarian concern for the most exploited and the most oppressed and the relative ease of penetrating these labor-intensive industries led church leaders to select the female-dominated sectors as a main target of their industrial mission. Most prominent was the role of Catholic youth groups (JOC) and the Urban Industrial Mission (UIM).[34] These religious organizations exploited their own international networks and their relatively secure standing vis-à-vis the state to provide shelters for women workers' labor-organizing activities. The UIM, for example, in addition to providing regular religious offices, offered workers a variety of educational programs and cultural activities, through which a number of labor activists were produced. Such trainees later played a vanguard role in forming independent unions in the garment and textile industries. According to one report, at least 20 percent of the newly organized independent unions of the 1970s were assisted by the UIM.[35]

Students also played an important role in raising workers' collective consciousness during the 1970s. Especially important in this regard were the night schools they operated near factory towns. Workers' night schools began to appear in the early 1970s just after Chun Tai-il's self-immolation, initially in response to young workers' strong aspirations for higher education. Gradually, however, the emphasis shifted from routine curricula to consciousness-raising programs. These classrooms provided an important arena where workers learned to articulate their daily experiences using a new political language and where they could

---

[34] For more information, see Seung-Hyuk Cho, *Han'guk konguphwa wa nodong undong* (Korean industrialization and the labor movement) (Seoul: Pulbitt, 1984); Jang Jip Choi, *Labor and the Authoritarian State: Labor Unions in South Korean Manufacturing Industries, 1961–1980* (Seoul: Korea University Press, 1989); George Ogle, *South Korea: Dissent within the Economic Miracle* (London; Atlantic Highlands, N.J.: Zed Books, 1990).

[35] Seung-Hyuk Cho, *Han'guk konguphwa.*

develop close links with dissident intellectual communities and labor activists in other areas.

Partly under these outside influences and partly out of their own self-learning from daily struggles with management, company unions (*oyong chohap*), thugs, and agents of the oppressive government, workers gradually focused their efforts on establishing independent unions, outside of and in active opposition to the government-controlled official union structure. This grassroots "democratic union movement," which began to gain momentum in the latter half of the 1970s, was marked by courageous and bitter struggles waged by female workers employed in textile, electronics, and other export industries. One of these struggles, known as the Y. H. incident of 1979, involved party politics. The female strikers, after being forced out of their factory, staged a demonstration at the headquarters of the opposition party. Political conflicts escalated and street demonstrations increased, culminating in the assassination of President Park Chung-hee by his intelligence chief.

The trajectory of the South Korean labor movement changed noticeably in the 1980s, however. By this period, the dynamism of Korean industry had shifted from the labor-intensive, light-manufacturing sectors to heavy and chemical industries. This structural change led to a significant shift in the composition of the industrial labor force: a growing proportion of it is made up of male workers employed in large-scale firms in the capital-intensive sectors, and most of these men grew up in the city and graduated from high schools. Concurrently, the center of labor conflicts shifted gradually from the female-dominant to the male-dominant sector and from small-scale industries to large-scale industries. Although the labor movement of the 1980s developed in a cyclical fashion, in close relationship with political developments outside the industrial arena, the level of organizational strength and the level of threat brought by the strikers increased continuously. Increasingly, strikes occurred in large industrial centers, and the leadership of the labor movement moved to the relatively well educated and politically conscious male workers.

The dominant trend of labor conflicts from the mid-1980s was toward interfirm solidarity struggles in which strike actions were coordinated among firms in the same industrial complex. These actions were facilitated by the concentrated pattern of South Korean industrial development, and, concomitantly, a high geographic concentration of industrial workers in a few industrial complexes (such as Kuro *kongdan*) or a few industrial towns (such as Masan and Changwon).[36] Equally important was the development of close social networks among labor activists across firms and the similar ideological and political perspective they developed through activities outside the industrial arena. The latter phenomenon is of critical importance in understanding the unique character of the South Korean working-class movement.

The *Minjung* Movement

Workers' struggles in any society are not a simple product of their experience at the point of production; those struggles are shaped intimately by the larger political and social processes that occur outside the industrial arena. One major reason why a much more active labor movement developed in South Korea than in other neighboring East Asian countries was the intensity of political struggles against the authoritarian regimes by students, intellectuals, and political dissident groups throughout the entire period of rapid industrialization. As mentioned above, student activism began to spill over into the industrial arena from the early 1970s. By the mid-1980s there were several hundreds (and possibly a couple of thousands) of students-turned-workers who quit their schools and penetrated factories to work as agitators and organizers of the grassroots democratic labor movement.[37]

Democratization struggles in South Korea influenced the labor movement directly by producing activist students who penetrated the industrial arena. But the effect of the political movement has been broader than this. A crucial phenomenon to understand in this context is the populist *minjung* movement, which exerted tremendous influence on the trajectory of the working-class movement in the 1980s.

The term *minjung* means "the people" or "the masses." The *minjung* movement emerged in the 1970s. Both internal political

---

[36] For a more detailed analysis of this industrial structure and its implications for the South Korean working-class formation, see Hagen Koo, "From Farm to Factory: Proletarianization in Korea," *American Sociological Review* 55 (1990): 669–81. Interesting contrasts between Taiwan and South Korea in this pattern are found in Yow-Suen Sen and Hagen Koo, "Industrial Transformation and Proletarianization in Taiwan," *Critical Sociology* 19 (1992): 45–67.

[37] Choi, *Authoritarian State;* Ogle, *Korea;* Hagen Koo, "The State, *Minjung,* and the Working Class in South Korea," in *State and Society in Contemporary Korea,* ed. Hagen Koo (Ithaca, N.Y.: Cornell University Press, 1993).

circumstances and external influences contributed to its development. The most significant factor was the hardening of the
authoritarian regime of Park Chung-hee and, more specifically, the
installation of a bureaucratic-authoritarian regime, called the
yushin (revitalization) regime, in 1972. The *yushin* intensified students' antiregime struggles and triggered strong opposition from
the intellectual community, religious organizations, opposition
parties, and a growing segment of the new middle class. Along
with this political problem, the issues of distribution of wealth and
widening class inequality came to the serious attention of the public in this period.

The political and economic reality of the 1970s thus demanded
an ideology that could articulate these problems and unite diverse
strands of struggles by students, workers, farmers, the urban poor,
journalists, writers, and so on. *Minjung*, a political language used
by both nationalists and leftists during the colonial period and in
the postwar years, suited the purpose eminently. It contains
strong nationalistic sentiment, it is not a Marxist language (which
is essential to avoid being labeled or persecuted as pro-
Communist), it is vague and broad enough to include all popular
sectors, and it is suitable to both political and cultural movements.
The *minjung* includes all those who are politically oppressed,
socially alienated, and economically excluded from the benefits of
economic growth.[38]

External influence also played an important role; it came in the
form of liberation-oriented theologies (especially Latin American
liberation theology), dependency theory, and other neo-Marxist
theories, which were very popular among students in the late
1970s and the early 1980s. Stimulated by these intellectual ideas,
Korean theologians developed *minjung* theology, while academics
proposed *minjung* sociology, *minjung* history, and *minjung* literature. Borrowing key concepts from these foreign sources, Korean
intellectuals, however, insisted upon Korean history and culture as
the ultimate source of their inspiration and their search for eman-
cipation.[39]

---

[38] Wan-sang Han, *Minjung sahoehak* (Minjung sociology) (Seoul: Chongro
Sochuk, 1984); Jae-Chun Yoo, ed., *Minjung* (in Korean) (Seoul: Munhakwa Jisung,
1984).

[39] See *Minjung Theology*, edited by the Commission on Theological Concerns of
the Christian Conference of Asia (1983).

At the core of the *minjung* movement is an ideology that claims that the *minjung* is the master of history and that Korean history is a history of the *minjung's* oppression by the dominant class and by external forces; hence, the real national identity and the authentic culture of Korea must be found in the culture and daily struggles of the *minjung*. With this broad ideological content, the *minjung* became a dominant discourse, slogan, and strategic tool for uniting and mobilizing diverse political and social struggles in the 1980s. To a great extent, South Korean politics in the 1980s was a series of continuous confrontations between the authoritarian regime and a loose, but highly active and strong, coalition of *minjung* circles.

The significance of the *minjung* movement, however, is not limited to its effect on political mobilization. The *minjung* movement is at once a political and a cultural movement. As a cultural movement, it stimulated serious efforts among intellectuals and artists to search for the essence of *minjung* culture, which has long been overshadowed by Western culture and neglected or even harassed by the authorities. These efforts led to reaffirmation and reappropriation of Korean culture and history from a fresh *minjung* perspective. Many of the best-selling novels in the 1980s belonged to the genre of *minjung* literature. Historical novels dramatized the agonies and struggles of the oppressed and tried to draw new historical meanings therefrom, while those with more contemporary themes sought to disclose the injustices suffered by the lower classes.[40]

One of the most interesting developments brought about by the *minjung* movement is the rediscovery and recreation of indigenous cultural forms practiced by commoners, such as the *talchum* (mask dance or play), *pungmul* (peasant band music and dance), *madang kŭk* (play performed in a village open space), and *madang kut* (shamanistic rites). Interest in these traditional cultural forms appeared first in the 1960s among a small circle of nationalistically minded, avant garde students at Seoul National University who demonstrated fiercely against the normalization treaty with Japan signed by Park Chung-hee's new military regime. At this time, students introduced old shamanistic rituals to their demonstrations to show their nationalistic sentiment. But with a greater articulation of *minjung* ideology in the 1970s, this cultural

---

[40] See Uchang Kim, "The Agony of Cultural Construction: Politics and Culture in Modern Korea," in *State and Society in Contemporary Korea*.

movement went beyond a mere reappreciation of traditional culture and made a serious effort to reinterpret and recreate *minjung*
culture. The 1980s saw a blossoming of all genres of *minjung* culture: *talchum*, *pungmul*, *madang kut*, and other peasant and
shamanistic rituals. There was hardly a college without a mask
dance group and hardly a student demonstration that wasn't
accompanied by a playful performance of *pungmul* or *madang kut*
or both. The dynamic dances and loud music of these rituals
played a very effective role in gathering students and stirring up
the collective mood for a violent confrontation with the police.

Changing Worker Identity and Consciousness

The South Korean industrial structure has undergone a tremendous change in the second half of the 1970s, accompanied by the
rapid proletarianization of its workforce. The number of manufacturing wage workers doubled in ten years, from 936,000 in 1970 to
1,904,000 in 1980.[41] In the 1980s, the industrial proletariat constituted about 15 percent of the total labor force, 23 percent of the
urban labor force. No longer were factory workers a novel
phenomenon, and no longer was a preindustrial image of servile
workers applicable to this large stratum of industrial workers.
Accordingly, the pejorative labels of *kongsuni* and *kongdoli* gradually disappeared from the vocabulary, giving way to a neutral
word, *nodongja* (worker). But the negative social image toward the
factory worker did not cease to exist, and the word *nodongja* was
still imbued with a connotation of a low, "dirty," and unrespect-
able person.

The working-class struggles in South Korea in the 1970s and
well into the 1980s were, therefore, simultaneously struggles to
secure better economic conditions and struggles to establish a
more respectable social identity for workers. For the majority of
workers during this period, and perhaps even today, concern
about status seems to be no less strong than materialistic concerns,
and class interest and status interest combined to form the basic
contours of their struggles.

The first important change to occur in the course of the
working-class movement in South Korea is, therefore, workers'

---

[41] Kwan-mo Suh, "Han'guk sahoe kyekup kusongui yonku" (A study of Korean
class structure) (Ph.D. dissertation, Department of Sociology, Seoul National
University, 1987), p. 65.

self-conception about being a *nodongja*. In this regard, a significant change began in the latter part of the 1970s. Workers came to realize that it was not shameful to be a worker, that many others were in the same position, and that workers make an important contribution to society. "I came to realize that being a worker is nothing to be ashamed of. What we eat, what we wear, where we live, is there anything into which workers' sweat has not been shed? Those pretty clothes and shoes college girls wear, our boss's limousine—they are all touched by our hands. There is no reason why we should be ashamed of being a worker."[42]

Exactly how such a change in the worker's self-conception occurred is difficult to document. The rapidly growing number of workers in a similar position, their concentration in a few industrial towns, rising wage levels, and most important, experiences drawn from many collective struggles must all have contributed to an awakening of workers' consciousness. But, as we have seen, a factor that demands close attention is the role of the students and religious organizations, for it was through attending worker schools or participating in small-circle activities—most of which are linked to or influenced by progressive churches and activist students—that many workers acquired a new perspective on themselves and their role in society.

Worker night schools provided a particularly important vehicle for promoting a new working identity. Those who attended these schools frequently report the same thing: "I hated the class whenever words like *minjung* and *nodongja* were mentioned. I couldn't help thinking that our teacher was ridiculing us because we were workers (*nodongja*). Until then, I had been reluctant to reveal my job to anyone because I was ashamed of being a worker." Another worker confessed, "I did not believe it myself when I first heard at the night school that 'the workers are the masters of society' or that '[workers] are the engine of history'." But most of the workers who attended night schools echoed their colleague who said, "Previously I was afraid to disclose that I am a worker. But now I can say to others with confidence 'I am a worker.' And now I have pride and satisfaction for being a respectable member of society as a worker."[43]

Overcoming one's inferiority complex as a "dirty worker" occurred conjointly with abandoning the aspiration for upward

---

[42] Chun, *Ingan tapge salja*, p. 49.

[43] Ibid., p. 77.

mobility. Workers realized that their dream for a middle-class life was unrealistic and that the real world was right there where they toiled day and night, far removed from the ideal that the commercial media portrayed. Female workers realized that they were most likely to marry other factory workers and that the cooking lessons or flower arrangement classes they attended to "better themselves" were nothing but a pitiful vanity on their part. With such a realization, workers developed a stronger feeling of solidarity with other fellow workers. They came to appreciate the commonality of their family backgrounds—all children of poor farm families—the common treatment they received from society, and the common fate binding them together in the wretched world of factory labor.

Developing a feeling of solidarity with other poor people is most commonly accompanied by a sharper awareness of the structure of social inequality in society. "There are people who earn a million won sitting idle using only their mouths, while we, working with blood and sweat, cannot escape poverty for a single day.... The world is really rotten."[44] People who share this feeling are angry; they want to kick hard at what they perceive to be a rotten society, and they want to share their bitter feelings with someone else.

A shared disposition to act is a crucial element in class formation, as many theorists stress.[45] Class is only an abstract construct apart from lived experiences of individuals and shared dispositions to act in a certain way. In his oft quoted definition of class, Thompson stresses the element of collective disposition:

> When we speak of a class we are thinking of a very loosely-defined body of people who share the same congeries of interests, social experiences, traditions, and value-system, who have a *disposition* to *behave* as a class, to define themselves in their actions and in their consciousness in relation to other groups of people in class ways.[46]

Similarly, Katznelson argues that shared disposition is a crucial "junction" point in the process of class formation, for it connects

---

[44] Dolbegae, *Kŭrŏna urinŭn*, p. 244.

[45] A clear exposition of this point is found in Ira Katznelson, "Working-Class Formation: Constructing Cases and Comparisons," in *Working-Class Formation: Nineteenth-Century Patterns in Western Europe and the United States* (Princeton, N.J.: Princeton University Press, 1986), pp. 3–41.

[46] E. P. Thompson, "The Peculiarities of the English," in *Socialist Register 1965*, ed. Ralph Miliband and John Saville (London: Merlin Press, 1966), p. 357. Emphasis in original.

class members' lived experiences to class actions. Class dispositions are shared experiences within a given cultural context: "They are formed by the manner in which people interact with each other. Thus dispositions are transindividual, not merely opinions or views of the individual actors. They are cultural configurations within which people act."[47]

A critical issue in class analysis is to explain how individualistic anger and resentment are translated into shared disposition or *class disposition*. It is easy to assume, quite erroneously, that class actions only follow class dispositions, or that shared dispositions are preconditions for class actions. Looking into the experiences of the South Korean workers, however, we see that some kinds of class-based actions seem to occur before any class dispositions; in fact, class-based actions often seem necessary ingredients in transforming individual-level dispositions into transindividual, class dispositions. That is to say, class dispositions are not likely to develop from routine daily experiences in the workplace or in the community, certainly not from the mere fact of occupying the same position within the structure of production. Class dispositions and class consciousness among Korean workers are the product of myriad small and large struggles as well as the consequences of participation in social networks of educational and cultural activities oriented to cultivate workers' critical consciousness.

As noted above, the majority of workers' collective actions in the 1970s and the early 1980s were concerned with immediate economic issues, most typically low wages, unfair layoffs, or delayed wages, but their involvement in such actions inevitably led them to confront the faces of the power structure that suppressed them—the police, thugs, company unions, co-opted male workers, and the media, as well as the employers and the managers. "Although the police must mediate from a neutral stance," workers often reported, "they always suppress and control our actions onesidedly. When we are questioned at the police station, they behave not like the police but like our company managers, scolding and threatening us as if we were criminals."[48] They reported the same experiences with the official union leaders. It was these experiences that led them to realize that they had to organize themselves, to create their own independent unions and destroy the company unions, which acted as arms of management

---

[47] Katznelson, "Working-Class Formation"; quotation at p. 18.
[48] Jung-nam Suk, *Kongjangui pulpit*, p. 155.

and the government. The level of collective consciousness varied significantly between those who participated in collective actions and those who did not.

It is this awareness of the importance of representative unions, the valuable product of previous struggles, that has propelled the "democratic labor movement" since the latter part of the 1970s. One worker expressed this awareness:

> Before knowing about unions, work was loathsome and hateful. We had to force ourselves to come to work and then would seek easy and less tiring job assignments as much as possible.... But at the union we find that work is not so hateful. No one who has not sweated in front of a machine is entitled to talk about the value of work. Hard, sad, and sometimes intolerably tedious [as our work is], it is at the union where we can discover that no one but our- selves can create a better society through work.[49]

Most likely, the level of class consciousness this worker expresses is not representative of ordinary workers, but by the mid-1980s, the number of workers who had acquired such a class disposition had risen significantly.

The "culture of solidarity," borrowing Fantasia's term, definitely grew and deepened in the 1980s.[50] It exploded into action in the fall of 1987, in the wake of the sudden political open- ing for democratization. Waves of violent labor strikes erupted and swept across all major industrial centers, demonstrating the enormous threatening power and solidarity of labor. Since then, however, the labor movement has fluctuated between strength and weakness, militancy and docility, solidarity and divisiveness. A critical variable determining the trajectory of the labor movement is still the strength of the state and its ability, even during periods of democratic transition, to debilitate and mold the activities of organized labor. After significant organizational gains through the "great worker struggles" in 1987 and 1988, the democratic labor movement began to show organizational weakness when the polit- ical and social atmosphere turned against it in later years.[51]

---

[49] Nam-soo Chang, *Bbaeatkkin iltŏ*, pp. 29–30.

[50] Rick Fantasia, *Cultures of Solidarity: Consciousness, Action, and Contemporary American Workers* (Berkeley: University of California Press, 1988). By "cultures of solidarity," Fantasia means "an emergent cultural form embodying the values, practices, and institutional manifestations of mutuality" (p. 25).

[51] See Jang Jip Choi, "The Working-Class Movement and the State in Transition to Democracy: The Case of South Korea" (paper presented at the conference "East Asian Labor in Comparative Perspective," Tahoe City, Calif., October 1993).

THREE

Class Identity without Class Consciousness? Working-Class Orientations in Taiwan

NAI-TEH WU

The problem of (working) class formation is one of the main foci in sociological studies of stratification. Under what conditions and through what processes will a class develop into a collective actor, or, at least, acquire a similar ideological disposition? That is, under what social, economic, and political circumstances do members of a class change from a "simple addition of homologous magnitudes, much as potatoes in a sack form a sack of potatoes"[1] into a class? Because the working class in industrial society is assigned by many theories a significant role in the process of social change as well as in the fight for social justice, the problem of working-class formation has attracted wide attention and research.

Various theories have been proposed to explain the formation or nonformation of the working class and its particular political disposition in various societies. The approaches include the cultural-historical perspective of E. P. Thompson as well as emphases on the role of the state; the effect of the mobilization of opposing classes; and the effects of social mobility, the status system, and economic development and income distribution, to list only a few.[2] Moreover, variation in the processes of class

The data used in this paper are from the project "Class Structure and Class Consciousness" sponsored by the National Science Council in Taiwan, series number NSC82-0301-H001-032.

[1] Karl Marx, *The Eighteenth Brumaire of Louis Bonaparte.* Cited from Jon Elster, ed., *Karl Marx: A Reader* (Cambridge: Cambridge University Press, 1986), p. 254.

[2] E. P. Thompson, *The Making of the English Working Class* (London: Victor Gollancz Press, 1963). On the role of the state: Ira Katznelson and Aristide R. Zolberg, eds., *Working-Class Formation: Nineteenth-Century Patterns in Western Europe and the*

formation among different countries has been called to our attention by other students of working-class formation.[3]

In the long history of research on working-class formation in advanced industrialized societies, numerous outstanding works have been produced. But studies of their counterparts in the newly industrialized societies are relatively few. One among them is the work of Frederic C. Deyo, who includes all four "Asian dragons" in his study.[4] Deyo tries to explain the failure of working-class formation in those countries. Specifically, he asks why East Asian working classes are relatively quiescent in the process of industrialization, as measured in terms of overt actions of labor militancy. Several "structural" factors are offered to account for labor's lack of militancy: an employment structure that emphasizes low-skilled work and generates a high turnover rate, a "nonproletarian" labor system with communal paternalism, and a lack of workers' communities with organizations to facilitate collective action. These structural factors allegedly work together to undermine the possibility of a labor movement.

Deyo may be correct. But one further question can be raised concerning the actual role of structural factors in working-class formation. In what way are those factors causally linked to labor quiescence? Do they constrain the development of working-class consciousness? Or do they have little effect on workers' social *attitudes*, yet limit the possibility of workers' collective *action*? Different answers to this question beget different theories of

---

United States (Princeton, N.J.: Princeton University Press, 1986); Gerald Friedman, "The State and the Making of the Working Class: France and the United States, 1880–1914," *Theory and Society* 17, 3 (1988): 403–30. On mobilization of opposing classes: Harold Perkin, "The Birth of Class," excerpt in *History and Class*, ed. R. S. Neale (Oxford: Basil Blackwell, 1983); Jurgen Kocka, "Class Formation, Interest Articulation, and Public Policy: The Origins of the German White-Collar Class in the Late Nineteenth and Early Twentieth Centuries," in *Organizing Interests in Western Europe: Pluralism, Corporatism, and the Transformation of Politics*, ed. Suzanne Berger (Cambridge: Cambridge University Press, 1981). On social mobility: Werner Sombart, *Why Is There No Socialism in the United States?* (London: Macmillan, 1976). On the status system: Seymour Martin Lipset, "Radicalism or Reformism: The Source of Working-Class Politics," in *Consensus and Conflict*, ed. Seymour Martin Lipset (New York: Transaction, 1985). On income development and distribution: Albert O. Hirschman, "The Changing Tolerance for Income Inequality in the Course of Economic Development," in *Essays in Trespassing: Economics to Politics and Beyond*, ed. Albert O. Hirschman (Cambridge: Cambridge University Press, 1981).

[3] Katznelson and Zolberg, *Working-Class Formation*.

[4] Frederic C. Deyo, *Beneath the Miracle: Labor Subordination in the New Asian Industrialism* (Berkeley: University of California Press, 1989).

working-class formation. For the first theory, we may assume, for example, that the small-scale enterprises dominating the economic structure of Taiwan hinder the development of working-class consciousness, and the underdevelopment of consciousness results in turn in labor quiescence. The reasoning behind this speculation is that workers' consciousness is largely a function of the interactions among workers themselves, whether in workplaces, in union activities, or in communities.

In the same vein, we may highlight another structural factor shaping workers' consciousness: social mobility. It is often proposed that socialization in the family is an important determinant of social attitudes: parents' social standing therefore exerts a significant effect on children's class identity. In a newly industrialized society where most of the industrial workers are from farmer families instead of worker families, we would expect an underdevelopment of working-class consciousness among the first-generation workers. If this theory holds, we should also witness a higher level of workers' consciousness among those workers from working-class families. Social mobility may also hinder the development of working-class consciousness in another way. Rapid industrialization often results in a high degree of upward social mobility through the enlargement of the middle class. Increasing chances of upward mobility for the lower classes is supposed to decrease their class consciousness.[5]

Another perspective sees structural factors not as determinants of subjective consciousness, but as constraints on collective action. The focus here is on the repression or the obstruction of workers' collective struggles. Among structural factors, the type of political regime is often stressed.[6] Additionally, we may propose that structural factors do not so much hinder formation of subjective consciousness as they hinder overt actions against employers. Workers employed in small firms, for example, are either more closely monitored by their employers or embedded in intimate social relations with their employers. In either case, it is more difficult for them to engage in collective action against their employers.

---

[5] For a review of the discussions by early socialist thinkers and later social scientists of the effect of upward social mobility on working-class consciousness, see John H. Goldthorpe, *Mobility and Class Structure in Modern Britain*, 2d ed. (Oxford: Clarendon Press, 1987), pp. 1–36.

[6] Deyo, *Beneath the Miracle*.

These two different perspectives on class formation may be compatible. We may assume that some factors work to shape the content of class consciousness, some to constrain actions, and yet others to shape attitudes and condition actions at the same time. The aim of this essay is not to provide a final answer to these complex questions. Rather, I try to examine the actual content of working-class consciousness in present-day Taiwan. The data used in this paper were collected in 1992 by a local Taiwan team affiliated with the International Project on Class Structure and Class Consciousness launched by Eric O. Wright.[7] The sample size was 1,491. Although the questionnaire closely follows Wright's original design, the definition of working class used in this study is somewhat different. The "working class" in our sample includes three groups: manual workers, service workers, and a smaller segment of self-employed workers.

I begin with the problem of working-class identity. Class identity is often taken as one dimension of class consciousness. Some students of working-class formation have focused their attention solely on this dimension[8] because probing class identity causes fewer measurement problems than does probing many other subjective social attitudes in a large-scale survey. The question format is brief (i.e., easily accommodated in most surveys) and standardized (i.e., allowing international comparisons).

In the discussion on working-class identity, I focus mainly on two problems. First, I examine the factors that explain the variation in class identity among workers in Taiwan. Previous studies of Western industrialized societies have found that class identification is largely an effect of class origins, that is, family background and educational attainment.[9] We will see if these factors also wield any significant influence in Taiwan.

---

[7] For a description of this project, see Erik O. Wright, "The Comparative Project on Class Structure and Class Consciousness: An Overview," *Acta Sociologica* 32, 1 (1989): 3–22.

[8] For examples, see John C. Goyder, "A Note on the Declining Relation between Subjective and Objective Class Measures," *British Journal of Sociology* 26, 1 (1975): 100–109; Knud Knudsen, "Class Identification in Norway: Explanatory Factors and Life-Cycle Differences," *Acta Sociologica* 31, 1 (1988): 69–79; Lynn W. Cannon, "Normative Embourgeoisement among Manual Workers: A Reexamination Using Longitudinal Data," *Sociological Quarterly* 21 (Spring 1992): 185–95.

[9] Erik O. Wright and Kwang-Yeong Shin, "Temporality and Class Analysis: A Comparative Study of the Effects of Class Trajectory and Class Structure on Class Consciousness in Sweden and the United States," *Sociological Theory* 6, 1 (Spring 1988): 58–84; Knudsen, "Class Identification in Norway."

Second, I take class identification as an independent variable and see if class identity is related to other dimensions of class consciousness. Class identification was found to be a strong predictor of other dimensions of class consciousness in other advanced industrialized societies.[10] We will see if this is also true for Taiwanese workers. Or rather, is class identity just a "hollow identity," as ethnic identities in some societies (e.g., the United States), not leading to particular ideologies and social attitudes? If the latter is the case, then in the study of the Taiwanese working class we may have to reconsider whether we should take class identity as an indicator of class consciousness. We may have to develop a new strategy for probing the meaning of class. This is an important question given that most surveys conducted in Taiwan have included a question on respondents' subjective class identity.

In exploring the issues outlined above, we will see whether theories proposed to explain the underdevelopment of class consciousness as well as labor quiescence in Taiwan are supported by empirical data. These theories include the temporary-female-worker thesis, the embourgeoisement thesis, the worker-concentration thesis, and the first-generation-worker thesis. One of the underlying assumptions of this essay is that in a newly developed country with a newly emergent working class and without any tradition of socialist thought, working-class consciousness cannot be taken as an integrated whole. Some of the factors or theories mentioned above may account for some dimensions of class consciousness but not others.

Class Awareness and Class Identity

Group consciousness plays a vital role in giving rise to similar social attitudes and political dispositions among people in the same group: racial, ethnic, religious, sex, or class. Under certain circumstances, it also motivates people with the same group membership to act collectively for social change or the protection of group interests or both. Students of working-class politics—among them, Bertell Ollman—have defined class consciousness in different terms. Ollman offered a maximalist definition. He distinguished nine steps in the development of working-class consciousness, from workers' knowing their own interests, seeing

---

[10] Wright and Shin, "Temporality and Class Analysis."

themselves as members of a class, and being able to distinguish their interests as workers from other, less important interests; through believing their class interests prior to their interests as members of a particular nation, religion, race, and the like and hating their capitalist exploiters; to the last steps of believing Marx's strategy to be the best means of changing their situation and being unafraid to act when the time came.[11] Admitting that class consciousness thus defined is hard to develop, Ollman nevertheless believes that these steps describe correctly the trajectory the development of working-class consciousness most often follows.

Without adopting Ollman's Marxist doctrine, Michael Mann offers a definition more suitable for empirical research. Mann distinguishes four elements of class consciousness: class identity, class opposition, class totality (defining one's total social situation and one's society in terms of the above two elements), and the conception of an alternative society.[12] More can be added to the list of definitions of class consciousness offered by various authors. Yet class identity is always a common element, or, as shown above, assumed by some to be the first stage in the development of consciousness. Without identifying oneself with others having the same group membership, one can hardly engage in collective action with them. The first step of surveying the content and development of working-class consciousness in a particular society is thus to examine working-class identity among its laborers.

But before we look into the identification of the working class in Taiwan, it may be useful to tackle the problem of class awareness. One may well argue that it is a self-fulfilling inquiry to ask the respondents to identify with some status group provided by the researcher. Among the choices, "working class" is often included. Many respondents may be induced by the interviewer to identify with a category that was never in their minds before the interview. The data collected thus are not a true reflection of respondents' attitudes. This kind of problem is inherent in large-scale interview surveys. Two remedies can help ameliorate, if not correct, this deficiency. First, before asking the respondents to

[11] Bertell Ollman, "Toward Class Consciousness Next Time: Marx and the Working Class," *Politics and Society* 3, 1 (1972): 1–24.

[12] Michael Mann, *Consciousness and Action among the Western Working Class* (London: Macmillan, 1973), p. 13.

identify themselves with a certain "class," we can try to measure the degree of awareness on class divisions among respondents. Second, we can see how respondents define and divide social classes. If most respondents are aware of class divisions in society, and if they also have a "correct" vision of how social classes are divided, then the data on their subjective class identification may be significant and useful. For the first endeavor, we asked "Which of the following two statements is a correct description of Taiwan society? (a) There are no class divisions in Taiwan society. (b) There are class divisions in Taiwan society."

If class awareness among our respondents is very low, then the data on class identity may be insignificant: it is absurd to talk about the class identities of people who are unaware of class divisions. Fortunately, the data show that our respondents are aware of them. As table 1 shows, 85 percent of respondents are aware of class divisions in Taiwan society. We also found that people of different classes do not show much difference in this awareness. It is important to note, however, that manual workers show the least awareness of class divisions, although the difference is not significant.

An awareness of class divisions, however, does not presume a coherent definition of classes. That is the next question to be tackled. How do people divide social classes? By what criteria do people define the memberships of classes: income, property, ownership of the means of production, social prestige, political power, or even ethnicity? Are common people more "Marxist" than "Weberian," or vice versa?

Previous studies conducted in the United States revealed that people usually use both economic and social categories to define social classes. Centers, in his famous study of social classes in the United States, asked what the respondent thought most important in deciding if a person belongs to his or her class. Four choices were given, with respondents free to choose more than one: family background, income level, educational level, and beliefs and attitudes.[13] Using the same design, Jackman and Jackman added two more items to the list of possible answers: occupation and lifestyle. Three of the items—occupation, income, and education—are

---

[13] Richard Centers, *The Psychology of Social Classes* (Princeton, N.J.: Princeton University Press, 1949). Cited in Mary R. Jackman and Robert W. Jackman, *Class Awareness in the United States* (Berkeley: University of California Press, 1983), p. 35.

Table 1: Class Awareness[a]

	Upper-middle bourgeoisie	Lower-middle class	Nonmanual worker	Manual worker	Self-employed worker	Total
Yes	367 (34.8)[b] (84.6)	231 (21.9) (91.7)	102 (9.7) (90.3)	262 (24.8) (79.9)	93 (8.8) (84.5)	1,055 (85.3)
No	67 (36.8) (15.4)	21 (11.5) (8.3)	11 (6.0) (9.7)	66 (36.3) (20.1)	17 (9.3) (15.5)	182 (14.7)
Total	434 (35.1)	252 (20.4)	113 (9.1)	328 (26.5)	110 (8.9)	1,237 (100)

[a] "Are there class divisions in Taiwan society?" was the question asked.
[b] Numbers in parentheses are percentages.

categorized as "objective criteria," the other three as "expressive or cultural criteria." The latter authors' findings were consistent with those obtained by Centers thirty years earlier: "class is indeed popularly interpreted as a social as well as an economic phenomenon."[14]

The survey on which this essay is based uses a different research design. After having asked our respondents if there are class divisions in Taiwan society, we asked those who expressed an awareness of class divisions to name the classes in society. Most respondents named three to five classes. Those names reveal the definitions used by the respondents. As expected, many respondents used multiple criteria to define classes. For example, the same respondent might have listed "the rich," "the poor," "the bosses," and "the professionals." In this case, criteria of income, ownership of the means of production, and education (prestige) are used simultaneously. We sorted these definitions into several categories: (1) wealth—rich/poor, property owner/nonpropertied; (2) occupation—manual worker/nonmanual worker, white-collar worker/non-white-collar worker, labor/nonlabor, *shi-nong-gong-shang* (literati-peasant-laborer-merchant); (3) gradation—upper/middle/low; (4) ownership of the means of production—employer/employee, boss/staff; (5) education—professional/nonprofessional, intellectual/uneducated; (6) authority in the production process—supervisor/staff; and (7) political power—the privileged, opportunists, the Kuomintang (KMT) ruling group, members of the legislative organs. The criteria of wealth, occupation, and ownership of the means of production clearly fit in the "objective" category, the criterion of education in the "cultural." But the criteria of gradation and of authority in the production process are ambiguous. The classification of upper/middle/lower does not tell us anything about the definition of class, just that people perceive classes to exist. Authority in the production process can be an objective criterion or an expressive (prestigious) one. For the moment, we put both these criteria into the cultural category to downplay the objective criteria (table 2).

But to our surprise, even when those two ambiguous criteria are put in the cultural category, it still accounts for only 22.4 percent. Nearly 60 percent of the definitions are in the objective category. Because different research designs were used, we are reluctant to say that people in Taiwan are much more inclined

---

[14] Jackman and Jackman, *Class Awareness in the United States*, p. 36.

Table 2
Criteria for Class Definition

Objective criteria		
Money (rich/poor; propertied/nonpropertied)	480	(30.9)
Occupation (manual/nonmanual; white-collar/non-white-collar)	297	(22.0)
Ownership of means of production (employer/employee)	80	(5.2)
Cultural criteria		
Gradation (upper/middle/lower class)	155	(10.0)
Education and professional	139	(9.0)
Authority (supervisor/staff)	52	(3.4)
Other criteria		
Political power (privileged; ruling party)	194	(12.5)
Other	111	(7.1)
Totals	1,508	(100)

Numbers in parentheses are percentages.

than Americans to define social classes in terms of objective economic position. But it is still striking that in a so-called Confucian society, which puts so high a value on education and culture, people overwhelmingly define class in objective economic terms rather than in cultural ones. For our present concern, however, it is noteworthy that further analysis does not reveal any significant correlation between one's class background and the criteria used to define classes.

Up to now we have found that people in Taiwan are aware of class divisions and that they overwhelmingly define class in objective economic terms. Given these two findings, we are in a better position to analyze class identification. Our questionnaire roughly followed the standard question format on class identity. Respondents were asked to identify themselves with one of three classes given by the interviewers: upper-middle, middle, or working class. The data show that objective class positions are significantly correlated with subjective class identities. Nearly three-fourths of manual workers and self-employed workers label themselves as working class, while only half of nonmanual service workers do so. By contrast, the lower-middle class and upper-middle class are more inclined to identify with middle and upper-middle classes (table 3).

Table 3
Subjective Class Identification

	Upper-middle bourgeoisie	Lower-middle class	Nonmanual worker	Manual worker	Self-employed worker	Total
Working class	173	77	56	243	79	628
	(41.5)	(30.9)	(50.9)	(74.8)	(73.1)	(51.9)
Middle class	199	143	45	65	24	476
	(47.7)	(57.4)	(40.9)	(20.0)	(22.2)	(39.4)
Upper-middle class	45	29	9	17	5	105
	(10.8)	(11.6)	(8.2)	(5.2)	(4.6)	(8.7)
Totals	417	249	110	325	108	1,209
	(34.5)	(20.6)	(9.1)	(26.9)	(8.9)	(100)

Chi-square = 150.23
DF = 8
P < .001

Lacking longitudinal data for comparison over time, we do not know whether patterns of class identification have changed during the process of industrialization. In some advanced industrial societies, it has been found that manual workers are increasingly identifying with the middle class (embourgeoisement thesis), while the nonmanual workers' identification with the middle class has declined. The gap between manual and nonmanual workers' identification with the middle class, however, is still wide.[15] We are not prepared to make temporal comparisons for Taiwan, but we note that at present, manual workers in Taiwan show a stronger tendency to identify with the working class.

A comparison with other societies may shed some light on the reading of these figures. Centers' study conducted in 1946 found that 51 percent of his American respondents identified with the working class. This figure is almost the same as in our study. More striking is the proportion of manual workers identifying with the working class: in Centers' study it was 77 percent;[16] it is 75 percent in our sample. In 1962–63, Runciman found that 52 percent of English manual workers identified with the working class; another 7 percent of them identified with the lower-middle class.[17] Compared with these figures for advanced industrial societies, identification with the working class is relatively strong in Taiwan. Ignoring for the moment the small differences in research designs of these studies, we tentatively conclude that workers in Taiwan today are no less class conscious, measured in terms of class identity, than were their counterparts in advanced industrialized societies a few decades ago. Can we thus say that workers in Taiwan already have had, or at least have begun to develop, a strong working-class consciousness? Does working-class identity have any bearing on class consciousness? Before answering this question, let us first examine the factors contributing to working-class identification.

Aside from the embourgeoisement thesis mentioned above, several theories have been proposed to account for the variation in subjective class identification. Some of them are especially relevant to a newly industrialized society like Taiwan. One

---

[15] Frederick H. Buttel and William Flinn, "Sources of Working-Class Consciousness," *Sociological Focus* 12, 1 (1979): 37–52.

[16] Charles W. Tucker, "A Comparative Analysis of Subjective Social Class: 1945–1963," *Social Forces* 46, 4 (June 1968): 511.

[17] W. G. Runciman, *Relative Deprivation and Social Justice* (Berkeley: University of California Press, 1966), p. 158.

approach argues that class identification is significantly influenced by family social standings. Those from working-class families are more inclined to identify with the working class, although the effects of family background fade as people grow older.[18] Inasmuch as industrialization in Taiwan has been under way for only three decades, fewer than 40 percent of our worker respondents (manual, nonmanual, and self-employed) whose family origins can be identified have a working-class family origin. We would expect those having working-class origins to be more inclined toward working-class identity, while those first-generation workers with peasant and other social class origins would be less so. This "first-generation-workers thesis" is a recurrent theme in the explanation by local social scientists of the lack of working-class consciousness among Taiwanese workers.

Another factor often mentioned to account for the lack of working-class consciousness in Taiwan is related to the particular pattern of economic development based largely on small-scale firms (concentration-of-workers thesis). In 1991, only 0.5 percent of enterprises in the manufacturing sector had more than 500 employees. Another 3.9 percent employed 100 to 499 people. The percentage for manufacturing enterprises employing more than 30 and fewer than 99 was 11.9 percent. That is to say, 83.7 percent of manufacturing enterprises employed fewer than 30 people.[19] Often it is argued that workers in such small-scale enterprises encounter more obstacles to collective action and unionization. The labor process and the personal relations between workers and employers in small firms also hinder the development of class consciousness. If large enterprises are the central location of working-class formation,[20] then Taiwanese workers are mostly situated on the structural periphery. This argument is empirically, and partially, supported by the fact that since the late 1980s, when the democratic transition was launched, most collective labor disputes have occurred in larger enterprises. But are large firms also the center of working-class consciousness? Are those workers employed in larger enterprises more inclined than those working in smaller ones to identify themselves with the working class?

---

[18] Knudsen, "Class Identification in Norway."

[19] Executive Yuan of the Republic of China, *Yearbook of Labor Statistics* (Taipei: Executive Yuan, 1991), p. 124.

[20] John D. Stephens, "Class Formation and Class Consciousness: A Theoretical and Empirical Analysis with Reference to Britain and Sweden," *British Journal of Sociology* 30, 4 (December 1979): 389–414.

In addition to the factors mentioned above, another proposed explanation for the variation in class identity is the sex of the respondent (temporary-female-worker thesis). It is argued that women are less inclined to identify with the working class on two counts. First, in advanced industrialized societies, female workers tend to conform to the class identity and social attitudes of their husbands. Many middle-class wives have gone into the employment market in recent decades, most of them being employed in the lower rungs of the service sector. This fact, it is said, has contributed to a decline in both working-class identity and class voting. Second, the young females employed in the manufacturing sector are mostly temporary workers. (See Michael Hsiao's chapter herein.) If they do not quit their jobs after marriage, they see their work as a secondary source of family income. Viewing their employment as only temporary or secondary, they tend less than the career male workers to join in workers' collective action. Isolated from interactions with other, male workers, their consciousness is less developed.

We used a logistic regression model that analyzes class identity as a dichotomous variable to test these theories. Because our purpose here is to analyze the factors contributing to working-class identity among workers, we selected from our sample only workers for analysis. The total number of cases in the analysis was 515. Because a great many respondents did not provide information on their income, the variable of income level was omitted from the model to increase the number of cases. A preliminary testing also showed that income level is not significantly correlated with class identification. The independent variables in the model are sex, educational attainment, age, family class origin (nonworker/worker), and employment status (service worker/ self-employed worker/manual worker). All but age were run as categorical variables and a dummy variable for comparison created for each factor: female for sex, primary school and below for education, nonworker for family class origin, manual worker for employment status.

The model reveals several interesting things. First of all, only sex, education, and employment status are related to working-class identity. Contrary to the conventional thinking of local social scientists and also to the findings in other industrialized societies, father's class position does not significantly influence children's class identity. Second-generation workers are not more inclined to identify with the working class than are first-generation workers. The thesis of the first-generation-worker is not supported by the empirical data. Neither is age correlated with working-class identity.

Second, as widely assumed, female workers do tend significantly less to identify with the working class. Our data, however, do not allow us to analyze the reasons for this result. In addition to the factor of sex, another factor explaining the variation in working-class identity is employment status. Compared to manual workers, service workers are significantly less inclined to identify with the working class, whereas self-employed workers do not show any difference from manual workers. The most significant factor explaining variation in working-class identity is education. College graduates (34 cases) in our sample identify significantly more with classes other than the working class than do those workers with primary school education or below. Compared with the latter, high school graduates also identify less with the working class. But the most striking finding as far as education is concerned is that workers with junior high school education identify more with the working class than do the less educated (table 4). Junior high school is the level of education that correlates most strongly with working-class identification. Similar to the findings for other societies, education wields a significant influence on the decline of working-class identity,[21] although the relation between these two variables is not linear.

The sample in this model includes self-employed workers, to whom two important variables do not apply: scale of enterprise and union membership. To assess whether these two theoretically important variables also wield any influence on working-class identity, we omitted the self-employed workers from analysis in a second model. We created two additional dummy variables in the new model. For size of firm, firms employing more than a hundred workers were made a dummy variable for comparison. Our finding from the new model is that neither union membership nor scale of firm has any significant influence on working-class identity. Similar factors influence working-class identity in the two models. The popular assumption that there is a close causal relation between the particular pattern of economic development and working-class consciousness is not supported by the data (table 5).

We have found in the above analysis that some factors often assumed to account for labor quiescence, or the lack of class con-

---

[21] Knudsen, "Class Identification in Norway."

Table 4
Estimates of Logistic Regressional Coefficients for
Model Predicting Class Identity (for Workers)

	Working-class identity	
	β	S.E.
Sex (male = 1)	.354 **	.110
Education[a]		
College	−1.380 ***	.304
High school	−.239	.190
Junior high school	.477	.195
Age	−.008 *	.112
Family origin (working class = 1)	−.016	.110
Employment status[b]		
Service workers	−.493 **	.171
Self-employed workers	−.493 **	.182
(Constant)	.615	.440
Chi-squares	73.755	
D.F.	8	
N	515	

[a] Primary school level and below as dummy variable.
[b] Manual worker as dummy variable.
* p < .05
** p < .01
*** p < .001

sciousness among workers, are not related to working-class identity. But the finding so far does not reject those theories. Can it
be that although those factors do not account for working-class
identity, they nonetheless do explain the variation in other dimensions of working-class consciousness? That is, is working-class
identity related to other dimensions of working-class consciousness? The following section addresses these questions.

Class Identity and Class Consciousness

In the introductory section of this essay, I mentioned Michael
Mann's definition of working-class consciousness; in addition to
class identity, this definition includes three other dimensions: class
opposition, class totality, and conception of an alternative society.
Our questionnaire contains several questions related to these three

Table 5

Estimates of Logistic Regressional Coefficients for
Model Predicting Class Identity (not including Self-employed Workers)

	Working-class identity	
	β	S.E.
Sex (male = 1)	.535 **	.133
Education[a]		
College	−1.561 ***	.409
High school	−.121	.233
Junior high school	.477 *	.240
Age	−.020 *	.150
Family origin (working class = 1)	−.135	.133
Service workers[b]	−.410 **	.140
Scale of enterprise[c]		
Small (1–29)	−.158	.174
Medium (30–99)	−.004	.215
Union membership (= 1)	−.120	.132
(Constant)	.895	.551
Chi-squares	55.690	
D.F.	10	
N	363	

[a] Primary school level and below as dummy variable.
[b] Manual worker as dummy variable.
[c] Large firm employing more than 100 as variable.
* p < .05
** p < .01
*** p < .001

dimensions. I use these data to see if working-class identity is related to these dimensions of class consciousness and also examine other factors influencing working-class consciousness.

It is important to note that factor analysis shows that factor loadings to the questions on different dimensions of class consciousness are dispersed. The respondents' attitudes on different dimensions of class consciousness are not consistent. Higher levels of consciousness on class totality, for example, do not ensure higher levels of consciousness on class opposition. Various dimensions of class consciousness do not crystallize into a coherent whole. This fact has an important implication for theoretical speculation. As far as Taiwan is concerned, we should not hope for a single theory, or a single set of factors, to explain class consciousness. When we explain class consciousness, we have first to single out which aspect of class consciousness we are talking about. Different dimensions of class consciousness may be explained by different theories or factors. It is important to note that when we do the statistical manipulation, the low consistency among various dimensions of class consciousness does not allow us to aggregate these data into a single scale of class consciousness. We thus have to analyze each dimension separately.

Let us first tackle the dimension of class opposition. Our questionnaire contains two sets of questions on this dimension. The first set concerns attitudes toward capital-labor conflict of interests, the second tests the degree of tolerance on income inequality. One question in the first set asks about attitudes toward capital-labor conflicts: "Imagining that workers in a major industry are out on strike over working condition and wages, which of the following outcomes would you prefer? (1) The workers win their most important demands. (2) The workers win some of their demands and make some concessions. (3) The workers win only a few of their demands and make major concessions. (4) The workers go back to work without winning any of their demands." To this question, 86.2 percent of our respondents chose the second answer; another 7.3 percent chose the first. With this high consensus, the question loses its validity for statistical analysis. The consensus does, however, show two important things. First, the prevailing climate of public opinion is not antilabor. Most people seem to be sympathetic to workers' demands, possibly because workers in Taiwan are still a weak force and seldom strike. These figures also reveal the low degree of radicalism among Taiwanese workers. Only 11 percent of manual workers want to see workers win most of their demands. Nearly 80 percent of manual workers think workers should make some concessions to capital in a strike.

Workers' low level of militancy is also shown by their response to another question. When asked if "striking workers are generally justified in physically preventing strikebreakers from entering the place of work," 89.3 percent of respondents do not agree. The percentage is nearly as high among manual workers—85 percent. It is also important to note that among those few militant workers within our sample, working-class identity is not related to labor militancy as measured in these two questions.

Another question allowing us to analyze workers' attitudes toward labor-capital opposition asks if "corporations benefit owners at the expense of workers and consumers." Manual workers perform "better" on this question, with 28 percent of them agreeing with it; this figure is about 10 percent higher than upper-middle class, lower-middle class, and self-employed workers and 5 percent higher than nonmanual workers. But the overall difference is not significant. Again, and more important, this attitude toward labor-capital opposition is not correlated with working-class identity. Those workers identifying with the working class are not more inclined to hold anticapital attitudes.

We use logistic regression models to evaluate more accurately the influence of class identity and other variables on this dimension of labor-capital opposition. Because the variables of firm size and union membership do not fit the employers and the self-employed in our sample, we run the regression in two different models. One includes all the working population in the sample without the above two variables. The other model includes these variables and analyzes the employees only. As table 6 shows, none of the objective factors of working-class position, family (working) class origin, and working-class identity are correlated with consciousness on labor-capital opposition in the first model. In the second model for the employed working population only, working-class identity is not correlated with attitudes toward labor-capital opposition. The only variable correlated with oppositional consciousness is concentration of workers. Those employed in small firms tend to have less oppositional consciousness. The concentration thesis seems to be supported by the empirical data, although the correlation is not significant. A more important finding is that working-class identity does not play any role in influencing anticapital attitudes.

In the above section, we found that concentration of workers is not related to working-class identity. Taking these two findings together, we come to a tentative conclusion that working experience in small firms has a negative influence on workers' anticapital attitudes, but not on their class identity. The structural pattern of economic development characterized by the dominance of small-scale enterprises accounts partly for the overall low level of class consciousness in terms of labor-capital opposition, but not in terms of class identity.

Another set of questions concerns attitudes toward inequality in capitalist society: degree of tolerance for income inequality and the explanation of such inequality. Tolerance for inequality is an important dimension of social attitudes, or more specifically, the notion of justice. As Barrington Moore, Jr., points out, people

Table 6
Factors Predicting Working-class Consciousness

	Labor-capital opposition[a]		Industrial democracy[b]		Socialism[d]		Inequality ascription[d]	
	All	Employees	All	Employees	All	Employees	All	Employees
Sex (male = 1)					+*			
Education								
Age						-***	-**	
Family origin (working class = 1)								
Class position (working class = 1)				+**	+***			
Class identity (working class = 1)								
Worker concentration								
Small firm (1–29)		-*		+*				
Medium firm (30–99)								
Union membership (= 1)								

[a] Corporations benefit owners at the expense of workers and consumers.
[b] Nonmanagerial employees could run things effectively without bosses.
[c] Modern society could run effectively without the profit motive
[d] Three questions on poverty-ascription in table 8.
* p < .05
** p < .01
*** p < .001

desire equality, especially when goods are scarce. But they may tolerate inequality if the inequality is a consequence of and in proportion to investment. Citing George C. Homans, Moore argues that the popular notion of justice is the proportionate relation between what one invests and what one receives: "Resentment arises very easily when persons doing roughly the same kind of work see that their co-workers are receiving higher rewards."[22]

Thus in measuring egalitarian ideology, it may be more appropriate to measure one's degree of tolerance for inequality than one's attitude toward absolute equality. To do this, we use the question format roughly following the one used in a previous study by Jackman and Jackman.[23] Respondents are asked to state the income levels they think people in several different occupations deserve. Some of the occupational categories are associated with lower income (e.g., skilled worker and typist), some with higher income (e.g., plant director of a large corporation). We calculated the preferred income ratio of low-income occupations to high-income ones for each respondent and used it as a measure of tolerance for income inequality. The score for each respondent is the mean of two individual ratios: skilled worker to plant director and typist to plant director. A lower ratio reflects support for a wider income gap. The score could range from 0.1 to 1.0. Over 90 percent of the respondents have scores between 0.25 and 0.81. Among them nearly 50 percent fall between 0.42 and 0.75. That is to say, about half the respondents think the low-income occupations should garner as much as one-half to three-quarters the pay of the high-income jobs. The mean score for all respondents is 0.48.

As the figures in table 7 show, people of different classes do have different degrees of tolerance for inequality. The differences, however, are not significant. The upper-middle class respondents prefer a wider income gap between the lower class and the upper class, whereas manual workers support a narrower income gap. As for the relationship between working-class identity and tolerance for income inequality, we found some variation between those who identified with the working class and those who did not. But again, the difference is not significant.

---

[22] Barrington Moore, Jr., *Injustice: The Social Bases of Obedience and Revolt* (White Plains, N.Y.: M. E. Sharpe, 1978), p. 43.

[23] Jackman and Jackman, *Class Awareness.*

Table 7
Preferred Income Gap

	Mean score	Working-class identity	Other class identity
Upper-middle bourgeoisie	.450		
Lower-middle class	.476		
Nonmanual worker	.494	.553	.443
Manual worker	.523	.531	.508
Self-employed worker	.511	.499	.532
Total	.484		

We come next to the analysis of ascription of inequality (i.e., how the lower classes explain their inferior economic positions). This is the dimension of "class totality" in working-class consciousness. Respondents are asked to choose from among five possibilities about the cause of poverty: "Do you agree that one of the main reasons for poverty is (1) that in every society some people have to be on the bottom and some on the top; (2) that some people are not intelligent enough to compete in this modern world; (3) that the poor lack education and job opportunities; (4) that many poor people just do not want to work; or (5) that government policies cause or perpetuate poverty?" Factor analysis showed that only the factor loadings to answers 1, 2, and 4 are on the same consistency level. Dropping answers 3 and 5, we aggregated these three answers into a single variable of poverty ascription. We gave a code of 1 to those who agreed with all three statements or two of the three without answering the third one. Those who agreed with two of the three statements and disagreed with the other, and those who agreed with one, disagreed with the other, and had no opinion on the third were coded 2. Those who agreed with one of the three statements and disagreed with the other two were coded 3. And those who did not agree with any of the statements were coded 4. A higher code means stronger inclination to ascribe the inequality to structural instead of personal factors.

The multivariate regression model presented in table 8 shows that the only factor influencing attitudes toward the ascription of poverty is age. Older people tend significantly to be self-ascriptive on inequality, while the young tend to ascribe inequality to structure. Except for age, no other variables are related to this attitude toward poverty. Neither working-class identity nor

Table 8
Multivariate Regression Model Predicting Attitudes
toward Poverty-ascription

	Ascription to structure	
	All	Employees only
Sex (male = 1)	.0030	.0338
Education[a]		
Primary school and below	−.1544	−.0458
Junior high school	−.0491	.0802
High school	−.0224	.0439
Age	−.0108 ***	−.0093 **
Family origin (working class = 1)	.0374	.0616
Class position (worker = 1)	−.0868	−.0078
Class identity (working class = 1)	−.0581	−.0242
Scale of enterprise[b]		
Small (1–29)		−.0671
Medium (30–99)		.0789
Union membership (= 1)		−.0081
(Constant)	3.4147 ***	3.0871 ***
R square	.033	.0247
D.F.	8	11

[a] College level and higher as dummy variable.
[b] Large firm employing more than 100 as variable.
** $p < .01$
*** $p < .001$

objective working-class position plays a role. Even education does not play any role in the subjective explanation of inequality.

The last dimension, or the highest stage, of working-class consciousness is the conception of an alternative system to capitalism. Two questions on the questionnaire inquire into this dimension. The respondents were asked if they agreed that "(1) if given the chance, the nonmanagement employees at the place where you work could run things effectively without the boss" and (2) "it is possible for a modern society to run effectively without the profit motive." Inasmuch as other dimensions of working-class consciousness are underdeveloped, as we have seen, we would expect that workers will not do better on this dimension. The statistical analysis meets our expectation. As far as the first question on industrial democracy is concerned, none of the variables listed in the model, including objective working-class status, subjective working-class identity, family class origin, or education, predicts the variation in this attitude. As to the second question on an alternative to capitalism, most of these variables wield no influence. The only exception is objective working-class status. The working class is significantly more inclined toward a socialist alternative. But again, working-class identity is not related to this ideology (see table 6).

Conclusion

We began this essay by presenting data on respondents' awareness of class divisions. We found a high awareness of class divisions among the Taiwanese population. We also found that people in Taiwan tend to divide classes along economic rather than cultural or political lines. When we examined the phenomenon of subjective class identity, we found that a great many workers identify with the working class. In comparison with the findings for some advanced industrial societies, we found in Taiwan a population highly conscious of class divisions and a working class with a relatively high level of working-class identity. Those phenomena are striking for a newly developed country with a reputation for rapid economic growth with equity.

As we looked into the factors influencing subjective working-class identity among workers, we confirmed several theories proposed to explain the variation in working-class identity. Female workers tend significantly less to identify with the working class. Service workers also tend less than manual workers to do so. Education plays an important part in working-class identification. The only factor often mentioned but failing to explain working-class identity is family class origin. Second-generation workers are not more inclined to identify with the working class.

Several puzzles emerged when we began to analyze the content of working-class consciousness, the relationship between working-class identity and other dimensions of class consciousness, and the factors influencing working-class consciousness. First, in spite of a high awareness of class divisions in society, class consciousness among workers seems undeveloped. Workers in Taiwan appear to conform to a great extent to the dominant ideology of capitalist society. They also show wide acceptance of the inequalities in capitalist society.

Second, although a high proportion of workers identifies themselves with the working class, the identity does not play any part in the formation of class consciousness. It is often assumed, and confirmed by empirical data for other societies, that class identity plays a role in influencing social attitudes. But our empirical data suggest that working-class identity among workers in Taiwan is close to a "hollow identity," leading nowhere. Anyone trying to take class identity as one dimension of working-class consciousness should be warned of this phenomenon.

Why is this so? Several possibilities can be proposed. The high degree of identification with the working class among workers shows the wide acceptance of the label of "laborer-worker" (*laogong*). In Taiwan the label of laborer-worker is not considered a humiliating term as it has been in South Korea. (See Hagen Koo's chapter in this volume.) "Sacred are the laborer-workers" has been a phrase in government propaganda since the 1950s. The workers may not take this propaganda seriously, but at least the term is not a label imbued with social contempt as is the terminology used in South Korea. Workers are not looked down upon in Taiwanese society and, unlike their South Korean counterparts, do not try to hide their status.

More important, the most significant welfare program in Taiwan is called the Laborer-Workers' Insurance Program. The program covers most employees in the private sector, including white-collar workers and even managers. Any person employed in any business, industrial, cultural, or nonprofit establishment employing more than five people is entitled to this government-sponsored program. Thus both manual and nonmanual workers are used to the label of laborer-worker. In addition to the insurance program, the government extends some house-loan programs exclusively to workers. These welfare programs help to construct a socially positive, if not privileged, label of worker among the working class.

The widespread working-class identification among the Taiwanese working class may be explained by the above reasons. They also explain why working-class identification is not related to other dimensions of working-class consciousness. Working-class identification, or more accurately, the label of "laborer-worker," is constructed socially and by public policies rather than in struggles between labor and capital. Workers who label themselves as workers do not necessarily see that label as implying interests opposed to those of other groups. This may explain why working-class identity measured in terms of self-labeling is not related to other dimensions of class consciousness.

We can also speculate that this disconnection between identification and other dimensions is due to the inadequacy of measurement. Working-class consciousness is created to a great extent by participation in larger political and economic struggles. If class consciousness is the consequence of class experiences, these experiences include not only objective position in the mode of production but also daily interactions, in personal life and work situations, in social and political arenas, among different classes. That is to say, instead of asking general questions on social and political processes and formations, we may have to formulate specific questions about the actual working and living experiences of the workers.

Another important finding of this work is that various dimensions of working-class consciousness have not crystallized among Taiwanese workers. There is a very low level of consistency among different dimensions of consciousness. Some workers are conscious of a particular dimension, whereas other workers are more conscious of other dimensions. In the present stage, therefore, we should not try to explain the development of working-class consciousness with a single theory or with the same set of variables. Different theories may be needed to explain the different dimensions of workers' social attitudes. Some factors exert influence on a particular dimension but not on others. The low concentration-of-workers rate, for example, which characterizes the pattern of economic development in Taiwan and is often proposed to explain labor quiescence there, influences different dimensions of class consciousness in opposite directions. It is often assumed that social relations in small firms make workers in those firms less sensitive to labor-capital opposition. Our finding confirms this speculation. On the other hand, workers in labor-intensive small firms, which do not require a high level of technology and management, are also more receptive to the idea of industrial democracy.

This leads us to an important theoretical as well as methodological question in the study of working-class consciousness. As E. P. Thompson observed, the working class makes itself through political and economic struggles. In a newly developed country with relatively equal income distribution, such as Taiwan, where the class struggle is yet to come or may never arrive, the content of working-class consciousness will be dispersed and fragmented.

FOUR

Changing Literary Images of Taiwan's Working Class

HSIN-HUANG MICHAEL HSIAO

Social science approaches to literature have received little
attention in Taiwan. The relevance of literature to social change
has therefore been ignored by most social scientists. Though
literary critics have attempted to relate the changing motifs and
themes of literature to external social and political transforma-
tions, a systematic analysis of this important subject is still un-
available. Our understanding of the dynamic ability of literature
to reflect as well as refract the changing social reality in different
phases of Taiwan's postwar development remains impressionistic,
though instructive.

Literature and Society

The conventional way in which literary experts analyze the
relations between literature and social change is to compare the
similarities and differences between writings produced by
different cohorts or generations of authors. In recent years, as
more and more collections of Taiwanese writers' works have been
published, this approach to Taiwanese literature is becoming
plausible. It is possible to detect a number of interesting
differences in the authors' social concerns, their views of how
society operates as well as their notions of how society ought to
be. Prior to the 1970s, before the younger generation of Taiwan-
born writers became influential, Taiwan's literature reflected very
little social concern, and most authors deliberately avoided any
sensitive social and political issues in their works. In the 1950s
and 1960s, under the hard authoritarianism of the Kuomintang
(KMT), civil society was completely demobilized and atomized;
hence the passivity of writers was understandable.

Before the indigenous literature movement of the 1970s Taiwan's literature was dominated by the "anti-Communist literature" and "mainland nostalgic literature" of the 1950s, followed by the "modern literature" transplanted directly from the West in the 1960s. In those literary works, images of Taiwanese social life were either ignored or distorted. Postwar Taiwan reality was subsumed under the shadow of the prewar Chinese legacy in "politically correct" anti-Communist and nostalgic writings.

Some of the famous modernist writings portrayed the Taipei experience in a biased way, describing only the life story experienced by a few prestigious mainland emigrant families. The characters in some of the most widely read novels were overseas students from Taiwan living in North America, who described themselves as "the rootless generation." In short, the realities of Taiwanese society were largely absent in literature. The profound changes in social and political life as experienced by the majority of the population, Taiwanese and mainlander alike, during those two decades had not been captured in any literary work. The collective memory of the important immediate postwar era was absent from literature.[1]

A countercurrent to the mainstream of antireality modern literature emerged in the late 1960s. A group of younger writers began to produce works that were socially realistic, with the intention of reflecting the multifaceted life experiences to be found in Taiwan's changing society. The *Literary Quarterly* launched in 1966 has served as a vehicle for those works to reach a wider readership. Taiwan's diplomatic setback in 1972 also inspired many intellectuals to begin a journey of self-discovery for themselves and for Taiwan as a whole. Liberal intellectuals began to demand political reform, though still on a limited scale, as a growing nationalist sense of crisis brought about an unprecedented collective consciousness to deal with the problem of survival then facing Taiwan. Because of external frustration on the diplomatic front, serious attention was directed to internal reforms, and Taiwan reality began to concern many intellectuals.

The indigenous literature movement was a deliberate effort by many of the second and third generation of postwar Taiwan writers to search for literary ideas from real people in real life, a

---

[1] H. H. Michael Hsiao, "The Indigenous Consciousness in Taiwan's Intellectuals: A Sociological Examination," in *The Taste of Sociology*, H. H. Michael Hsiao, 185–211 (in Chinese) (Taipei: Dung-Da Books, 1988).

conscious attempt to move away from modernism to social realism. The movement reached its high point during the period of controversy over "indigenous literature" in the mid-1970s; since then social realism has established its legitimate status in Taiwan's literature.

The redirection toward indigenization or Taiwanization also took place in other cultural and academic fields. The social science community, especially in sociology, psychology, and history, became more reflexive about its research questions and more anxious to make social science relevant to Taiwan's social reality. Taiwanese popular culture such as Taiwanese opera, temple-related music, and other indigenous art forms received new appreciation, and steps were taken to restore and revitalize them.

Popular songs were rewritten to be more reflective of how Taiwanese people, especially the youth, live and think. "To sing our own songs!" was the slogan of the new breed of "folk singers" who sang not only about romantic love, as in the past, but about youth, family, workers, and society. Taiwanese-language songs were once again widely received with enthusiasm. New Taiwanese singers emerged, and their songs were more socially realistic than Mandarin-language ones. The voice and feelings of the common people and lower-class elements—for example, female workers, bar girls, dancing girls, street peddlers, gangsters, and sailors—were expressed in many of the revitalized Taiwanese-language songs.

The performing arts and movies experienced similar indigenization. The trend has continued in the 1980s and 1990s.

Under the cultural trend since the 1970s, many real stories of Taiwanese life have been told. Most of them concern the less pleasant aspects of life in modernizing Taiwan: impoverished farmers and fishermen, migrant workers from the countryside, divorce, extramarital affairs, family conflicts, workers without job security, the underworld of prostitutes and punks, corrupt businessmen and speculators, the loves and hates of middle-class women, and the changing faces of rural life. The stories dwell on the trials and tribulations of the lower classes and the conflicts and disintegration of Taiwan's complex social life. This literature can provide social scientists with information and insightful human stories of what really occurred in society while the Taiwan economic miracle was being made.

This essay focuses on how the working class has been constructed in Taiwan's literature since the 1970s. No attempt is made here to quantify the extent to which the theme of the working class has been adopted in Taiwanese fiction. As mentioned above, many social groups have been portrayed as main characters in works since 1970s. My crude impression is that, although workers appear prominently in these stories, they are not the dominant theme.

There is no clear sign that worker literature has grown in size over the years, and there has been no significant development of professional worker writers either from the ranks of workers themselves or from among intellectuals and writers. It seems that the political and cultural constraints imposed by capitalist ideology have greatly limited the growth of progressive literature in Taiwan.

To determine my sample of works to be analyzed, I have relied on the opinions of writers, literary critics, and my own reading and research experience in tracking down writers and stories in which the working class figures prominently. Because this essay is interested in analyzing changing images of the working class as portrayed in fiction, substantive discussion of the ways in which various aspects of the workers' lives and their characters are manifested is crucial. Five writers have been selected according to the above considerations: Yang Qingchu, Chen Yingzhen, Zeng Xinyi, Mo Shangchen, and Zheng Junqing. Yang has established himself as the representative of working-class literature. Mo and Zheng have also concentrated their writings on workers. Chen and Zeng cannot be labeled as writers specializing on workers.

In all cases, their works have portrayed different generations and different types of Taiwan's postwar workers. The following discussion is therefore organized in such a way that the images of different generations of the working class since the 1960s can be highlighted based on the characters and their stories as illustrated by different writers in their respective works. It should be pointed out that the notion of class will be dealt with in a broader sense throughout the main part of the discussion, and the writer's ideology of class and working-class consciousness as revealed in his or her writings will then be analyzed in the conclusion.

The Image of Taiwan's Working Class in the 1960s and the Early 1970s

Yang Qingchu is often classified as a working-class writer, but his work as a whole is itself a telling story of Taiwan's transition to industrialization. Thomas Gold, who has translated five of Yang's short stories into English, calls him a writer of modernization.[2] One can learn more about Taiwan's postwar development problems in the 1950s and 1960s from Yang's literary works than from many social science studies.

In most of Yang's stories, the farm families have experienced a process of disintegration, with the younger generation eager to leave the land to search for new lives in the townships and cities as wage workers in offices and factories. They are objects of envy, in large part because many young women prefer workers to farmers when choosing a husband. The more land a farmer owns, the less chance he has of finding a suitable girl to marry.

In "Twilight in the Fields" (1972), Shirong, a high school graduate who just finished his military service, has to stay on the farm to help his father with the farming so that the younger children can receive advanced education in the city.[3] His decision to remain in the countryside is to many fellow villagers and childhood friends a terrible mistake. His girlfriend, a former classmate of his sister's, is the daughter of an "idle and educated family" in the village: her father is a retired office clerk, her eldest brother an employee in the county government office, the second brother an office worker in a state enterprise, and her married sister a teacher in an elementary school. The girlfriend does not like the idea of Shirong's remaining in the countryside either, telling him that he should go to the city and look for a steady job or get some money from his father to start a business, as other young men would normally do.

When Shirong's mother asks the matchmaker to go to his girlfriend's parents to propose marriage, the proposal is declined on the grounds that Shirong does not have a job. Farming in the fields is not considered a real job. A job is the kind of work his girlfriend's brothers have. Shirong is angry, but he cannot change anyone's mind. He feels that his family is unlucky to own so much land. His three uncles all have left the farm and established textile and spinning mills in the city whereas his father, the eldest in the family, decided to continue the family tradition of farming the largest landholding in the village.

---

[2] Thomas B. Gold, *Selected Stories of Yang Ching-Chu* (Taipei: Dun-Li, 1978).

[3] Yang Qingchu, "Twilight in the Fields," in *The Virgin Girl* (Taipei: Dun-Li, 1978).

At the end of the story, Shirong's father is poisoned by insecticide, and his uncles have finally persuaded his father to let Shirong leave the farm. The uncles contribute funds to start a new spinning mill for Shirong to run; Shirong's father withdraws the family's entire savings, which were to be used for children's weddings and tuition, to help out the new business. A farmer is thereby turned into a factory manager. The family's huge landholding is converted into a profitable fish pond.

This story is a lively depiction of the changes in many Taiwanese farm families in the 1960s. Shirong's tale does not end in this story, however. Yang continues the saga of Shirong's journey into industrial life in *Virgin Girl* (1978), a collection of stories. Shirong fails in business and incurs huge debts. Once again, his family extends a helping hand to solve his financial crisis, but this time he is completely lost.

Other characters in Yang's stories are not as fortunate in their social origins, and none comes from a family with huge landholdings. Their fates in the changing society are, however, equally frustrating. Sadness and agony accompany their new lives in industrial factories.

Three groups of Taiwan's first generation of workers are adopted as characters in Yang's various stories of working-class life: temporary workers who enjoy no job security and no benefits, permanent workers with regular and steady salaries and a chance to be promoted into the rank of foremen, and teenage female workers in various private manufacturing industries. The temporary workers of both sexes in the stories are concentrated in a few large public enterprises; the permanent and teenage female workers can be found in both public and private sectors.

Most of Yang's workers are of rural origin; working in a factory is their first career change or even their first work experience. Regardless of their age, the first-generation workers all have inherited from their past rural experience the characteristics typical of post–land reform small farmers: passivity, fatalism, low expectations, and ignorance about their rights as workers. As Shirong's story shows, in 1960s Taiwan holding a steady and permanent job in a factory or office was a dream come true for many young people from farming families.

Compared with the kind of work and income available to a farmer at that time, a worker with a steady income and a hope for promotion felt fortunate indeed. But not everyone could acquire such a job in either private or public industry. Many ended up being hired as temporary workers in public enterprises, where they received low wages and had no job security, no benefits, and very little opportunity for promotion. This was particularly true for those with minimal education.

Temporary factory workers are treated as an underclass in Taiwan. They are evaluated periodically by their superiors to determine their rank and salary. Their hopes of being promoted to permanent worker status are constantly frustrated, and their experiences of asking for higher rank are humiliating. Their wives are also forced into casual labor in order to support the family. Not surprisingly, the family lives of these temporary workers are not happy. That unhappiness forms the dominant theme of Yang's early writings on workers. Many of these sad tales are recounted in Yang's first collection of stories, *The Factory Man* (1975).[4]

Winning promotion to a permanent position in the production line, it is believed, depends more on exploiting personal connections and giving gifts to superiors than on skill and performance. In "Promotion" (1971), Lin Tianming, in his sixteen years as a temporary worker, plays by the rules waiting for his day to be promoted but fails time and again. Finally, as his workmates advise, he tries to succeed by volunteering for extra gardening work at his manager's house. Through his connection with the manager's wife, Lin is given a chance for promotion. One passage vividly describes Lin's excitement: "Promotion! Promotion! Permanent worker! Permanent worker! I am a permanent worker now! Viva! I waited for sixteen years, and I am finally a permanent worker!" He draws a deep sigh, and tears fall from his eyes.

He shares this good news with his wife, a temporary worker who polishes rusted iron boards for a local subcontractor, thinking she will no longer need to work outside the home but will be able to stay home and take care of their children. His wife replies that she hopes the days ahead will truly be better because her life of following him has been difficult for a long time. The couple then tries to cash in their contributions in a rotating credit association in which they have participated, hoping to collect enough money to use as a gift for his manager. Finally, her parents borrow enough money from relatives and neighbors. But at the end of the story, Lin's promotion is denied on grounds that he tried to gain promotion by bribery. He realizes that he has made a terrible

---

[4] (Taipei: Dun-Li).

mistake in bypassing his immediate superiors. The denial was decided by his department head. The ending is another tragedy.

In another story, "The Underclass" (1971), the character is a sixty-five-year-old worker who, after thirty years of working as a temporary janitor, is forced to retire without any pension. Worried that after his retirement he will not be able to support his aged and blind father, he decides to die on the job so his father will have his accidental death compensation to live on. Before his death, a painful smile crosses his face, as he thinks he has finally accomplished one thing in his life.

Shi Jiansong is another temporary worker in the short story "The Confined" (1973). In this story, the protagonist is frustrated by repeated failed attempts at promotion. Furious about the continuous rejections by his superior of his requests for a transfer to another unit or a better rank in the same unit, he finally kills his boss in a severe quarrel. Even after the murder, Shi cannot escape from the boss's control. The boss's ghost insists, "Your fate is still in my hands. I control your destiny!" In the end, Shi is arrested and imprisoned. In the factory, he had felt humiliated among permanent workers and other temporary workers with higher ranks; now he loses his freedom completely.

There are other tragic characters in Yang's world of temporary workers. A temporary worker pretends to be a foreman with a decent salary. He is introduced to a fellow worker's sister, a former temporary worker who had an impossible love affair with the son of the factory owner. The owner, of course, disapproved of the romance and bought off the girl's brother to find another man for her to marry. After the worker rapes her, she is forced to have an abortion, a heartbreaking experience that makes her emotionally unstable.

However, she marries the worker anyway, believing him to be a permanent employee, and gives birth to a child, expecting to move into the company housing complex. Before autumn festival, she asks him about the bonus that the company customarily gives all its permanent employees on that occasion, only to discover that he is just a temporary worker. Shocked by that horrible truth and haunted by the recurring memory of the earlier rape, she becomes even more unbalanced and is confined to a mental hospital for the poor. The home is then without a wife and mother. The worker's unfortunate situation attracts sympathy from his superior, and with the help of his boss, he is finally promoted to the status of permanent worker a year after his wife's confinement.

On the day of his promotion, he goes to see his mentally battered wife, who does not recognize him. The doctor informs him that his wife has no chance of recovery and offers to issue a medical certificate if he wishes to remarry. But he has made up his mind to bring her back home and give her the life a permanent worker can afford. The ending is touching but tragic.

Compared to his many stories about the sorrows of temporary workers, Yang did not write much about regular and permanent workers in *The Factory Man*. Only through the eyes of temporary workers do we see that regular workers are better protected and able to maintain their families in a humane way. In some stories, a few regular workers do show sympathy to their less fortunate temporary workmates and even render a helping hand in their quest for promotion. But most of the ordinary regular workers in these stories come across as obedient, passive, and busy taking care of their own problems of livelihood. In one story, a permanent worker tries to get close to his company's general manager by going to the barbershop when the manager does. In another, a temporary worker turned regular employee seeks revenge on the superior to whom he gave gifts for his promotion when he learns that his boss is to be transferred to another new factory.

In only one story do some active regular workers try to strengthen their labor union. Although the factory management is very upset and uses all kinds of stratagems to stop them, still they succeed. These heroes are a tiny minority of articulate workers who believe in workers' rights and know how to mobilize their co-workers. The focus, however, is on the active individuals rather than the union. In the story, the general manager who tries to stop the workers from running in union elections finally recognizes that his workers are genuinely nice people and begins to feel attached to them emotionally. Although this realization comes only after he is assigned to a new position, his resentment toward the union does melt away.

In his later collection of short stories, *The Circle of Factory Girls* (1978),[5] Yang relates many similar life experiences of the other half of the first generation of workers—the teenage factory girls. Some of them are temporary workers and some are regular employees; some are new on the job and some have spent quite a long time in the factory. But all of them entered factory life right after their

---

[5] (Taipei: Dun-Li).

graduation from primary or middle school. Most of them sought factory jobs with the hope that they could earn enough money to send to their parents or to save for their own dowries, or even to meet new friends of both sexes. Their mobility was usually high, but some did remain at the same job for many years. These female workers had to put up with sex discrimination imposed from both management and their male co-workers.

"Zhaoyu's Youth" (1976) portrays a young girl who has spent twenty-two years in the factory. Although she has been transferred from the production line to office work, she is still a temporary worker. At one time, she turned down the marriage proposal of a young man who was also a temporary worker and encouraged him to continue his high school studies at night. Zhaoyu did not want to be a temporary worker's wife. She broke off a two-year relationship with a young engineer when she discovered that he had another girlfriend. She finished middle school by studying in the evening after work, but she was already twenty-eight, and unmarried. Ten years later, Zhaoyu still has not been promoted, and she is told that many younger girls with higher education are in line for promotion. Finally, at the age of thirty-eight, she is promoted after submitting a petition to the general manager. Yet she feels no gratitude, having traded twenty-two years of her youth for this position.

Love and hatred, hard work and injustice characterize the life experiences of many female workers in Yang's stories. Some of these teenage girls endure accidental pregnancy, some are seduced by male superiors promising promotions, and some are forced to quit after injuries on the job. In one case, a young girl is forced by her boss to kneel down in humiliation simply because she touched his luxury car with her wet and dirty hands. Female superiors are not necessarily more sympathetic; in some cases they are even tougher and more demanding. The managers are equally cruel to the female workers, and even the foreign owners wonder why local managers so openly exploit their own workers. When confronted with exploitation or labor disputes, these factory girls know that their union cannot provide any help; they can exert pressure on the factory only by threatening to quit collectively. Some actually do undertake "wildcat strikes," and the whole production line is forced to shut down for a time. That is the sole recourse of these teenage girls in response to the injustice all around them.

The Image of Taiwan's Working Class in the 1970s and the Early 1980s

A large portion of the literature on workers was published in the late 1970s and early 1980s. Stories produced in this period reflect a wide range of life experiences drawn from more diverse groups of Taiwan's working class. Not limited to temporary workers and teenage girls, the protagonists include many other figures: mainlander veteran workers, foremen, union activists, female workers with high school education, sympathetic managers, unreasonable department heads, groups of activist factory girls, salesgirls in department stores, bar girls, miners, and the like.

More aspects of working life are also touched upon in the stories written in this period: vivid descriptions of the acute conflict of interests between workers and management, the naive dream of a young salesgirl to be a singer or of a factory girl wishing to be independent, the guilt of a foreman who feels responsible for the illness of his son, the deep resentment and anger of a worker who suspects his wife of having an affair with his superior, or the struggle of a union official to resist the bribe of the company. In other words, these more recent stories present much richer and more colorful dimensions of working-class lives.

Mo Shangchen's writings on workers are collected in a single volume of short stories entitled *Nightmare 99* (1983).[6] Eleven of the twelve stories are insightful illustrations of Taiwan's workers in the 1970s and 1980s.

As in Yang Qingchu's stories on the 1960s, workers' difficulties remain important themes in the works of Mo Shangchen. However, the characters in Mo's stories are portrayed as less fatalistic, more conscious of their rights, and more inclined to take action to change the situation, though seldom in an effective and collective manner. The difference is significant and should be highlighted at the outset.

The hero of Mo's "Ladder to Heaven" (1983) is an unnamed veteran mainlander worker who still cannot afford a wife and tries to reject social conventions by climbing to the top of a tower in the city. The story tells of the confusion, resentment, fear, guilt, and paranoia in the inner world of this old worker who is under great pressure in the workplace, where he is seen by his superiors

---

[6] (Taipei: Vanguard Books).

as useless. In response, he fantasizes that he is a savior, linked to Almighty God. But clearly he can do nothing to save the corrupt world. Far from being a savior, he is really a sacrifice to modernity.

Although Mo hints that the worker has been treated by a doctor for severe paranoia and mental disorder, he does not spell out explicitly why the protagonist acts so strangely. But the causes are implicit in Mo's portrayal of the character as a confused worker resentful that he cannot afford to get married and fearful that he might end up wandering around homeless in the street after his retirement. The story ends when the worker is rescued by firemen and sent away in an ambulance. Before he is taken to the ambulance, he expresses the belief that God must still be waiting for him at the top of the tower, ready to listen to his endless accusation.

"Death of a Goldfish" (1983), another tragic story of a resentful middle-aged worker, describes the combined problems of work and family faced by a typical frustrated worker. You Zhengwian suspects his wife is having an affair with a neighbor and co-worker recently promoted to foreman through flattery and personal connections. Unable to stand it any longer, You follows his wife in hopes of catching the couple in dalliance. He even calls a policeman, but ends up by making a fool of himself. Finally, he kills the suspected foreman during a quarrel at the harbor. For the rest of the day You tries very hard to keep calm. Without that man, his wife remains his, and the family can be kept together he thinks.

That evening, he is surprised to see that his goldfish has died in its aquarium. Suddenly, the dead fish turns into the body of the man he has just killed, jumping from the water toward him. He breaks the aquarium and sees the dead fish lying on the broken glass. The goldfish had been a gift from the foreman to his wife. During the night, the image of the dead body is transformed into a huge black curtain, which drops from the sky to enshroud him.

In "Son's Sky" (1983), Qiushan, leader of a factory construction team, is happily married with one healthy three-year-old son. Busy with a heavy schedule set up by the company and threatened with severe punishment if he refuses to work overtime, Qiushan ignores his son's persistent high fever. It is too late when he finally sends his son to the hospital after ten days; his beloved son has lapsed into a vegetative state. His company promotes him to foreman when his superiors hear of his misfortune, but his co-workers remark that Qiushan has paid too high a price for his new position. He shows no excitement about the promotion; instead, his personality changes, and he no longer works hard for the company.

Deep feelings of guilt haunt Quishan for five years after that incident. One day he dreams that his son is standing in front of him with flowers in his hands. After he is awakened by the sounds of his son, he cries out loudly, "Help! Save my son!" A terrible thought suddenly comes into his mind; his face turns ugly and mean, and he sees his son's weak body being consumed by a huge worm. Qiushan kills the worm in a vain attempt to save his son. The dead worm changes into a snow-white cocoon from which a beautiful butterfly flies toward the sky outside the windows of his house. Standing by the window watching the butterfly flutter freely toward the vast expanse of green nature, Quishan has never felt so relieved. A smile comes his face, his first smile in many years.

Mo's roots as a poet are evident in the liberal doses of symbolism in his stories: the high tower, the dead fish, and the fluttering butterfly all symbolize the inner feelings of the workers. The three stories mentioned above reveal the complex interior world of the Taiwanese industrial worker. Whereas the emotions expressed by workers of the 1960s in Yang Qingchu's works were straightforward fear and anger, those expressed in Mo's works add a dimension of complexity to the equally sorrowful psychology of workers in the 1970s.

Mo's other stories also portray the social characters of his workers, though in a different way. In "Voting" (1983), Luo Qingxian, a council member of the union, is strongly against the company's plan to force every union member to pay NT$300–$400 into the Mutual Aid Fund. He does not trust the management of the company, suspecting the manager has something up his sleeve with respect to the fund. Although many workers also feel the same way, they do not know how to bring the plan to a halt. Luo, feeling compelled to take action to change the company's mind, persuades some other council members to join him in voting against the proposal. A former council member who had been active in fighting on the workers' behalf comes with the manager to Luo's house to ask him to compromise on this matter. Luo screams at the former council member and the manager and chases them off. His wife tries to dissuade him, but he insists on his course of action and refuses to compromise himself or the other workers' welfare.

Before the council meeting, the company arranges a week-long tour for all union council members. Luo is not going to join the tour until his good friend, also a council member, advises him to go ahead and have a good time and then still vote "No." He goes along, but he is very unhappy, feeling he is receiving a bribe from management. Luo cannot contain his anger at the first stop of the tour, Beitou, a tourist spot famous for its hot springs and prostitutes. He openly charges that the tour is a bribe by which the company is trying to buy out the union. He then leaves the hotel and returns to the south, to his factory and home.

On the day of the final vote, Luo is riding his motorcycle to the company when he is hit by a motorbike coming out of the main gate. He is sent to the hospital, but runs back to try to cast his "No" ballot in the meeting. The story ends there. It seems that the result of the meeting is not as important as the emergence of a new kind of worker. More accurately, it is the new leadership among the workers that concerns this writer.

Mo also portrays several other labor leaders who possess different attitudes and styles from those depicted in Yang's stories.

The hero of "Fire Shower" (1983) is a team leader in a shipyard. Li Guizheng has a normal and happy family life and deeply appreciates what his wife has done for the home and for him. Although from time to time he still thinks of the girl in the teahouse with whom he once fell in love in his bachelor years, he is determined to keep his family together.

His attitude toward his co-workers is also very positive; he even defends an arrogant young worker before management. That young worker is a fast learner, yet he holds a very negative perception of management. He feels that all superiors are enemies, constantly finding fault with the ordinary workers. The young worker comes to work late, leaves work without prior permission, and chooses to be idle as a way of passive protest. Li Guizheng understands this young man well and hopes he will change someday. He tells his manager that the mistrust and struggle among workers themselves is more serious and detrimental than the conflict and distrust between labor and management.

In this story, Li's foreman is also a very considerate and humble superior. He speaks up for the team leaders under him when company management complains that he has been too easy on them. Li himself is kind to an older worker who labors diligently and seldom complains. This "familial feeling" among worker, team leader, and foreman is probably overly idealized in the story, but it is intended to point to the kind of relations that can guarantee high morale in the workplace. In this story, the brotherhood works. During a fire, the troublemaking young worker saves his team leader and other co-workers.

In another story, "Climbing up to the Top" (1983), a young worker who studies high school after work is encouraged by his many co-workers, but his foreman is not at all happy about the activity. One day the worker learns that the company has a policy of paying for any worker who passes the qualifying exam to attend the technical college. He asks for permission from his foreman but is turned down, so he goes to the director for help and is finally approved. The director reprimands the jealous foreman for discouraging the young man's studies. Times have changed and the thinking of management has to change too. The young man passes the exam and successfully enters college.

His co-workers are excited to hear the good news and share his happiness as though they themselves had achieved something spectacular. After two years of hard study, this young man returns to the company to assume a higher position. In a welcoming ceremony, the director introduces him to all the workers and encourages other workers to take him as a role model. The director also emphasizes the importance of new knowledge in upgrading the quality of both production and management. The humbled foreman stands quietly in the crowd.

It is clear that at least some enlightened managers have come to realize that they must keep pace with the changing world. Under such progressive leaders, the workers can thrive.

During the 1970s, "workers" came to include more and more women, and authors came to include them in their writing. The following stories concern female workers in the 1970s and the early 1980s.

Mo's short story "Nightmare 99" (1983) tells of a girl's ninety-nine days in an export-processing-zone factory where the majority of workers are females. After having failed the college entrance exam, this girl decides to work during the day and study in a tutorial school at night to prepare for the next year's exam. Her family does not much like the idea, but she is determined to proceed with her independent life. The first day on the job, she notices a big sign saying "Take the factory as home." She is heartened, believing she has joined a new family.

However, in the following ninety-nine days before she is fired, what she sees and experiences convinces her that the factory is no home after all. She witnesses a forewoman's mistreatment of an elderly woman in the production line. A young girl tells her about being raped by a man working with her in the restaurant where the girl works at night to make extra money to send home. She makes friends with a nice young male worker, but thereby becomes the target of jealousy of another girl. In one incident, her boyfriend is injured when he tries to protect her from being hurt by the jealous rival. After that incident, she is fired. Stepping just outside the main gate of the factory she sees that the big slogan is still there. It is beautiful outdoors. She counts the days of the nightmare she has endured: ninety-nine.

In "The Cloud" (1983), a work by Chen Yingzhen, the story is told through a young female worker's diary.[7] She works in an American-owned manufacturing factory, a new feature of Taiwan's economic scene since the 1970s. She likes to write and is noticed by a young manager who then encourages her to contribute to the company's monthly magazine. She is very excited about the recognition she has received from the manager.

The company's general manager is an American who wishes to make the Taiwan branch a part of the global policy of the American mother company, complete with industrial democracy and workers' rights. Therefore, he asks one young manager, Chang, to help establish a union that truly belongs to the workers. A group of female workers decides to take the initiative to reform the existing union controlled by the factory management. The diary relates day-by-day events of this unionization effort, describing the reformist sentiments shared by many workers.

The factory management uses every conceivable means to stem the tide of change. Feeling threatened, the incumbent union officials join with management in a common effort to kill the reorganization of the existing union. For a time, two unions exist side by side in the factory: the new union backed by the American general manager and manager Chang in the Taipei headquarters, the old union in the hands of local factory personnel.

The showdown finally arrives. Contrary to expectation, the U.S. headquarters discourages the new general manager from supporting the new union. The factory general manager, it seems, is backed by a Chinese partner who is a retired air force general and

---

[7] In *Cloud* (Taipei: Yuan-Jing, 1983).

still has power in the overall operation of the company. The activist girls are abandoned in the fight for an independent union. In one vivid scene depicting the fight between the women revolutionaries and the conservative men, a girl tears off her blouse and exposes her breasts, screaming at the man who tries to chase her and her fellow female workers away from the voting booth. Some male workers then join them to protect the ballot box. The majority remain bystanders on the other side of the lawn in front of the office building. The girls are sobbing and beseeching their fellow workers to show their support by raising their company hats. Quietly, hundreds of hats of different colors representing different departments begin to wave in the air. But that ends the revolution. The new union is aborted and all of the activist girls forced to leave.

Later, the American general manager passes along a message from the U.S. headquarters to manager Chang. It reads, "The safety and interest of the company are more important than human rights considerations." Chang, the naive Taiwanese manager who has all along believed fully in the company's global philosophy of industrial democracy and human rights, suddenly feels ill. He soon leaves the company to start his own small trading business in Taipei.

This story documents the rise of collective action led by a new breed of energetic, intelligent, and conscious female workers. The stereotypical image of the passive, disorganized, and ignorant female worker is challenged in this powerful work. It also raises the curtain on the unfolding drama of Taiwan's labor movement. According to government statistical data, in the 1970s the total number of labor disputes grew more than tenfold, and the proportion of disputing workers in the total employed population jumped from 0.07 percent to 0.4 percent, a fivefold increase. Entering the 1980s, the incidence of labor disputes increased with even greater momentum. From 1981 to 1988, some 10,441 cases were registered.[8]

Zeng Xinyi writes of another kind of urban working girl. In "The Princess from Wulai" (1976) she describes the experiences of Lucy, a bar girl.[9] At age thirteen Lucy leaves her aborigine village

---

[8] H. H. Michael Hsiao, "The Labor Movement in Taiwan: A Retrospective and Prospective Look," in *Taiwan: Beyond the Economic Miracle*, ed. Denis F. Simon and Michael Y. M. Kau, 151–67 (Armonk, N.Y.: M. E. Sharpe, 1992).

[9] In *The Collected Works of Zeng Xinyi* (Taipei: Vanguard Books, 1992).

of Wulai to work first in a teahouse as a waitress, then as a bartender, and finally as a bar girl—a prostitute. She was cheated by the two women who enticed her to run away from home and who, it turned out, were prostitutes. She married three times and was beaten by all three husbands. Now approaching thirty, Lucy feels she has no luck with husbands. Moreover, she has to go home often to take care of her parents because her two younger sisters have married. She feels weighed down by her heavy burden.

The heroine of "Chaifeng's Dream" (1977) is a salesgirl in a department store who dreams of becoming a famous singer. She is recommended by her company to compete in singing contests that offer the possibility of becoming a professional singer. Through the course of many contests, Chaifeng has to socialize with and please her vice–general manager and sponsoring businessman, both of whom try to take advantage of her. The businessman even asks her to be his mistress, promising her ample money every month.

At last she wins a contest, and the owner of a restaurant–piano bar offers her a job as a singer. It is a high-class, expensive restaurant, and she can't resist the temptation of the high salary and comfortable life, so she quits her job in the department store and begins to sing in the restaurant. Many of her friends envy her new job and the bright future ahead of her.

But soon Chaifeng realizes she cannot escape unwelcome advances from men. One day, she is asked by her boss to entertain a Japanese businessman. Alone with the Japanese visitor inside the private VIP room, she realizes what is wrong with this restaurant. Her dream has not come true after all.

Zeng's girls are a particular kind of city worker. From the 1970s, more and more girls have been either forced into or voluntarily involved in the sex industry in Taiwan. (For the comparable trend in mainland China, see Gail Hershatter's chapter herein.) One account estimated that in the late 1980s there were at least forty thousand establishments involving the sex trade and that about 4 percent of Taiwan's women were prostitutes.[10] From various journalists and human rights groups, we know that Taiwan's sex industry has recently gone underground, and accurate figures are nearly impossible to obtain. Literary accounts of bar girls,

---

[10] See Charles McCaghy and Charles Hou, "Career Onset of Taiwanese Prostitutes" (paper presented to the Annual Meeting of the Society of Social Problems, Berkeley, California, August 6–8, 1989).

dancing girls, and prostitutes thus often provide more insight about this emerging social problem than do the reports of social scientists.

From the above discussion we see that literary depictions of workers in the 1970s and the early 1980s differed from the depictions in previous decades. More varieties of workers were introduced, their inner worlds revealed, and more progressive activists presented. The literary works also hint at a changing relationship between labor and management in this period.

The Image of Taiwan's Working Class since the Mid-1980s

Working-class literature has received greater attention since the mid-1980s, and many colloquial and literary reviews on this topic have appeared. For example, at the beginning of 1985 *Taiwan Literature* published the papers from the seminar "Workers' Literature: Retrospect and Prospect"; more recently, in May 1993, *Literary Notes* organized a regional literature symposium focused on worker writers.

Few novels on workers were actually produced in the same period, however, although social scientists began to study the labor movement and workers' collective actions. The development of tension and confrontation between labor and management became overt in the 1980s, though labor disputes had been on the rise since the 1970s. In the mid-1980s the working class in general was mobilized through many incidents of organized collective action. The rise of reformed and independent unions and the surge of the labor movement are significant developments of this period. As my previous studies have shown, it is only within the context of the overall changing state-society relationship and the dialectic dynamic between social movements and political liberalization that the origins, formation, and significance of the 1980s labor movement in Taiwan can be fully understood.[11]

In this critical juncture, Zheng Junqing's *Angry Workers of a Mountain City* (1989) is of particular relevance.[12] It is the only lengthy work devoted entirely to workers. Commissioned by the Taiwan Labor Legal Assistance Association (changed in May 1988 to the Taiwan Labor Movement Assistance Association) in the summer of 1987, it is a novel based on the documentary accounts

---

[11] See Hsiao, "Labor Movement in Taiwan."

[12] (Taipei: Vanguard Books).

of the labor disputes and ensuing collective actions that took place in the Hsin-Chu Glass Company beginning in the summer of 1985, the most significant labor movement incident before the actual lifting of martial law in July 1987.

The story begins with the chairman of the board having run off with a large sum of money from the company coffers. The financial plight of the company quickly becomes a serious problem for all its employees. The main character of the story is the plant general manager, Heng, who has been working for more than eighteen years. Heng started as a regular worker, then was appointed foreman, department manager, and finally general manager of the plant. The majority of the employees are farmers turned workers who have lived for generations in the villages and townships near the plant. It was a reputable company, and the workers took pride in being part of the plant. But in recent years, as a result of internal struggles for control over company operations through stock manipulations, the company has been constantly faced with managerial and financial problems. The older workers who joined the plant at its inception became victims whenever the power center of the company changed.

Because of their experiences under authoritarian control during the 1940s and 1950s, the elderly workers recoil in fear when faced with conflict or injustice. The younger ones have inherited this conservatism and apathy, believing it to be the best way to keep out of trouble. Work is their whole life, and they have given their all to the plant.

After Heng and some other plant managers learn of the chairman's embezzlement and the ensuing cover-up by the company's chief executive officers, they are extremely upset. Having repeatedly tried in vain to get the company leadership to solve the financial mess, they come to realize that the current company management is part of a bigger conspiracy that is putting all workers in jeopardy. Led by Heng and a few others, the workers take over the management of the plant. Every worker agrees to contribute a capital share to the total sum needed to restore the plant operations according to his or her wage. Workers then begin to take out their own money to save the plant from closure.

The process is not easy. Resistance from the existing company management is strong; financial and legal support from the county, provincial, and national unions is almost nonexistent at the beginning; and the local politicians for whom the workers voted in past elections are all reluctant to take sides. The workers are forced to adopt their weapon of last resort: to go out on the streets to demonstrate. When a decision to stage a street demonstration is reported, the public security forces monitor the leaders and even warn them to stop the demonstration. But the workers are determined to ignore the threat. Finally, their voices are heard by the central government, and an agreement to reorganize the management of the plant is reached. Afterward, the workers are surprised to realize that the government does "dig deep only on soft dirt": three months of law-abiding petitioning prove less effective than one day of illegal street demonstrations.

The novel describes how Heng and his fellow workers changed their attitudes from fatalism and passivity to consciousness and activism and, more important, organized behind the new leadership headed by Heng. When Heng is indicted on charges from the company that he has misused public funds to favor the workers, virtually all workers side with him. The story details the process by which workers tried hard to understand the law and sought help from the Taiwan Labor Legal Assistance Association, an emerging grassroots progressive labor organization. Through self-help as well as outside assistance, employees at this local plant developed into a collectivity of class-conscious workers, mobilized against the company and its capitalist-class leaders.

Missing from the work is a discussion of the internal struggle that occurred within the preexisting union before the decision to take over managerial power was made. In fact, the activist workers had to undertake a virtual "revolution" to reorganize the union. It is unclear why the author omitted these events. But to social scientists studying Taiwan's labor movement at the time, the successful reform of the "old" union must be seen as a crucial factor in the development of a successful organized labor movement.[13]

---

[13] Hsiao, "Labor Movement in Taiwan"; see also Jenn-hwan Wang, "The Formation of Working-Class and Collective Action," in his *Capital, Labor, and the State: Taiwan's Political and Social Transformation,* 189–217 (in Chinese) (Taipei: Radical Quarterly in Social Studies Publishers).

Recapturing the Stories

To what extent have these insightful literary works reflected the actual situation of workers in different phases of Taiwan's postwar development? What is the ideological structure underlying these fictional portraits of the working class?

The breakdown of the postwar era into the three decades of the 1960s, 1970s, and 1980s should not be taken too literally, as they are used simply to represent the three general phases of Taiwan's industrial and economic transformation and political change: the rapid industrialization of the 1960s, the deepening capitalist development of the 1970s, and the beginning of political liberalization of the 1980s.[14]

It is clear from the illustrations above that the literary works do portray the images of workers differently in different decades. Yang Qingchu's many works on temporary workers presented the suffering faces of a special underclass within the first generation of the working class during the dual process of rapid industrialization and rural-urban migration. The less sharp portrayal of permanent workers suggests that they belong to a different category, though they still have to struggle for their own survival in the workplace. How to climb the occupational ladder while keeping themselves out of trouble seems to be the dominant concern of almost all workers in Yang's stories. That image can equally be applied to the female workers who have constituted a significant part of Taiwan's workforce since the 1960s.[15] They are more or less fatalistic, self-pitying, and unaware of their rights. The most common way to change their situation is to change themselves to accommodate to the environment imposed on them. It is unthink-

---

[14] See H. H. Michael Hsiao, "Explaining the Taiwan Development Model: Lessons to be Learned," in *The Role of Market and State: Economic and Social Reforms in East Asia and East-Central Europe*, ed. Dalchoong Kim et al., 127–47 (Seoul: Institute of East and West Studies, Yonsei University, 1991); and idem, "The Rise of Social Movements and Civil Protests," in *Political Change in Taiwan*, ed. Tun-Jen Cheng and Stephen Haggard, 57–72 (Boulder, Colo.: Lynn Rienner, 1992).

[15] See Yung-Mei Tsai and H. H. Michael Hsiao, "Women Factory Workers in Taiwan Today: A National Profile," in *Conference Record of the Seventh Annual Science Engineering and Technology Seminar*, ed. S. C. Lou (Houston, Tex.: Association of American Chinese Professionals, 1985). The percentage of women in the labor force increased from 28.7 percent in 1955 to 34 percent in 1965; by 1982 almost half the women fifteen or over held income-earning jobs. In comparison, the male labor force participation rate has always been higher.

able for them to do something collectively to change the behavior of their bosses or the rules arbitrarily set by the company.

The workers of the 1960s as portrayed in the stories share in common a sense of victimization caused by unfair treatment. The stories told by Yang Qingchu are the concrete reflection of the sentiments expressed by atomized and demobilized individual workers.

The images of the 1970s workers painted in a number of works by Mo Shangchen, Chen Yingchen, and Zeng Xinyi are different. The common feature is still the problems faced by the workers, and the root of their problems stems from their work situations. The workers are no longer perceived as one-dimensional working individuals, however, but are treated as multidimensional human beings. Beyond the direct illustration of the expressed frustration of the workers, their inner world of anxiety, fear, hope, and love is also explored. Also, a new kind of worker and a new style of leadership among the workers emerges in various stories as the workers of the 1970s begin to think of themselves as a group sharing similar fates and hopes. The changing relationship between labor and management is also hinted at.

Moreover, the possibility for workers to change the world of the factory is implicitly introduced in the stories, though the probability of success is still very low. The abortive revolution of a group of enlightened female workers is praised, and the option of organizing workers into a potentially cohesive force is also suggested. The rise of workers' collective action, though liable to end in failure, is already recognized by the writers.

The single work devoted to a successful workers' collective action of the 1980s illustrates the complete process by which the workers can change their fate through self-learning, self-organizing, and self-mobilizing efforts against a powerful company. The sentiments of the workers are no longer expressed in individual terms, and certainly not in a self-defeating manner. Hope and anticipation characterize this novel. Zheng suggests that the future of industrial democracy lies in the collective identity of workers led by a functioning union. The workers of the 1980s as portrayed in this novel are more than a group of workers sharing similar experiences: they have begun to see themselves as a social class with the same interests. In this novel, the overt conflict of interests between workers and management is clearly manifested, and beyond that, the state, the legal system, and the security apparatus are viewed as opposing the workers. This work traces the rise of working-class consciousness among many of its characters.

In the stories reviewed in this paper, the perception of workers has changed: atomized individuals acquire a group identity and finally become a social class. The role of the union also changes in the minds of the workers in different decades. Since the late 1970s, labor unions have been seen by the workers as a potential tool that they themselves should try to control. And since the mid-1980s, workers have fully acknowledged the critical role of labor unions to the protection of their own rights in the workplace and in society. Many reformed unions have published internal newsletters from which we can clearly sense such growing consciousness.

Finally, it is interesting to detect a commonly shared acceptance of the objective divisions in society, an acceptance that finds embodiment in the stories. No suggestion is ever made to question or reject that existing social structure. Even in cases where acute confrontations and conflicts are manifested in workers' collective action, the intention is to improve the working-class position within the social class structure rather than to reject it. Even the idea of class as an objective division in Taiwan society of which the working class is an integral part is not evident in the fiction until the mid-1980s. Moreover, as Nai-teh Wu's empirical study of the early 1990s suggests, in spite of a high awareness of class divisions in society, the level of working-class consciousness among Taiwan's workers remains low; they generally seem to conform to the dominant ideology of the capitalist social system and to accept the inequality of that society (see chapter three herein). It is therefore unlikely that Taiwan's emerging labor activism will develop in a radical direction in the near future.

FIVE

Owner, Worker, Mother, Wife: Taibei and Chengdu Family Businesswomen

HILL GATES

Let labouring men stride in the streets.
Let radiant columns file through the squares.
> Ah Ch'ing (Bold 1970:339)

In delight I watch a thousand waves of growing rice and beans,
And heroes everywhere going home in the smoky sunset.
> Mao Zedong (Bold 1970:176)

They tease one another in coarse accents.
An occasional joke helps to banish fatigue.
The lingering flavour of rustic stories
Puffs rings of smoke that lengthen in the air,
Recalling to mind many a summer night at home in the backyard.
Once, twice, a thousand times—it never grows stale.
Now it is being brought to fresh life in this city landscape
To make its listeners nostalgic.
This vast building brings them together from all over the land;
Strangers have now become brothers.
. . . . . .
Whose shoulders are cast in bronze
That they can sustain knocking against slabs of stone or iron?
There are also family worries and illnesses
That blur their vision of the colours of the toiling seasons.
An instant of dizziness or carelessness
Will end in a heap of blood and flesh,
Or the usual striking out of a name
From the register of Heaven!
> Ts'ang K'e-chia (Bold 1970:333–34)

Worker-heroes in the militant struggle for class liberation, peasant-soldiers self-liberated and doubly heroic as veterans and growers of rich crops, villager high-steel men balancing family troubles and bodies at risk—a trio of Chinese poets celebrates Labor. These excerpts make a series, from facelessly egalitarian revolutionaries to men with particular accents, concerned for family members and for the radical individualism of death.

For me, an anthropologist who has spent all of my field time with Chinese and Taiwanese working people, the series anticipates a fourth instance.[1] My memory flashes images of the worker at home, safe in familiar routine, yet under demanding discipline; a shareholder in familial property while still a laborer upon it. Trying to epitomize "labor" in the broader Chinese context, I look for a poem that celebrates the worker—who might well be a woman—tied to a frame-knitting shop, a household piggery, a hot-pot restaurant. But she is not, it appears, an appropriate subject for poetry. Nor is she seen as a laborer in more prosaic genres. Indeed, as I have learned from talking to such women, she perceives herself as carrying a puzzling and contradictory identity. If we seek to understand Chinese forms of labor, and the intentions of Chinese laborers, we cannot examine only the classical industrial proletariat. We must focus as well on the women and men who produce commodities in their homes and on their farms. They form the majority of China's workforce and a very substantial proportion of Taiwan's.

Because the two Chinese genders mutually constitute each other, it is impossible to talk about women without implicating men—just as the reverse is always true. Here, however, I will focus on women as best I can, for women's worker identities are especially interesting, always on the brink of dissolving into those of kinship. Many of the failures of Chinese socialism may be attributable to the social failure to create a political-economic structure that encouraged stronger worker identities for women. Many of the recent successes of Chinese women may be nurtured, however, by the high value placed on work for women both under socialism and beyond it.

---

[1] For the sake of brevity, I use the term "Chinese" as an ethnic supercategory to include those of Han ancestry who now live in many parts of the world and those of imperial times. Only when it is plainly contrasted with a category of citizens of other nation-states, as here, will it refer to citizens of the People's Republic of China.

In a very special subset of women, 1980s owner-operators of small businesses, worker identity is preserved in a delicate glace of self-esteem that comes from work itself. Under analysis, that icing quickly melts; but it holds its shape long enough for us to glimpse the complexities that people face when they must not only create commodities, but produce selves that are sufficiently sturdy to withstand the haggling and negotiation that characterize class status, market transactions, and family life (v. Gates 1993). Below, I sketch the political-economic parameters that structure these petty capitalist lives, giving shape to their identities as workers, as private owners of means of production, and as women.

Petty Capitalism

Commodity production has a long history in China, where markets have been an important part of economic life for at least a millennium (Gates 1995). Over the centuries, Chinese people have fashioned structural and cultural repertories that give their societies substantial expansionary dynamism. These repertories are not merely survival strategies. They organize and reproduce classes that have been essential both to the slow growth of the past and to twentieth-century economic success. Producing outsourced goods for larger firms, rearing children who as adolescents are lent to the formal sector as capable and low-cost labor, supplying cheap goods and services for each other and low-wage workers in all sectors, petty capitalists have much in common in present-day Taiwan and China. Their commonalities help explain *Why the Emperor's New Clothes Are Not Made in Colombia* (Morawetz 1981), but in Hong Kong or Shanghai. Petty capitalist households of current and future owner-operators form an important and theoretically problematical portion of Chinese working classes.

In Taiwan, the ruined post-1945 economy was resuscitated by local and immigrant petty capitalist household firms. Myriad shops, small building firms, and tiny factories recovered prewar living standards and supplied the growing population with food, housing, and clothing. These owner-operators found themselves living under a labor regime suddenly restructured by geopolitics along lines that pruned away most nonmanual jobs for Taiwanese while simultaneously giving many of them access to small-scale means of production. Great numbers of educated Taiwanese were dispossessed from state- and capitalist-sector employment; land reform homogenized rural society into small farm households

producing increasingly for market. But this small-producer economy, politically feeble and dependent on easily taxed agricultural
products for its income, lost much of the wealth it created to the
powerful Kuomintang state.

Taiwan's economy from 1945 to about 1965 was dominated by
noncapitalist state production, employment, and forms of circula-
tion. Rural and urban petty capitalism were kept firmly subordinated, though essential. Only as the 1960s "liberalization" took
hold did corporate capitalism begin to play a major role in
Taiwan; Kuomintang leaders of the 1940s and 1950s were as suspicious then as Communist ones are now of unconstrained and
large-scale capitalism. Even after a new wave of multinationals
began to create expanding wage employment in the later 1960s,
petty capitalism continued to employ a great many Taiwanese.
The goal of running one's own business has come to be seen
locally as a mark of culturally specific national character—as we
see in Hsieh Guo-hsiung's 1992 study "Boss" Island.

Although Taiwan remains politically independent of China, its
economic fortunes are increasingly imbricated into the fabric of
the continent's growing coastal development. There too petty capitalism is important. As the result of the reforms of the past
fifteen years, it can be argued that classes engaged in petty
capitalism—owner-operators, unpaid family labor, informal
apprentices, and hired hands who often graduate to small
businesses of their own—constitute the numerically largest and
politically most influential working class in postrevolution China,
as well as in Taiwan.

The political influence of petty producers in China is not direct,
nor does it date from the recent reform period. Rather, petty producers have been a major force in post-1949 politics by virtue of
the stubborn tendency of householders, rural and urban, to turn to
private production for the market whenever central controls on
such behavior were relaxed. After the few genuinely capitalist
institutions of the pre-1949 political economy were eradicated,
officials continued to attempt to quash what they saw as resurgent
capitalism in town and country. They aimed to wilt sprouts of
capitalism, to cut off capitalist tails, and generally to extirpate a
deep indigenous complex of household production, informal
finance, local and regional marketing, and their ideational supports.[2] Virtually all of the PRC's political-economic movements—

---

[2] Fei Hsiao-tung stressed the importance of this complex for rural and small-
town economies in his early work, especially in *Peasant Life in China* (1939) and

most notably the Great Leap, the early Cultural Revolution, and the 1980s privatizations—were responses to the persistent pressures of households toward petty capitalist production. Daniel Kelliher sees the 1980s reforms as having been driven far beyond state intentions by unorganized but unanimous rural strategies centering on petty production (1992). The political-economic vision of a vast class of actual and potential owner-operators, family workers, and informal apprentices regained an important niche. Now, in the 1990s, the mix of state, capitalist, and petty capitalist modes of production is remarkably similar in Taiwan and the PRC.

Market transactions and a highly commoditized way of life are important elements in Chinese culture. These are not new phenomena, engendered by the pressures and fantasies of the West. But the capitalist-like tendencies of imperial-period Chinese were, and continue to be, reined in by the intimate connection that the state has enforced between economic activity and kinship organization. Kinship relations became extremely significant relations of production, defined and protected by state management of inheritance and family law.

The petty capitalist mode of production emerged historically as both a convenience and a form of resistance to a dominant state mode of production. It is reproduced in the present for the same reasons. The tendency of people acting in this mode to create full-blown capitalism has been firmly subordinated by most Chinese states to official kinship and property controls, to the state's power to extract taxes and tribute, and to state competition for the production of unusually strategic or profitable goods. At the same time, in true Gramscian style, petty capitalists have colluded in their own subordination by the ambivalent honor they pay to the norms and practices of the bureaucratic ruling class. A single-minded bourgeoisie would have gone further in dismantling state and Party ownership in both Taiwan and China; but it is in the nature of subordinated classes to be unable to be single-minded in their own interests.

Threatened more by the state than by unfettered and legally protected capitalist competition, petty capitalists find virtue in secrecy and in smallness. They pursue highly personalistic

---

Earthbound China (with Chang Chih-i as coauthor, 1948). He has returned to this theme, with a group of younger colleagues, in recent years (e.g., *Small Towns in China—Functions, Problems, and Prospects* [1986]).

business strategies; firms are usually small in scale, networked rather than pyramided, and difficult to perpetuate over generations. Unlike capitalists, whose accumulation depends heavily on the waged employment of free labor, petty capitalist accumulation depends heavily on the exploitation of personal ties, especially those of kinship, and on evading the clutch of the state. Waged work is important, but in complex ways is assimilated, if often only superficially, to personal ties. Young women are peculiarly susceptible to this kind of exploitation; their labor and marriage exchanges play a large role in enabling the flexibility and dynamism of family firms.

In times of economic expansion, whether stimulated by a state-funded building project or by capitalist demand, petty capitalism as a complex of material practices and ideological supports is effective at mobilizing production. The energetic operation of petty capitalist subcontracting and satellite systems that undergird export production in Taiwan and China is a response to the opportunities offered by both capitalism and the state mode. Capitalist and state production, although fundamentally different, both potentiate a multitude of economic niches and encourage their colonization by household firms. Where a patriarchal state dominates, these household economic activities can claim the protective shelter of kinship norms, can evade the state's efforts to tax industry, and can join capitalist ventures or compete with them as opportunity beckons.

Petty Capitalism versus Capitalism in Chinese Contexts

Chinese struggles of the past half-century have not been fought out between a socialist proletariat and a renascent capitalist bourgeoisie. They have been battles between those favoring a *ganbu* (cadre)-managed tributary mode of production (with some ill-digested socialist features), and those who preferred ever-updated versions of the indigenous petty capitalist mode—the default position of the *laobaixing* (commoners). In Taiwan, Kuomintang "bureaucrat capitalism" has played a strikingly parallel role in stimulating and managing small-firm production. To make matters interesting, many households have clear interests in both the tributary and the petty capitalist system, as well as, increasingly, in capitalism proper.

Is there in fact a distinction to be drawn between "capitalism proper" and the Chinese forms of petty commodity production

that I here term "petty capitalism"? Is such a distinction support-
able and, even more important, useful?

Let me first clear some conceptual ground on the subject of
capitalism itself. I think it essential to essentialize capitalism, to
see it as a positive feedback system of accumulation of re-
investable surplus value with a historical tendency to enable a politically dominant class to define the principal conditions of social
reproduction. Although human agents enact capitalism in a wide
variety of historically conditioned settings, it is not necessary to
abandon the idea of a unifying structural dynamic that can be dis-
cerned beneath the surface of events. To do so is to give up the
insight that can be obtained by juxtaposing cases that are structur-
ally similar, though historically differentiable. Marx formulated a
complex and difficult analysis of capitalism as a materialist structuring of recent world history. It is imperfect, incomplete, and
subversive, and in some particulars plainly wrong. It remains,
however, enormously useful, and the only available analysis is
both coherent and critical.

Wherein lies its utility? First, Marxism defines capitalism as a
mode of production that comes into existence only when most
relations of production in society take the form of wage employment by private owners of means of production. It makes the
social relations of getting our livings central to the periodization
of human events and points out the extraordinary historical
significance of the shift to societies based on the private and
unconstrained ownership of capital and labor. When we look at
the sometimes drastic realignment of relations of production for
Chinese people in this century, we see important changes, but not
in a clearly capitalist direction.

Neither Taiwanese nor Chinese seem to me to be assembling
social structures in which the majority of relations of production
are in the form of wage labor for private employers. Both countries employ huge numbers of workers in state enterprises,
bureaus, schools, and military establishments; this is not capitalism. Both countries produce much of their wealth privately, but
through the actions of unpaid family members. Kinship is not a
capitalist relation of production. And in both countries, wage
work for private employers is often a sort of apprenticeship aimed
at setting up a family business of the worker's own, rather than a
life sentence to the proletariat. Young people who work for far
less than their labor is worth, learn the business, and then set up
as owner-operator petty capitalists are almost the statistical norm,

and certainly a normative ideal, for Chinese. In short, most Chinese workers are not wage laborers in impersonal private capitalist firms, as they are under capitalism.

A second insight from Marxism into the structure of capitalism is the importance of the interaction of the market and the class-biased legal arrangements that grew up among Europeans to protect private ownership. An extraordinarily important corollary of capitalism has been the legal force that secures contracts and financial institutions. Absent these, personalistic ties are the best, if not always fully satisfactory, means that Chinese firms have to protect themselves from internal and external predators. Chinese petty capitalists have invented a colorful suite of credit and interest-producing mechanisms almost entirely outside the reach of the state. Kin groups and communities are capital pools into which appropriately positioned firms may dip.

In the West, history has stressed the single legal individual— person or corporation—as society's molecular actor. In Chinese political economies, households act, rights over their labor secured by kinship to household heads. In neither Taiwan nor China are the actions of ruling officials moving toward the kind of legal individualism for persons and corporations that has long been characteristic of—and essential to—capitalism. Taiwan is certainly more liberal in this area, and the current multiparty, multiethnic polity may come to choose institutionalized legalism as its governing style. Nevertheless, in Taiwan as in the PRC, state and custom continue to maintain the patrilineal household as the principal private-property-holder and to make members of economically joint households legally and politically responsible for each other. For administrative ease and to escape responsibility for welfare costs, Chinese officials prefer to reproduce kinship collectivities, which are obliged to assume major economic and political functions. Chinese do not meet the market as artificially individualized selves but as kinfolk from officially defined registered households. State-mandated kinship mediates in extremely powerful ways between persons and their productive roles in strikingly noncapitalist fashion.

Third in any list of the characteristics of capitalism is the matter of the productive balance between direct human labor and the use of laborsaving technology. The tendencies toward positive feedback in capital accumulation create pressures for constant revolution in the techniques of production—the condition of modernity. As yet, neither Taiwan nor China has contributed greatly to the world's store of new technology. Indeed, it is characteristic that a great many excellent Taiwan and Chinese products are made with simple equipment and high labor inputs—quite the reverse of the general tendency of capitalism. Taiwan has been promising high-tech breakthroughs to a new phase of industrialism for decades, and China longs for these. But the wish is not yet father to the child.

Finally, capitalism has provided the political-economic logic behind the past few centuries of Euro-American world domination. Compared to Central and South America, the Caribbean, Africa, and Southwest and Southeast Asia, foreign imperialism in China was brief and shallow. Who can compare what has been done since the sixteenth century to Zaire, to Haiti, to Bangladesh, or to Indonesia with what foreigners, for a century, did to China's outer fringe? Even Japan's direct control over Taiwan lasted only fifty years. Most previously imperialized countries must still struggle with their former masters for control over their raw materials, foreign policy, and financial dealings, making the term "postcolonial" a coarse joke. By contrast, at present, in both China and Taiwan, a powerful ruling class of purely domestic officials, backed by large state production systems, controls public ideology, limits the operation of private producers, and prevents external capitalists from extracting impoverishing quantities of wealth. Indeed, China and Taiwan have expanding economies whose momentum is recalibrating all possible world futures. This historical trajectory of internally controlled development sets the Chinese sharply apart from the world's colonialized peoples. It will be a long time before either Taiwan or China permits the virtually free flow of international capital that would put them in the position of a Canada or a Mexico. China and Taiwan produce for a worldwide capitalist market, but they are almost uniquely successful in filtering capitalist inputs and restraining the political energies of indigenous capitalists.

In their low proportion of privately employed wage-workers, their continued administrative use of kinship to manage labor, their slowness to initiate high-technology/low-labor production innovations, and their historical tendency to escape exogenous capitalist control, Taiwan and China seem not to fit well into the framework of fundamental capitalist structure.

What then is the place of capitalism proper in today's Taiwan and China? Plainly, many firms operate there in ways indistinguishable from capitalist operations in any other Third World

country. Their influence, especially in Taiwan, spreads far beyond
the export processing zones and other special arrangements made
for foreign investment. I would argue, however, for an ultimate
state control to which capitalists must submit as the price of doing
business. Most foreign (and joint) investment is elaborately (even
maddeningly) managed by state officials. Along with allotments
of land, electricity, water, labor power, permissions, currency
transfers, and tax abatements, large, highly visible corporate capitalist enterprises owned by noncitizen capitalists are offered the
somewhat illusory protection of legal and administrative documents that they themselves have sometimes written. Labor is
hired—impersonally, as far as the capital-owners are concerned—
and exploited in exemplary fashion. But such firms are, propor-
tionately, extremely few.

Many of the smaller firms generally labeled capitalist in
Taiwan and China might better be categorized as petty capitalist.
In China's most productive region, the southeastern coast, small
firms are often capitalized through informal means by
entrepreneurs making use of previously existing social ties to
guarantee a higher degree of business probity than the limited
legal context can enforce. Overseas Chinese, from Taiwan and
elsewhere, are predominant among these entrepreneurs in China.
They help secure reliable cooperation with local managers and
workers through emphasizing common ancestral ties, through contributing to local social services (such as schools, temples, and
infrastructure construction), and through manipulating official
regulations favoring outside investors. Local businesspeople make
strenuous attempts to attract nonnational partners so as to work
this and other tax fiddles; but such collusion requires trust and
personalism throughout the firm. Kin ties are seen as the most
effective and secure for these purposes. Such firms often eschew
advantages of scale in order to remain inconspicuous to the state
and to support the nonwage incentives and sanctions that characterize petty capitalism.

Taiwan and China entrepreneurs operate in similar fashion in
their own countries, often setting up production in rural areas
with good transport, supplies of labor, and raw materials. Excellent studies of Taiwan business networks, large and small, are
now available (Numazaki 1986, 1992; Skoggard 1993; Shieh 1992;
Ka Chih-ming 1993). My work in Chengdu and Xiamen suggests
that similar patterns are common in China as well.

The widespread involvement of small Chinese firms with local ritual, informal financing, characteristic methods of reliance on kin, and the personalizing of even waged labor relations argues for a distinguishable cluster of political-economic relationships. This petty capitalist pattern takes its form as much from small-scale producers' domination by the state as from their subaltern role in capitalist production. Ka Chih-ming, comparing the commodity production of rice versus sugar in Japanese Taiwan, sees this behavioral clustering as a matter of class within a capitalist mode of production. His arguments, however, are replete with references to the ultimate determination of many economic processes by the state and in the interest of cameralist (Rebel 1991) concerns that transcend capitalist interests (Ka 1994). One could easily make parallel arguments for Taiwan today and for some parts of China where capitalism has power over entire regional systems. I think the triad of three interacting modes of production (tributary, capitalist, and petty capitalist) offers clearer and less Eurocentric insight, however. This is almost certainly true for Sichuan, where corporate capitalism has a very feeble foothold, while state-run production remains extremely strong. I think it is also true for most, if not all, of the rest of China and for Taiwan because of the dominant, noncapitalist state sectors in both. There is plenty of room for argument about ultimate determination and about the appropriate language for discussing petty capitalism. Here, I will focus simply on the structural consequences for entrepreneurial women of their embeddedness in political economies where sexist states are strong economically as well as politically and ideologically and where corporate capitalist activity is monitored by those states far more efficaciously than in countries with less powerful centralizing sectors (Pyle 1990).

Women in Petty Capitalism

Petty capitalism is a system of commodity production by firms organized in the idiom of kinship, embedded in a dominant tributary mode managed by state officials who put their requirements for reliable revenues, stable class relations, and continued hegemony above any perceived need for economic expansion. State officials define kinship relations as relations of production; by maintaining kinship orthodoxy (and, of course, through other means), they regulate labor and set limits to the private accumulation of resources. The unavoidable implication of sex as an aspect of kinship puts the gendered division of labor at the very center of petty capitalist production.

Positioned as inferior to their male kin by the dominant structures of a hierarchical tributary system, women are apportioned less access to the society's and the household's resources. Under the commoditization of their labor (and persons) that takes place with powerful surges of petty capitalist production, their degree of subordination is often exacerbated. They become not only a massive reserve army for capitalist industrialism, but a source of primitive accumulation for their household corporations as their labor is exploited even more fully than that of their male kin. The oppression of Chinese women, still in place despite the industrialization and socialism that might, in their different ways, have alleviated it, is well known.

Yet petty capitalism also offers women opportunity for wealth, autonomy, and social power. Whereas the subordinate position of woman is fixed under the hegemony of tributary hierarchy, petty capitalism offers property owners the equality of the market. A woman's frame-knitting factory is as valuable on the market as a man's; her share in a rotating credit society is accounted only in currency, not in gender characteristics. A woman who can control means of production gains equality with a man of equal means in her economic dealings. The same petty capitalism that commoditizes the labor and even the persons of her propertyless sisters allows her to own, to employ, to dominate. In the commoditizing economies of 1980s and 1990s Taiwan and China, her property ownership may enable her to smuggle the values of the marketplace even into her relationships with her husband, parents-in-law, and children. Whereas a woman's subordination in the tributary mode is assured and reproduced by customary and official practice, her equality in the petty capitalist mode can be attained through ownership of means of production.

Chinese women entrepreneurs produce their identities as workers from a complex set of interacting dichotomies. Within the petty capitalist sphere of commoditized experience, they are both owners and direct production laborers. Within the tributary sphere in which they are classed as privately employed citizen-commoners, they rank below the classes of state employees. In the gendered division of labor on which these two modes of production differentially depend, they are "only" women, deprived by custom if not always by law of equality with men. Yet from this tangled web of possibilities, female property owners often overcome the limitations that Chinese hierarchies of class and gender have set them in. Successful businesswomen are everywhere in today's China and Taiwan, creating new female/nonstate/worker identities of substantial social power and esteem.

In this, they are aided by a valuable ideological weapon: that work, even manual work, deserves respect, at least for women. Under Chinese socialism, the respect due to labor ideally is not gendered, but it is plain in daily life that women gain more from this view than men when the work is heavy, dull, or troublesome. The tenet that labor is the source of all value restates the "traditional" position that women are judged not only in their roles as mothers and wives, but as household workers as well. In Taiwan, where women are not officially encouraged in socialist gender equality and love of labor, they can still expect respect for their material contributions to their households and for their dedication to work.

Businesswomen of Chengdu and Taibei

In 1988, 175 businesswomen in two surprisingly similar cities took the time to let me watch a portion of their work lives and to talk to me about them. Having begun this work in Taibei, where I have done previous fieldwork, I chose Chengdu for parallel interviews because Chengdu is much like Taibei in size and political placement. With about two million in population, each is a center of industry, administration, and military power. In Chengdu, de facto capital of southwest China and Tibet, provincial-level officials often subtly convey their taste for independence from Beijing. The hinterland on which its government draws, and which its businesses can service, is immense, Sichuan alone having a population of more than a hundred million. Taibei, capital of an essentially independent Taiwanese nation, has a much smaller internal hinterland: the island is home to only about twenty million people. In addition, however, the city produces and supervises a huge external trade with China, Hong Kong, and other countries. As in Chengdu, a large and powerful part of the Taibei population works for and depends on the complex of national, provincial, and city "units." In Chengdu, I find much the same mix of proud, hierarchically minded officials and hustling, money-conscious petty capitalists as in Taibei. Chengdu is even divided spatially into neighborhoods that effectively segregate those who work for the state from the more commercially minded older residents, as Taibei so visibly was in the 1970s. Taibei's petty capitalists were greater in number, richer on average, and, by 1988, far more politically influential than those of Chengdu. To my eyes, however, as I peer beyond the glitz of East Taibei or Renmin Donglu to the workaday streets of shops and household factories, the two cities are remarkably alike.

In each, I sought interviews with women who ran or worked in family businesses employing no more than ten people, spending at least two hours with each. To the seventy-five from Taibei I added an additional twenty-five women whom my assistants and I had talked to in 1986. After setting aside those now retired from income-earning work, I was left with 75 active petty capitalists for each city. I was accompanied in 1986 and 1988 by recent college graduate field assistants in Taibei, and in 1988 by cadres of the Sichuan Provincial Women's Federation in Chengdu.[3] My modest fluency in Mandarin and Taiwanese enabled me to be an active, though sometimes puzzled, participant in these open-ended discussions. Many of the Taibei women were old acquaintances, or have come to be so since the interviews. In Chengdu, I have since revisited a dozen of our subjects, some repeatedly, checking and revising my initial impressions and observing change. During the initial fieldwork in Chengdu, I took the precaution of interviewing an additional twelve subjects without the presence of an accompanying cadre (and found my impressions unaffected). My data

[3] In 1986, I shared the interviewing with the energetic and competent Lu Meihuan, Li Anru, and Chen Weirong. In 1988 Chen Xiaowei and Lu Hana were tireless and imaginative assistants in Taibei; Hu Cuizhen, Hua Xinghui, Jiang Yinghong, Li Jufang, and Wang Rong were resourceful and companionable colleagues in Chengdu. The fieldwork was as much their projects as my own, and I am grateful to all of them. I owe special thanks to Director Chuang Ying-chang of the Institute of Ethnology of the Academia Sinica (Taiwan) and to Professor Qin Xuesheng of the Sichuan Committee for the Preservation of Cultural Relics for facilitating introductions and for generous Chinese hospitality. This fieldwork was supported, in 1988, by the Rockefeller Foundation's program on women's status and fertility; in 1989, 1990, and 1991 by the Luce Foundation (under the direction of Arthur P. Wolf); and in 1992 by the Harry Frank Guggenheim Foundation's program on the causes and consequences of violence and aggression. I am most grateful to these bodies for funding and to the All-China Women's Federation, Sichuan Provincial Branch, Xiamen City Branch, and their excellent grassroots cadres for extraordinarily helpful and competent cooperation in large survey projects. My thinks go too to many fine colleagues at Xiamen University, most especially Drs. Zheng Ling and Shi Yilong. Arthur Wolf has my gratitude for inviting me to join his project and for going trekking in Sichuan to take part in mine.

remain those of an opportunity sample, but, especially for Taibei, they are reasonably representative.

"Accumulators" and "Housewives"

The image of Chinese small business owners as perspicacious workaholics intent on making their family's fortune is not without foundation. During my second interview in Chengdu, I was grilled hard by a round, lively woman whose rabbit meat snacks were having great success in the city. She was planning to start distribution elsewhere in Sichuan but was more interested in the prospects of selling in Guangzhou or Hong Kong. The barrier to the latter possibility was the necessity of international-standard vacuum packaging.

"What do you know about vacuum packaging? Is it true that American housewives use a machine to heat-seal plastic bags for home storage? Are they hard to use, expensive to run, do they break down a lot? Do they need a lot of electricity?" she rapid-fired.

As so often happens in these exchanges, I was forced to admit near-total ignorance of home vacuum packaging and its shortcomings. My offer to try to learn and pass on useful information was waved off politely: "Never mind. I'm going to Guangzhou on business next month, and I can find out all about it there."

She was paralleled, in Taiwan, by a woman who had found a gold mine in the underserved market for child care that weighs heavily on working women. I interviewed her mother-in-law, who was generous with praise for the younger woman's initiative:

> She started with just a little day-care center here at our house a few years ago. Now she has three, and employs more than a dozen teachers, as well as cooks and a driver. She bought a van and owns a building; she still rents in the two other places, but she keeps expanding. The teachers all have the most up-to-date training. This daughter-in-law of mine knows all the modern ways to make money!

As the Chengdu snack-producer concluded, "Modernization and expansion are the routes to success, you know."

So Marx said. But a substantial number of women in both cities do not see their businesses as seeds of great enterprises. Chengdu and Taibei are full of tiny stores and service businesses that women run on much more leisurely principles. A Taibei neighborhood hairdresser told me that after our daughter entered primary school, I was terribly bored and lonely at home. We live in one of the housing blocks that belong to the Ministry of Forestry, so the wives all live rather quietly and privately. We don't know our neighbors, and my relatives and school friends are all in the south, so I needed something to fill the time. My husband didn't want me to work outside, because that looked bad—as if he couldn't support us. But he finally agreed to let me open my beauty shop in our front room. I have a small, regular clientele now, so I still have plenty of time to take care of household duties. I don't make much over the costs of the materials and equipment, to tell the truth. But when I want to buy something for my daughter, I don't need to discuss it with my husband, and there is always someone coming and going to chat with.

Some women are prodded out of an indolent life at home by an older woman or by their own increasing maturity. A Chengdu house-front storekeeper pointed laughingly at her small stock of cigarettes, liquor, toilet paper, soy sauce, and the like:

You can see I'm not much of a businesswoman! I sell only a few RMB's worth of goods a day—I don't think I make 100 in profit in a month. But it's not much work, and I have to be here anyway with the baby. Before I had this child, I just watched television and slept a lot. Mother finally said to me, "You're a married woman now! Why don't you do something to make some money and help your husband? Who will pay for your child's education? Your living room is right on a good street; it would be easy to set up a *ganza* [grocery shop] there. Don't you see you are wasting that good shop front? People pay hundreds a month to rent a room like that for business! Your father-in-law is still strong; he can help you with the big boxes. It is bad for your mind to sleep every day, doing nothing!"

I started the store, and I should thank my mother. It's really not much trouble, and I can afford more treats for the child. It's quite suitable for our family.

The beauty shop and the *ganza*, like a great many small businesses, will never make their owners rich, never result in the reinvestment of profits that begins the process of capitalism. This is the sort of petty production that fills the alleyways of stagnant Third World cities, producing a vast "informal sector" literature, but no economic growth. By contrast, I would not be surprised, on my next visit, to learn that Ms. Zheng's expanded and mechanized factory now ships hot rabbit cubes to Vancouver.

Early on in the fieldwork, I began to think of these women as "housewives" and "accumulators." Housewives do what Chinese women have always done when they can. They use the time left from home and child care to bring in a supplemental income that the family consumes. These are semiproletarians, or even peasants, swapping cabbages for pigs' feet or homespun yarn for red-dyed cloth through the simplifying media of money and market. Their small transactions familiarize even housebound women with the initial mysteries of buying and selling. Only when commodity production flourishes because of more general economic dynamism, however, will it be possible for many of them to become accumulators.

Postreform Chengdu and the booming Taibei of the 1970s and 1980s provided such buoyant environments. It is not surprising that many of our interview subjects had expansive plans for the future. Based on their statements and the history of their businesses so far, I found that close to half of the Chengdu and about one-third of the Taibei women were reinvesting profits for expansion.[4] The other half and two-thirds respectively intended to putter along with tiny capitals, drawing what was more a return for semiproletarian labor than a profit, strictly speaking. These returns were typically consumed rather than saved or reinvested.

We turned up a few failing businesses as well: a spiced-goose seller, whose product my Women's Federation associate tactfully suggested was below par, a newsstand keeper with a bad location in one of Taibei's quiet lanes. These were few, however, as our sampling technique was not designed to capture the almost or recently bankrupt.

Small businesses fail frequently, as I have learned from taking women's work histories. But here, too, the distinction between housewives and accumulators seems relevant. A failing housewife business trickles off. The family consumes the stock and requisitions the furniture for other purposes, the living room reverts to its former use, and that is that. An accumulator is more likely to sell off what she can and convert her assets into a more promising line of work. In failure as in success, individuality accounts for much.

Between the dynamism of the current economy and the variation in individual taste for entrepreneurial risk lie a host of variables. How much start-up capital could a woman tap? What

---

[4] Figures on income and profits are so closely held that my associates and I had to judge profitability ourselves from a broad range of factors. Although I have confidence in our judgments, they do not warrant the spurious accuracy of a few percentage points here and there.

skills did she have? Did kin or other personalistic ties provide valuable assistance? Does education count? I hope to have firm figures to answer some of these questions for a future publication.

At the anecdotal level, however, I remain impressed with the apparent unimportance of these intervening variables. Given the will of individual determination and the way of a steadily growing market, some people became remarkably successful accumulators on the basis of nothing but self-exploitation—working for less than the market rate for labor. To profit in this means working protracted hours. Telling how they had come to run a substantial tea business in the city's rail-side wholesale market, an elderly Chengdu couple took pride in having started with empty hands. The woman speaks:

> Start-up capital! That's a laugh! I gleaned a basket of peanuts from the commune fields, walked along the railroad tracks till I got to the market, and sold them. After a few trips like that, my husband and I could buy peanuts from his relatives. He traveled around, buying and transporting, and I stayed in the market to sell them. We soon saw that tea was a much better business, so we got into that. The business grew because we sweated.

In Taibei, where petty capitalism has been the majority option for many families for decades, competition makes such empty-handed starts less likely. By the early 1990s, Chengdu people too were beginning to complain of the fierce competition that kept beginners out and made doing business more like gambling. In both cities, however, the wealth that trickles from the hands of prosperous petty capitalists, professionals and the privately salaried, and the better-paid civil servants still creates the conditions that tempt the underemployed to employ themselves.

Lingering on Taibei's Nanjing East Road at business lunch time reveals much about strength of household production on the very doorsteps of multinational capitalism. Amid the banks, airlines offices, and import-export companies, a high-noon army of sturdy Taiwanese women appears, laden with box lunches. An hour later, they are home, resting from labors that began at dawn with buying trips to central markets. Lunches cost about US$1.50. Taking home the equivalent of US$0.50 for each of a hundred lunches, five days a week (office workers go home or out for lunch after the Saturday half-day) nets an average producer about US$1,000 each month. She has her afternoons and evenings free, can take days off whenever she chooses, spends most of her work time in her own kitchen, and pays no taxes. Startup capital of US$100–$200 is accessible to virtually anyone, just as setting up a shoe-manufacturing workshop can be managed on as little as one year of an average household's savings (Skoggard 1993:214). If everyone did that, the market would be unbearably crowded—but not everyone, apparently, is an accumulator at heart.

A box-lunch seller who comes and goes in an hour is virtually untaxable. People calculate to the *mao* the cost-benefit ratio of sinking rent into a permanent restaurant, which can cope with an all-day clientele and a higher-priced menu. But, in addition to the rent, a fixed location entails a host of taxes, fees, kickbacks, paperwork, and trouble. The informal group or single individual, evading the costs that greater visibility results in, may make a better profit. The smaller the enterprise, the more direct and complete the return to labor. If you are going to exploit yourself, you want to be paid in full. As long as a strong state can tap the income of highly visible businesses, people will be tempted to invent businesses that are hard to see, or at least to catch.

Networks: The Next Step in Accumulation

There are obvious limits to the capital that a single accumulator can amass in a lifetime.[5] To bring accumulation to a higher level, Chinese avoid some of the visibility of large-scale, formally organized corporations by generating informal networks to spread risk, assist in production, and pool capital. This, in a very un-Marxian way, "socializes" a good deal of the wealth generated in production across a petty capitalist class of owner-operators and small investors. In interviews with small firms in both Chengdu and Taibei, I constantly saw the process through which even relatively large firms gain advantages of scale while keeping a low profile. At its most primitive, this takes the form of putting-out or subcontracting systems.

In Chengdu's periurban fringe, putting out is especially prevalent in the manufacture of garments, in machine-embroidered clothing and bedding, and in frame knitting. These are the commonest production activities and ones in which women are especially active. Frame knitting is modestly capital-intensive, each hand-powered knitting frame costing about RMB1,200 secondhand. Electric machines are not used because the power supply in Chengdu is unreliable, especially in the dry winters.

---

[5] That limit is nonetheless large. Wang An of computer and Wang Foundation fame did not do badly.

A frame owner can use her own labor to turn out preshaped pieces for sweaters and woolen underwear or set up several and supervise the low-skilled task of providing motive force for the simple machines. The frame owner has the edge over any additional workers with whom she may jointly produce, by virtue of her machine's high cost. The frame owner is thus the putter-out, supplying bulk yarn or knitted pieces to subcontracting women and paying them at piecework rates for their labor. To use frames efficiently, however, she needs the assistance of yarn winders and finishers, who sew pieces together into complete garments. Yarn winders, using a simple hand-cranked bamboo reeling wheel, shift yarn from factory spools to those used on the frames. Both finishing and yarn reeling are conveniently put out to neighbors and relatives; many women own sewing machines, and reelers are cheap.

The three Chengdu frame knitters we interviewed have organized factories on family premises, but the majority of their hands work scattered in their own houses. The largest employs more than forty people; only ten of them work in the firm's household factory. Many garment-trade producers (including those who specialize in children's clothing and machine-embroidered bedding) do the same.[6]

The pattern of maintaining a low business profile for defense against state interference repeats at every level of scale. Ichiro Numazaki's careful investigation of Taiwan's business networks (1986:517; 1992) shows its operations, as does Ian Skoggard's fine study of the many-layered pattern of shoe manufacturing for Taiwan's domestic and international markets (1993). So too, apparently, do those most "informal" of petty capitalist undertakings—the unambiguously criminal enterprises such as gambling, drugs, prostitution, and labor smuggling.

---

[6] The atomistic style of petty capitalism is frequently attributed to a sort of family cycle in its reproduction (e.g., Greenhalgh 1984:541–44). This may vary with the scale of the business (Wong 1985:64; Numazaki 1986:522–23). Because the present paper focuses on labor processes that are most typical of household firms, I leave this debate for another occasion. I will only observe that "the family cycle" is not something that can be automatically assumed, but is a pattern rooted in more fundamental political-economic forces.

The Search for Dignity

Frank Pieke, who anthropologized among the Beijingese during 1988–89, found that

> unlike most workers or cadres I got to know, private entrepreneurs were very hesitant to talk to me, afraid as they were that this would draw the attention of the authorities. Given the bureaucratized nature of society and the restrictions still imposed on private entrepreneurship, all private entrepreneurs had practically no option but to evade taxes or break state laws and regulations in the course of their business operations. (1992:102)

In Chengdu and Taibei as well, petty capitalists display alarm at the threat of official attention and often structure their work to avoid it. People hope and plan to evade the claims, legitimate or illegitimate, that officials levy on commoners' material resources; such claims, they well know, constitute the basic tributary relationship between their rulers and themselves.

The best way to be inconspicuous is to limit all official contacts. Businesses are left unregistered when possible. Apart from the commonplace wish to limit taxability,[7] people prefer not to register for a variety of reasons. In Chengdu, registration is an unpleasant process. It may take months before all the paper has been shuffled and stamped. Each visit to a government office for documents and permissions is an exercise in petty humiliation as well as in wasted time. Generally, too, registration requires substantial gifts to cadres at the Gongshang Ju, which oversees industrial and commercial activities. Registration also leads directly into involvement in a theoretically obligatory small business association, which many prefer to avoid.

In Taibei, unregistered industries can draw water and electricity at household rates rather than higher industrial rates. "Underground factories" are a frequent newspaper subject, part of the huge informal sector that so worries government planners. In both cities, sanitation rules, labor regulations, and building codes are more easily contravened when one's business remains unregistered. The only advantage to registration in either city, as far as I could determine, was the possibility that existed in Chengdu's periurban fringe for recognized businesses to get low-cost capital

---

[7] Officials too have reasons to avoid the accurate recording of taxes. The total tax bill for entrepreneurs in a Sichuan survey sample amounted to twenty-three times the figure given in official county statistics and five times the sum officially recorded by the township (Odegaard 1990/91:38).

loans from rural bank branches. As people learned during the tax crackdown that followed Tiananmen, however, government loans brought surveillance and ownership claims on extremely successful businesses (Gates 1991a:235).

Whether evading registration and taxation or conforming to them, petty capitalists are frequently reminded of the limitations on their social status. As taxes or as bribes, money flows "up" out of their coffers, leaving those who pay the losers in the unending struggle over surplus. Some entrepreneurs respond to these demands with self-confident anger, as did one Chengdu trader:

> The worst officials are the Gongshang Ju people. They do nothing but sit in their offices and take people's money. Just look at them if you meet them, wearing a gold ring on every finger! They look so satisfied with themselves! I work sixteen hours a day, travel away from my family all the time, have to think and worry until my head swells up. Then they take my profit. They are really parasites, trying to keep us small. Deep in my heart, I hate them.

This anger cannot be displayed, of course. The necessity of concealing it, and even of flattering and cajoling those in authority, makes the relationship still more distasteful and destructive to dignity. In encounters with state officials, it is plain to both sides who is on top.

In Taibei in the 1980s, such petty corruption had diminished. In the late 1960s and 1970s, though, doing business required the same essentially defensive posture and resulted in the same reassertion of conventional tributary hierarchy.

This ultimately economic control is experienced also as class inferiority in a much broader sense by petty capitalists (and other subaltern classes). Women petty capitalists may internalize this inferiority differently from men, but both describe their work as lacking in worth or in self-justifying, defensive terms. Pieke describes a Beijing businessman in the following terms:

> Despite his obvious success, Ye was not altogether satisfied with his life. Although it was possible to make a lot of money fast, there still was a limit to what that money could do. Despite his wealth, Ye thought of himself as a simple man without any real power, education, or status. People looked down upon private businessmen like him....Ye still found himself living at the fringe of society, merely being tolerated....
>
> Ye...had ample money but knew no way of somehow translating it into influence or prestige....To [two cadres] the official socialist morality did at least provide a solid frame of reference which, if nothing else, provided them with a baseline for their complaints

and criticisms. Ye, however, did not even have that. (Pieke 1992: 104–6)

Having bought a house and car and having paid the fines to have second and third children, Ye wanted to travel abroad but feared to invite investigation into his financial affairs by applying for a passport. "[G]reener pastures were still grazed abroad and by the leading cadres within the planned sector" (1992:106).[8] In major capitals like Beijing and Chengdu, where so many of the best jobs are with the state, class snobbery toward the private sector is rampant.

A Chengdu grocer, talking with me two years after the fact, was still appalled that she had fallen from the position of forewoman in a state factory to someone with no unit membership. The grocery brought in much more than her factory job in monthly salary, bonuses, and benefits; the loss lay elsewhere. She spoke with passion of her failure, a decline from respectability and self-worth to marginality and degradation. The reason for her sharp response to what was, in material terms, at worst an even trade became apparent when her mother joined the conversation. The older woman's strained voice reminded me of aging Taibei opera singers, harsh and habitually loud from a lifetime of projecting over fortissimo orchestras and noisy outdoor crowds. And such she turned out to be, a performer in a rootless profession still seen as spatially promiscuous, belonging nowhere, and hence disreputable. Our grocer, who had grown up backstage and on the road, had loved the discipline of her factory, had admired its chain of command, and had reached a pinnacle of ambition on her promotion to forewoman.[9]

---

[8] Writing in a very different analytic tradition, Frank Pieke has much insight to offer about the operations of the tributary/planned mode/sector and the interactions of those within it with each other and with petty capitalists.

[9] I was reminded on hearing her of the words of a Jiangxi man who had spent the 1930s peddling cloth and notions before joining the Nationalist army:

My training as a mechanic was easy. I worked in a group where each person learned a certain part of the aircraft and was responsible for replacing it if there were defects. Each person did his own part and didn't learn about anyone else's. We didn't have to make any judgments.... The whole system worked like this, with equipment carefully checked and responsibility divided in an orderly way....

During the war, life was good for me. Food was ample, the conditions of life were orderly. I went to the airport to work every day as dawn broke, and came back to barracks every evening at eight or nine o'clock. It was physically much easier than peddling or farming. (Gates 1987:137)

Here was respectability itself, after a youth filled with embarrassment at her chain-smoking, foul-mouthed, raddled mother. Scrabbling for a living in her private exile, with no workmates, no dignified pension, no "worker" identity still made her cry.

Among our Chengdu subjects, only she had actually lost a high-value job as defined by the socialist system. Most of the younger ones had failed before the job was theirs. Closed off from the educational credentials necessary for state employment by lack of talent, Cultural Revolution mistiming, class background, or youthful indiscretion, the high road for white-collar or labor aristocracy was the road not taken. No one ever spoke of dropping out as an opportunity, a happy chance, not even those who twinkled with gold jewelry or one extraordinary "boss-lady" who employed a handsome bodyguard. Sincerely or not, even the energetic accumulators noted with regret that they had not achieved success via education and promotion through a socially sanctioned hierarchy.

Chinese in the People's Republic, of course, have had forty years of emphasis on the relative status of officials and state workers versus those in less-favored classes—especially of petty capitalists. In Taiwan, where the propaganda campaign for tributary values has been less strident and petty capitalism the mainstay of the numerically dominant ethnic Taiwanese, entrepreneurs have more self-confidence. Their apologetic comments on their limited schooling and, hence, state-sector opportunities are quieter and less compulsive. Perhaps in Taiwan the status relationship has changed, and bourgeois virtue is coming into its own? One line of evidence suggests that few families value their entrepreneurship to the point that they prefer it to the post-Confucian alternative. My informants all wanted a "better" future for their children.

In asking about the employment of children, Taibei women were at one with their Chengdu sisters. Although numerous women with grown daughters and sons employed them, those with relatively young offspring all insisted that they expected no help whatsoever from school-age children. Whether I asked about work in the family firm, housework, or babysitting for siblings, the women preferred not to use their children's time. Children needed every moment for homework (and a few stylish accomplishments) in the demanding and competitive schools of both cities. The possibility that a teenager might be well served by learning the business young, as her mother's hired apprentices were doing, was absurd. Nothing should stand in the way of a child with a talent for the educational road to the state and corporate sector. The rough-and-tumble of juggling creditors, pleasing customers, and bribing authorities was necessary work, but it was not good enough for one's son or daughter. Later, perhaps, when a daughter reaches her academic limit, she will keep books for her mother. After the son has closed out higher options and got an MBA, he will offer his expertise to the family's informal business network. People who can afford to have their children try to climb the educational ladder into the heights of government service continue to do so, showing where their strongest aspirations lie and how they disvalue their own class and its opportunities.

Those who have spent time in Taiwan and China recently will be aware of how commonly Chinese people discuss the relative value of money and a market-oriented life. Although it is indisputable that the same discussion, in much the same terms, has gone on for centuries, the 1980s and early 1990s have been a period of worldwide laissez-faire for market forces. We have seen stock market crazes in both countries, the outrageous commoditization of babies and brides in China, the popular lunacy over wealth and its fetishes in Taiwan (remember the Wealth Toad? Da Jia Le? Shiba Wang Gong? I especially enjoyed New Year's decorations in the shape of enormous NT$1,000 bills, a gilded *fu* sharing top billing with—magnificent irony—the face of Jiang Jieshi.) Even those who literally worshiped money during those years sometimes seem deeply concerned about whether money has got out of control as a dominant force in society.

Petty capitalists do, sometimes, assert the overriding value of money and those who have much of it. Frank Pieke's state sector informants had the usual things to say about the growth of petty capitalism. For them, "money was not a measure of success, but only a reason for jealousy or a ground for condemnation" (1992:238). Nevertheless,

> among entrepreneurs...an independent market-sphere morality and self-esteem is gradually growing. Entrepreneurs, whether they are former cadres who have contracted a company, or owners of a small vegetable stall, all stress that money means more than a high standard of living. Entrepreneurial activity, and the money which comes with it, means freedom from the state, freedom to do what you want without having to get permission for it. (238)

Ian Skoggard argues for Taiwan that

> entrepreneurs are esteemed in Taiwan society because of the gen-

eral respect accorded intelligence, efficacy and money. The entrepreneur's ability to organize production and attract outside capital
is seen to benefit the whole community and fits in with traditional
ideology which encourages work in the interest of the group.
Plaques hanging in a temple...proclaimed..."serve the multitude
(*fu-wu jen-ch'un*)" and "build up the people's wealth (*tsao jen-min
fu*)." (1993:212)

He quotes the saying "If you are rich everyone earns" (*yu-ch'ien
ta-chia chuan*) (1993:212).

Taibei businesswomen especially relish the expression *Shei you
qian, shei jiu shi lao da* (whoever has money is Number One). They
say this mostly, however, about the relatively equal playing field
between wife and husband. When it comes to officials, they know
that even a low-ranking civil servant can destroy the fortunes of
even a rich entrepreneur. Money does not dissolve all difficulties
in a Chinese political economy, where markets remain englobed
within strong and persistent tributary systems.

The Dignity of Labor?

Petty capitalists face another difficulty in their search for dignity in systems where they are still a clearly subordinate class.
Their work spans the great cultural divide between mental and
manual labor; owner-operators operate as well as own. In small
factories and shops, this often means hard and dirty work as well
as supervision and accounting. In larger enterprises, it means
knowing the business from the ground up and taking ultimate
(and usually immediate) responsibility for every decision taken.

Unlike pure capitalists, whose capital "works for them" in
ghostly partnership with their hired (and also disembodied)
"hands," petty capitalists work themselves, contributing the value
of their physical labor, managerial presence, and other necessary
skills to production. Whereas a capitalist risks principally capital,
petty capitalists, subordinate in dignity and class standing to state
workers, must often take serious legal and political risks as well.

Chengdu knitting-frame owners have the arduous jobs of
obtaining bulk yarn, for which they travel personally to Xian, and
of finding transport to distribute their goods. Unlike the frame-
knitting operations in 1970s Taiwan described by Stevan Harrell
(1981:37–41; 1982:66–73), Chengdu frame owners do not subcon-
tract from larger factories that facilitate the work with truck
deliveries of yarn and patterns and pickup service. This situation
is due in large part to a distant decision to make Xian, not

Chengdu, the woolen textile and woolen and artificial fiber yarn center for the western provinces. It is due also to the notorious scarcity of transport and the heavy pressure of freight on such transport as exists. Many producers told of pulling heavily laden carts of materials through the streets themselves to get their businesses started. After expanding to the point that direct purchases of raw materials from the source become possible, garment producers find it necessary to travel to Xian, Guangzhou, or Shanghai for yarn, fabric, and patterns.

The trip must be made in person both to obtain the materials and to arrange for their transportation on overcrowded trains. In practice, this means developing a relationship with someone in the railway freight department who can assure the shipper that the goods will travel the same train as the petty capitalist. Getting the goods back from the railway is almost as difficult as getting them on. These costly arrangements cannot be left to an inexperienced or untrustworthy assistant.

Also difficult to arrange is the actual purchase of raw materials from the state factories that produce them. Small buyers must compete with the demand for materials from other state enterprises, which during the 1980s were eligible to purchase at fixed state rates. Although the selling unit prefers not to sell at these lower rates, the buying (state) unit has a powerful incentive to acquire a valuable commodity, which it may then re-sell in some form. State units, women told me, prefer to sell to large private buyers; "little fish" like themselves must develop a connection, and they often pay the highest market rate along with the costs of generating *guanxi* with their supplier. Here, too, the petty capitalist is unwilling to risk delegating purchasing authority by turning over the necessary wads of cash to a subordinate who might prove inept, disloyal, or merely careless of the criminals who also ride the trains. As long as the private entrepreneur must obtain a substantial proportion of the necessary means of production from state sources, she is wise to follow the classical petty capitalist pattern of personalized management. In Taiwan, such problems are now mostly confined to occasions when a producer needs to negotiate the barriers to obtaining foreign currency and imported raw materials or to export finished goods—large exceptions in Taiwan's export-driven economy. Until the 1980s, they remained costly business bottlenecks, fueling corruption at every level.

In the petty capitalist division of labor, the owner has a dirty job, even if it does not literally blacken her hands. Against this overwhelming cultural criticism, women may have an easier riposte than men. Capable efficiency—*nonggan*—is a much-admired female trait. Women's work has always been largely manual, even among the elite (Mann 1992). Women entrepreneurs in Taibei and Chengdu appear to take the grubby bits of their job more in stride—though they are not above pushing off the heavy transport on any available male relative or worker. A willingness to do visibly manual work was more marked in Chengdu, where an ideology of encouraging women to adhere to socialist standards in this regard has existed since the 1949 revolution. I admired especially a lovely, black-around-the-edges printshop owner who was delighted to be praised for her work in this traditionally male field. She sprang into action with wrenches and oilcans to show me her favorite press, receiving nearly worshipful attention from her male and female apprentices. Few of the Taibei women had chosen dirty work (unless you count child care), though many worked hard physically at moving stock. The single exception, a Taibei motorcycle repairwoman, gave me a hasty handshake that took two days to wash off.

Cadet Labor

I have focused thus far mostly on the owner-operator, the managerial fraction of the petty capitalist class, and plainly a worker herself. She generally does not work alone; if she plans to accumulate resources, she cannot go far singlehanded. Her most usual assistants, whom we may call "cadet labor," are the family worker from a junior generation and the informal apprentice. As petty capitalist businesses enlarge, they hire adult wage laborers whose circumstances may oblige them to remain classic proletarians for long periods. Even they, however, are affected by the small-scale origins of many firms.

Family workers and informal apprentices personify the forms of East Asian labor power whose circumstances are most difficult to theorize and who are an essential source of the "primitive" or initial accumulation of capital for an expanding family firm. The yet more problematic relationship between spouses will be dealt with separately.

Family workers in junior generations and informal apprentices are similar and dissimilar in important ways. Both are employed for particularistic reasons and through personal ties, paid more in room, board, and training than in cash wages, likely to work only a few years under their employer, and likely too to acquire skills and contacts through their work that will enable them to set up businesses of their own. In small firms, they may be treated much alike. Of his life in a Qingdao peanut-oil shop in the 1920s, a Kuomintang veteran once told me:

> Seeing I was no student, my father started me working in the business. He thought I should learn everything from the bottom up, because he feared I would become spoiled and wasteful of money. So I worked with the other two apprentices at the lowest work— sweeping up, running errands, moving stock—while my father, elder brothers, and two uncles managed the accounting and the customers. When things went wrong, if the other apprentices got beaten, I did too. I ate with them most of the time, but I slept inside with the family, not out front in the shop with the hired workers. (Gates 1987:158)

Today, with primary education universal in both cities, and higher levels extremely common in Taibei, a young petty capitalist's children are spared the rigors of an apprentice's life. Nieces, nephews, and more distant kin, who are favored as workers for family firms, are not. Chengdu and Taibei restaurant keepers and small manufacturers often rely on such more distant cadet labor. Sleeping, eating, and working together with hired nonkin, they appear to receive similar treatment in terms of their physical well-being and work expectations.

Junior family workers are unlike apprentices, however, in a very important way. They are more completely controlled than apprentices by their kin senior "employers." Parent-employers can bind children-laborers tightly to the family corporation with the ties of affect (both love and fear), material dependence, custom, and law. Just as important, parent-employers may also sever their children-laborers from the family by reallocating their labor elsewhere. A cadet's labor can be temporarily reallocated by arranging for her or his employment elsewhere. The reallocation may be made permanent, however, through mechanisms like marriage, divorce, adoption, and (more strikingly in the past) sale. Arthur Wolf has demonstrated how dramatically north Taiwan households once reshaped their workforces by marrying out infant girls and bringing in infant daughters-in-law in ratios that suited the household's reproductive strategies (Wolf and Huang 1981) and, I would argue (Gates 1989:814–18), its production strategies as well. To a far lesser degree, adoption of male children and the choice of arranging or not arranging marriages for sons also enabled households to balance labor power–capital ratios.

Although their employers may stand partially in loco parentis to young informal apprentices, their labor power is not so completely alienated from their parents that employers gain the parental right of its permanent reallocation through kinship mechanisms, at least in the present. In the past, parents might contract to dispose of even these rights over their children's (and wives') labor to persons who made use of them as bondservants, slaves, or concubines (Watson 1980; Jaschok 1988).

The problems of analysis of cadet labor are compounded by the realities of gender: unmarried daughters and the household's daughters-in-law are more like apprentices than are sons in the matter of ownership of family means of production. Women become shareholders in family corporations only under exceptional circumstances: a paraplegic folk artist, for example, received one-third of the proceeds from the family house when her father died because her work had supported the household for many years (Gates 1987:164–74). Men are automatic shareholders in their father's ancestral property and in whatever wealth their labors add to it.

Junior women are also expected to work harder than junior men, or at least to contribute proportionally more of their labor time or earnings. Unmarried daughters can be expected to contribute more of their premarital earnings to their parents' household, or to work for no wage, when compared to sons. Greenhalgh's explanation for this phenomenon as it appears among young women who work outside their own household holds, I believe, for those who work within it: because a daughter's postmarital economic obligations are to her husband, children, and parents-in-law, she has only a short time to contribute to her parents' and brothers' economic needs and plans. A son, who is obliged to his parents for life, can give them less of his outside wages, especially during his unmarried youth (1985).

Cadet labor is an important source of surplus value in petty capitalist firms. In the short run, all working cadets can be rewarded with less value than their work creates, leaving surplus value in the petty capitalist's hands. The restoration of etiquette, filial piety, and respect for age that were so vociferously demanded by adults after the Cultural Revolution are parts of a regime of labor regulation absolutely central to the emergence of the present petty capitalist economy.

The Female Advantage

In Chengdu, where private production has reappeared for less than fifteen years, we may be seeing only an immature pattern of petty capitalism. Tiny firms abound, unemployed potential labor teems, and an insatiable market for useful and inexpensive consumer products sucks goods out of shops almost before they are on the shelves. Taibei producers face a much more competitive situation. The box-lunch women show us that even there, however, petty capitalist start-ups keep finding profitable niches. I have suggested that the exploitability of the young, and especially of girls and young women, is the fount and source of petty capitalist growth. Let it be admitted that without an articulation with capitalist or abundant tributary resources, petty capitalism is a zero-sum game. But given the advantages of one of these *and* a culture that constrains the young and women with special vigor, petty capitalists capture enough of the available surplus to continue to reproduce themselves and often to expand.

Unlike Frederic Deyo (1989) I think petty capitalism is not on the brink of surrendering to a hegemonic, proletarianizing capitalism. It is too well protected by the state's need to make male heads of families its lieutenants in the struggle to maintain social order. Kin seniors are too well advantaged by their right to command young labor to give up the family firm model. In economic terms, though not necessarily in terms of affect or intrafamilial power, males are too smoothly channeled into control of resources to find gender equality acceptable. As long as this primary dynamic has the additional advantage of readily available, docile wage labor, we should expect to see petty capitalism persist as a powerful counterstrategy to tributary or to capitalist dominance.

It is of extraordinary interest, therefore, to look at the relations of production practiced by women. They reveal three areas in which women have positive advantages in petty capitalism: a woman's right to privately held money; a mother's special power over her daughters; and the relatively egalitarian relationships that are possible with husbands. These cultural loopholes in a political economy that is otherwise so plainly biased against women may be a little larger in China than in Taiwan. Chinese official support for gender equality, however wavering and weak it may have been, has been stronger than any such tendency in Taiwan. But it might also be true that the greater openness that Taiwan's people have experienced to global currents may have affected gender relations in ways that are positive to women.[10]

---

[10] The long relationship with Japanese culture and the ugly tide of Japanese and

Custom based more on petty capitalist than on tributary logic permits married women to exercise a right unique in domestic economy. Unlike all other members of a household, who are supposed to pool and share resources, married women may own *sifang qian*—private money. This right is of immense significance. A woman who can obtain even a mite of private money can hope to increase it in the informal financial system of petty capitalism or use it as means of production. One of the most profitable of the small companies I investigated in Taiwan, a dentures-manufacturing concern, was founded on the *sifang qian* that was part of the woman's dowry. It constituted the sole founding capital for the business, which now has islandwide scope. Numazaki describes how a woman in one of Taiwan's very large firms became an individual, participating partner on the basis of "her own money and her future earnings" (1992:120–21).

How women obtain such money and the complex negotiations they must undertake to keep it from being pooled with that of parents, parents-in-law, or husband are among the great silent dramas of Chinese family life. Given *sifang qian*, however, a woman has an important prerequisite for becoming a petty capitalist in her own right. And given children, she has the other.

The atmosphere of households in which grown children work for their mothers as opposed to their fathers is often markedly different. Mothers and daughters are often warmly affectionate; sons who work for an especially competent mother hung around our interviews to put in a word, to make jokes, to give their mother an occasional pat. When father heads the business, sons are more reticent. Margery Wolf has told us why (1972). It is often the case that while Chinese fathers rely on authority and sternness to keep their domestic workforce in line, Chinese mothers can draw on a more lively affection, which they cultivate assiduously, even at the father's expense.

A woman's daughters and sons can also be differentiated, if perhaps not so reliably, in terms of their value as assistants. Young women are often the workforce of choice (such as in frame knitting and restaurant keeping) because daughters work so well for their mothers. They provide motivated labor when young and trustworthy management skills when older, especially when they are managing other women. Sons are far harder to manage. Much as sons may love their mothers, women often complain that

---

Western pornography and other forms of sexual exploitation work in the opposite direction, however.

"now that girls can earn money, they are better to their mothers than boys." A woman whose superb cooking I have often enjoyed in private failed at running a small restaurant, she thinks, because she had only males to help her:

> I tried to teach my son how to choose the best meat and vegetables, how to make dumplings, and how to treat the customers. My husband helped a little, but his manner is very rough. When you run a restaurant, you have to talk nicely to customers and treat them right. My husband just says, "Take it or leave it," and walks away. He's no help. My son is too much like his father. Besides, he doesn't want to learn anything from me. He worked for a few months, and then said he wouldn't work any more. (Gates 1987:129)

What is the source of the relative independence of sons? Sons will inevitably inherit most of what their mother accumulates; daughters, as always, must "earn" what they are given through hard work and maintaining pleasant relationships. People often naturalize this difference as inherent in sexes of their children. Women choose daughters to help in their businesses "because they are *guai* (docile, controlled, well-behaved); boys like to fool around." In the intimate arrangements of many small firms, one sees something of the same gender difference between *laobanniang* (boss-lady) and her female and male hired workers.

Women play a special role in reproducing petty capitalism because they often manage the money their unmarried (and married) daughters earn. Whereas an unmarried daughter should turn over money she earns outside the family to her mother for pooling, the mother may well keep some or all of it back as part of her own *sifang qian* or in a kind of separate account for her daughter. In either case, it may be invested profitably and increase, if the mother is capable. When the daughter marries, she has an informal moral claim on at least some of this money, unless it has all been consumed by a needy family. When a woman works for her mother, either before or after marriage, they arrange between them how she will be paid: directly and openly; some of her earnings paid directly, the rest kept discreetly by the mother, safe against the daughter's husband's and parents-in-law's claims; or perhaps not at all, but with the daughter having a standing claim on her mother's resources.

These separate female circuits are a source of considerable anxiety to Chinese men and mothers-in-law—who know all too well what often transpires between mother and daughter. References to *sifang qian* are usually greeted with nervous laughter; suspicions that a woman is slipping her mother money make husbands uneasy and irritable. Such suspicions are an extremely rewarding, though difficult, subject of study because they reveal so vividly the falsity of the unified front that patrilineal families try to present to themselves and the world.

About half of the women in both Chengdu and Taibei worked in partnership with their husbands. The degrees of a woman's independence from her husband and of his assistance to her are not easily determined by one-off interview methods. Marriage implies and requires economic partnership, but different official stances toward women's rights encourage Taibei women to present themselves as subordinate to their husbands and Chengdu women to stress their independence from them. And even husbands who contributed none of the initial capital and who do not take part in day-to-day operations may still be crucial to business success, especially in China. The most obvious case of this is the woman who runs a beer stall in Chengdu with beer supplied at a low price by the state brewery for which her husband works. Unable to reemploy my informant after she and her husband returned from years in the countryside, the company offered this help to her both as a former worker and as her husband's wife. Men, more likely than women to work in the state sector, provide contacts for obtaining a number of resources, including transport, raw materials, and stock for stores. In Taibei, husbands are needed for occasional heavy work—to move stock, to act as bouncers, and the like.

In contemporary Taibei and Chengdu, a married pair comes closer to having an egalitarian relationship than any other Chinese dyad. A woman who marries with affection, who brings the seeds of a family business in her *sifang qian*, and who works reasonably harmoniously with her husband in their common venture has a strong chance of creating an enterprise in which ability outweighs gender as a factor in decision making. The wife-husband partnerships in our samples were about evenly divided among three kinds: wife plainly dominant, but with some participation by the husband; wife and husband sharing work and decision making about equally; and wife working essentially alone, "partners" with her husband only insofar as all couples form economic unions. Our sampling method biased selection away from partnerships in which women took a minor role with low visibility; these, quite properly, are not perceived as businesses run by women.

Husbands who merely "allow" their wives to work, like the hairdresser's husband, or who offer neither interest nor support, like the husbands of many small shopkeepers, may be factors in a woman's decision to retain a housewife rather than an accumulator approach to work. One Taibei hairdresser, who admitted in an agony of humiliation that she had formerly been a prostitute, worked unwillingly to support her worthless husband as she had from puberty to support her equally worthless father. Such examples underline the degree to which a woman gains an invaluable ally in a husband who is an equal partner or one who cheerfully accepts a subordinate role, deferring to his wife's superior energy, skill, acumen, or material resources.

One of the fullest and most positive partnerships I encountered was between a thirty-something couple running a three-story jewelry factory in a Taibei suburb. Employing eight young workers from among neighbors and relatives, wife and husband also worked at their noisy electric drills and polishers when business was brisk. Wife kept the accounts, husband arranged for the physical movement of products, son and daughter studied hard, although their parents expected them to learn the business when they were older. This partnership had produced more than Taiwan jade bracelets and two dutiful children, however. Their fourth-floor family residence was the most interesting house I have ever visited in Taiwan. With an imported European kitchen, a Japanese tatami room for guests and chess playing, and an emphatically Taiwanese-Chinese living room, the couple had crowned their industrial success with a self-designed, self-conscious statement of cultural identity. Their mutual pride and pleasure in explaining its provenance revealed much about their business success as well.

Chengdu couples who support each other strongly also often display their unity in household decor. I was entertained in the bedrooms of a number of wife-husband pairs who seemed especially compatible and effective as working teams. It was the fashion to paper a wall or two with floor-to-ceiling photo-murals of natural scenes. In residences largely given over to often very grubby businesses, the couples' private rooms were oases of color and style. Such expense on personal luxury was frequently identified as "something that women like"; its presence announced that the wife had substantial control over the family's income. In such households, one has a very strong sense of the positive value of something that comes close to being unalienated labor, at least for those in charge.

Women who claimed their business to be completely their own had what appeared to be very considerable power over their husbands. A Taibei restaurant keeper who had combined capital with her younger brother was allowing her husband to work his way into partnership with them by paying back some of his monthly wages for a fixed period. This round, pretty mother of two small daughters was openly acknowledged by her husband, mother, and father, all of whom she hired for wages, to be exceptionally capable. The husband told me that his own family was so poor that he would have had no future without his wife. A Chengdu husband, clearly an assistant in his wife's thriving *jiaozi* parlor, admitted ruefully that if she had not brought his smoking and drinking under control, the family would have been headed for ruin. "She saves it all, every cent, and puts it all back in the business. As long as she controls the money, we do really well." A Taibei flower-arranging teacher put her husband into a small business after he had been swindled out of the much larger one into which he had sunk his inheritance. "I owe her everything; she's been the one that made it possible for our son to study, keep up his music, and even play for the city symphony. I hate this restaurant of ours, but it paid my debts and keeps us making money. I really owe her everything."

Female entrepreneurs thus have three important advantages in the petty capitalist context: the right to hold capital separately; when they employ their own children, a truly dedicated workforce; and access to a woman's subset of the resources that circulate among petty capitalists. In addition, if they are equal or superior to their husbands in their input into the business, they have a strong chance of achieving the perfect unity of purpose that makes any effort thrive. These advantages are hardly adequate to offset the many disadvantages female entrepreneurs experience in Chinese societies, but they level the playing field a little.

It is, I think, one of the splendid ironies of the Chinese world that women, who are so thoroughly exploited there, can sometimes turn the conditions of that exploitation into charters for the improvement of their lot. Women turn kinship principle to their own use when they can and consciously exploit their kin juniors—though not with the freedom possible where labor comes primarily from the market as "free" individual workers. Women rely on a complex of managerial and financial skills honed through keeping secret their money sources and channels; the structure of state and family keeps their accumulations petty, but it is sometimes enough to make them the equals of men.

Women operate within petty capitalism in parallel to the way petty capitalists in general operate in Chinese societies that are dominated by state-centered political economies. Out of all these wheels within wheels comes a very great deal of the dynamism of East Asia. From this complex political-economic machinery, many women manage to spin not only money and social esteem, but a worthy identity as workers in a culture that honors work. That accomplishment should, somehow, deserve a poem.

References

Bold, Alan. 1970. *The Penguin Book of Socialist Verse*. Harmondsworth: Penguin.

Deyo, Frederic C. 1989. *Beneath the Miracle: Labor Subordination in the New Asian Industrialism*. Berkeley: University of California Press.

Fei Hsiao-tung. 1939. *Peasant Life in China*. New York: E. P. Dutton.

Fei Hsiao-tung and Chang Chih-i. 1948. *Earthbound China: A Study of Rural Economy in Yunnan*. London: Routledge & Kegan Paul.

Fei Hsiao-tung and others. 1986. *Small Towns in China— Functions, Problems, and Prospects*. Beijing: New World Press.

Gates, Hill. 1987. *Chinese Working-Class Lives: Getting By in Taiwan*. Ithaca, N. Y.: Cornell University Press.

_____. 1989. "The Commoditization of Chinese Women." *Signs* 14, 4:799–832.

_____. 1991a. "Eating for Revenge: Consumption and Corruption under Economic De-Reform." *Dialectical Anthropology* 16:233–49.

_____. 1991b. "'Narrow Hearts' and Petty Capitalism: Small Business Women in Chengdu, China." In *Marxist Approaches in Economic Anthropology*, ed. Alice Littlefield and Hill Gates, pp. 13–36. Monographs in Economic Anthropology, no. 9. Lanham, N.Y.: University Press of America.

———. 1993. "Cultural Support for Birth Limitation among Urban Capital-owning Women." In *Chinese Families in the Post-Mao Era,* ed. Deborah Davis and Stevan Harrell, pp. 251–74. Berkeley: University of California Press.

———. 1995. *China's Motor: A Thousand Years of Petty Capitalism.* Ithaca, N.Y.: Cornell University Press.

Greenhalgh, Susan. 1984. "Networks and Their Nodes: Urban Society on Taiwan." *China Quarterly* 99:529–52.

———. 1985. "Sexual Stratification in East Asia." *Population and Development Review* 11, 2:265–314.

Harrell, Stevan. 1981. "Effects of Economic Change on Two Taiwanese Villages." *Modern China* 7, 1:31–54.

———. 1982. *Ploughshare Village: Culture and Context in Taiwan.* Seattle: University of Washington Press.

Jaschok, Maria. 1988. *Concubines and Bondservants.* London: Zed.

Ka Chih-ming. 1993. *Market, Social Networks, and the Production Organization of Small-Scale Industry in Taiwan: The Garment Industries of Wufenpu.* Taipei: Institute of Ethnology, Academia Sinica (in Chinese).

———. 1994. "Land Tenure, Development, and Dependency in Taiwan (1895–1945)." Ms.

Kelliher, Daniel. 1992. *Peasant Power in China: The Era of Rural Reform, 1979–1989.* New Haven, Conn.: Yale University Press.

Mann, Susan. 1992. "Household Handicrafts and State Policy in Qing Times." In *To Achieve Security and Wealth: The Qing Imperial State and the Economy, 1644–1911,* ed. Jane Leonard and John R. Watt, pp. 75–95. Ithaca, N.Y.: East Asia Program, Cornell University.

Morawetz, David. 1981. *Why the Emperor's New Clothes Are Not Made in Colombia: A Case Study in Latin American and East Asian Manufacturing Exports.* New York: Oxford University Press.

Numazaki Ichiro. 1986. "Networks of Taiwanese Big Business." *Modern China* 12, 4:487–533.

———. 1992. "Networks and Partnerships: The Social Organization of the Chinese Business Elite in Taiwan." Ph.D. diss., Michigan State University.

Odegaard, Ole. 1990/91. "Inadequate and Inaccurate Chinese Statistics: The Case of Private Rural Enterprises." *China Information* 5, 3 (Winter): 29–38.

Pieke, Frank N. 1992. "The Ordinary and the Extraordinary: An Anthropological Study of Chinese Reform and Political Protest." Ph.D. diss., University of California, Berkeley.

Pyle, Jean Larson. 1990. *The State and Women in the Economy: Lessons from Sex Discrimination in the Republic of Ireland.* Albany: State University of New York Press.

Rebel, Hermann. 1991. "Reimagining the *Oikos:* Austrian Cameralism in Its Social Formation." In *Golden Ages, Dark Ages: Imagining the Past in Anthropology and History,* ed. Jay O'Brien and William Roseberry, pp. 48–80. Berkeley: University of California Press.

Shieh Gwo-shyong. 1992. *"Boss" Island.* New York: P. Lang.

Skoggard, Ian. 1993. "Dependency and Rural Industrialization in Taiwan: The History and Organization of Taiwan's Shoe Industry." Ph.D. diss., City University of New York.

Watson, James L. 1980. "Transactions in People: The Chinese Market in Slaves, Servants, and Heirs." In *Asian and African Systems of Slavery,* ed. James L. Watson, pp. 223–50. Berkeley: University of California Press.

Wolf, Arthur P., and Huang Chieh-shan. 1981. *Marriage and Adoption in China, 1845–1945.* Stanford, Calif.: Stanford University Press.

Wolf, Margery. 1972. *Women and the Family in Rural Taiwan.* Stanford, Calif.: Stanford University Press.

Wong Siu-lun. 1985. "The Chinese Family Firm: A Model." *British Journal of Sociology* 34:58–72.

SIX

The Chinese Cultural Revolution in the Factories: Party-State Structures and Patterns of Conflict

ANDREW G. WALDER

During the 1950s the Chinese Communist Party established a new regime of labor relations that anchored workers to their workplaces, within which Party-state organizations would play an active political role. As the movement of labor between urban factories was restricted to a bare minimum, factories became the focal point for the establishment and funding of a wide range of benefits, from apartments and meal halls to medical insurance and treatment and pensions. Party organizations within factories (as in other organizations) exercised control over the allocation of raises and promotions and could influence employees' access to other benefits (especially housing).

Factory Party organizations sought to develop networks of loyal rank-and-file Party members and other "political activists" and "backbone elements" who were given preferential access to career opportunities and benefits in exchange for their loyal support of the Party organization and its labor policies. Indeed, the primary way in which workers could aspire to promotion off the shop floor was through active participation in Party-sponsored political activities: in the Party organization, Communist Youth League, union organization, the factory militia, or by working for factory security departments by observing and reporting on the

The research for this paper was funded by grants from the John Simon Guggenheim Memorial Foundation, the Wang Institute for Chinese Studies, and the Luce Foundation. Eugene Wu of the Harvard-Yenching Library kindly lent us his personal copy of the compilation of red guard materials cited frequently in this paper. Gong Xiaoxia provided invaluable research assistance. The arguments and interpretations offered here are my responsibility alone.

activities of their co-workers. It was from among activists in these organizations that candidates for promotion to various positions would be selected: group or shift leaders, office jobs in the union or youth league or in such staff offices as the propaganda and security departments.

These Party-sponsored networks cut across all the offices and workshops and all the occupational groups within a factory. Through time, some of the relationships within these networks came to embody personal loyalties as well as more abstract loyalties to the organization and its doctrine. As part of the new Party-state's strategy of industrialization and labor control, these networks were to provide a reliable base of mass support among a minority of workers and to cut across the kinds of occupational loyalties among the workforce, or more accurately specific subgroups within it, that in past decades had served as the basis of an active labor movement. In addition, these networks themselves were used as part of the Party's continuous effort to monitor opposition and dissent and to head off labor protest before it could reach the point of collective action. This fact was evident to rank-and-file workers who were not part of these official networks and who typically resented activists, viewed them with disdain and suspicion, and often harassed and intimidated them in those times and places where such acts could escape retribution. The divisions within the labor force created by these political networks were just as real as those based on differences in skill, pay, or geographical origin and dialect group that had served as focal points of labor mobilization in an earlier era of the labor movement and that in many cases were still potential bases of mobilization.

To say that these political networks cut across other bases of group affiliation among workers is not to imply that such networks obliterated all other bases of collective mobilization in the workplace. It is to say, instead, that they existed in tension with them, and that they provided competing bases of loyalty and affiliation. Moreover, to say that these official networks served to demobilize collective labor protest is not to say that such collective protest could under no circumstances emerge. To the contrary, with the exception only of Poland, China's working class has mobilized for collective protest more often than any other Communist regime's. The years 1956–57, 1966–68, 1974–76, 1980–81, and 1989 have seen large waves of collective action by workers.

Such protest has expressed occupational grievances that were in other periods suppressed by the Party organization.

This observation leads directly to the following question: under what circumstances did this system of labor control, built around the creation of workplace-level networks loyal to the Party organization, fail to prevent the emergence of labor protest? One evident possibility is derived from the fact that these networks acted collectively under the direction of their leaders. Unlike occupational groups, they are hierarchies of authority that connect people of different occupations and statuses. If the leaders of these local hierarchies do not move to oppose emerging collective protest, such networks will not act to do so. Each of the periods of active labor protest mentioned above was also a period in which factional divisions at the top of the national hierarchy transmitted contradictory or ambiguous messages to local Party leaders, thereby disorienting or immobilizing them. One unique characteristic of intra-Party political struggles in China, in fact, is that workers and other ordinary citizens have not merely been permitted, but often encouraged for a period to voice independent criticisms of the conduct of local Party officials or even to mobilize collectively to further the aims of a faction within the national leadership. Such a call from above to criticize or mobilize in defense of a Party faction characterized the Hundred Flowers period of 1956–57, the labor unrest of the mid-1970s, and especially the Cultural Revolution. Indeed, conflicts within factories during the Cultural Revolution were shaped heavily—though not exclusively—by divisions created in the workforce by the Party's political networks.

Previous research on the Cultural Revolution has emphasized that the movement unleashed an unexpected upsurge of protest among workers and others that derived from long-suppressed economic demands. That such suppressed grievances existed is hardly surprising; workplace authority relations were generally unresponsive and harsh, loyal workers were publicly given privileges and preferences, and the high accumulation development scheme of the regime left little slack for the satisfaction of local labor demands. For a period in late 1966 and early 1967, China was swept by a wave of labor demands. This episode, however interesting, was fleeting, and it was repressed with a severity that has not been fully appreciated outside China. Although highly suggestive of a subculture of resistance beneath the orderly facade of Party rule, this incipient labor movement, in the end, was swamped by other waves of conflict and political mobilization during the period.

The Cultural Revolution illustrates the ways in which the collective action of workers could be shaped by the Party's networks even as those networks were under attack. These political networks divided workers into factions and factional struggles around which conflict revolved at the outset of the period, and successive efforts to defend and attack Party networks led to escalating cycles of persecution and cruelty of a kind rarely associated with labor movements anywhere in the world, including China before 1949. Certain identifiable interest groups within the workforce are clearly visible in protests during a certain phase of the Cultural Revolution, but the main conflicts of the period are not easily explained as the pursuit of interests by distinct categories within the labor force. The politics of the Cultural Revolution in the factories—and in other institutions in China—is one shaped by attacks against local networks of power and counterattacks in their defense, by the eventual unraveling of the Party's grassroots networks, and by a subsequent draconian offensive by a Party-army faction that employed unbridled repression and terror to construct new networks along similar lines.

Mobilization and Countermobilization: Party Networks and Factional Cleavages

The political premise behind the launching of China's Cultural Revolution revived the central tenets of 1930s Stalinism. This is the idea that socialism is beset by enemies abroad and at home, that class struggle continues under socialism, that this struggle becomes more acute as socialism is on the verge of final victory, and that it takes the form of hidden conspiracies by remnants of former exploiting classes and hidden domestic agents of foreign imperialists.[1] Because opposition to socialism works through conspiracy, it is difficult to detect, and vigilant "proletarian dictatorship" is necessary.

---

[1] I elaborate this argument more fully in "Cultural Revolution Radicalism: Variations on a Stalinist Theme," in *New Perspectives on the Cultural Revolution*, ed. William A. Joseph, Christine P. W. Wong, and David Zweig, pp. 41–61. Harvard Contemporary China Series, no. 8 (Cambridge: Council on East Asian Studies, Harvard University, 1991).

The ambiguity of these tenets leads to a characteristic arbitrariness. How does one recognize the outward signs of opposition and conspiracy? Insufficient adulation expressed toward the great leader? A lack of enthusiasm toward, or doubts expressed about, some aspect of the Party's current policy? Does the fact that one has lived abroad, was educated in a Western university, or has relatives overseas make one a prime suspect? Does the fact that one or one's parents were from a capitalist or landlord class before the revolution or were members of organizations connected to the Nationalist regime (unions, youth organizations, party, police, army) mean that one is likely to harbor inner doubts about communism that make one prone to participation in conspiracies? It is not possible definitively to say who is beyond suspicion.

What made this conception so explosive in late 1966 and early 1967 is the threat that it represented toward local Party apparatuses in factories and other organizations, as it became clear that officials within the Party organization could be suspects themselves and that ordinary citizens could make accusations against them and demand their removal. Party organizations in workplaces were often disoriented by political developments and sometimes unsure how to proceed, but they and their clients consistently took an orthodox interpretation of the sources of opposition and conspiracy—that it came from outside the Party in the form of former class enemies and imperialist agents who sought to worm their way into positions of importance in the new society. They therefore tended to direct attacks outward, away from the Party networks and toward individuals with "historical problems" or suspect associations. Opponents of Party organizations in workplaces, who had a wide variety of motivations, took a more unorthodox interpretation of the sources of opposition and conspiracy—that it was bred within the Party apparatus itself as officials seized privilege and turned into oppressors of the masses. The opponents of factory officials therefore tended to direct their attacks toward the Party leadership and its network of clients. The Cultural Revolution commonly began in factories as a process of mobilization and countermobilization along a cleavage created by the Party's clientelist networks—those who remained loyal to these structures of power versus those who were critical and for various reasons opposed to it.

These factional struggles did not spring into existence automatically; their origins were organizational, and the impulse came from the top. The Cultural Revolution came to some factories during June to August 1966 in the form of "work teams" of officials dispatched by higher Party organs to take control of the factory and conduct investigations and purges before certifying the factory as politically clean.[2] These work teams combed through the personnel files that contained the political histories of all employees, consulted with the top officials in the factory, and collected intelligence and accusations from ordinary employees. In most cases they also appear to have stimulated or encouraged the formation of red guards (organizations of rebels) among young, politically active workers, especially those already admitted to the Party or who were active in the Communist Youth League. Once the work teams had decided upon an appropriate list of targets for the movement, they suggested likely candidates to the activist workers (now forming red guard or rebel groups), often leaking information from the personnel files that could be used in accusations from these "revolutionary masses."

Work teams instructed sections and work groups to hold meetings to examine the behavior and background of their members, sometimes providing each group with a quota of one or two victims. As targets were served up in accordance with instructions, "struggle sessions" were organized in which the targets were put on a stage and subjected to shouted accusations, rough treatment, and often severe beatings. Afterwards they were removed from their posts (if they were office personnel) and put under surveillance, prevented from leaving the factory compound, sometimes put into makeshift cells where they were required to write a full self-criticism. A wide variety of individuals found themselves under attack: office personnel, heads of staff sections, factory accountants, section chiefs, shop foremen, and ordinary workers. Two kinds of "problems" appear to have stimulated the charges against them: "historical problems," or the fact that a person had been targeted or criticized in a past campaign or had a suspicious background—for example, a foreign education or relatives abroad; or that a person had committed an "error" with political overtones—an accusation that could range from real or imagined slanders against socialism to being caught in petty corruption or an extramarital affair.

---

[2] Unless footnotes are provided to specific documentary sources, the account below of the activities of work teams draws on interviews with the following informants interviewed in Hong Kong in 1979 and 1980 (see appendix): nos. 1, 2, 3, 12, and 64.

Some work teams fulfilled their task with unusual zeal. The work team sent to the Shanghai No. 15 Cotton Textile Mill concluded that the Party committee was "rotten" and that 90 percent of the middle-level cadres were bad. They organized struggle and criticism sessions against some six hundred cadres and workers, 18 percent of the employees. One worker was targeted because his vegetarianism was interpreted as a subtle attack on the Party; another worker attempted suicide repeatedly and went insane as his interrogators sought to extract a confession through torture.[3] Although this work team was an unusually militant one, the teams appear in all cases to have left behind a trail of victims both within the Party's organization and without who invariably felt wronged and who would seek shortly thereafter to reverse their verdicts. The fact that work teams were withdrawn from factories at the end of the summer and publicly denounced as a plot by a disgraced Party faction to obstruct the Cultural Revolution and suppress the "revolutionary masses" would encourage these attempts.

The Defense of Party Networks

Whether work teams entered a factory or not, factionalism originated among factory employees out of a dispute over who had the right to form popular organizations and participate in the movement. The dispute was also, from the outset, over the definition and aims of the movement. Factory officials, not surprisingly, interpreted the purposes of this renewed search for enemies of socialism in a way consistent with Party purges of the past. Loyal members of the Party's organization and network of activists would be mobilized to attack people with suspicious backgrounds or a history of trouble with the Party leaders or who had expressed dissatisfaction with socialism.

Often the first mass organizations to emerge in factories formed at the instigation, or with the blessing, of factory Party officials or the work teams. Reliable members of the Party's youth league, activists and small group leaders and section heads on the shop floor, model workers, members and leaders of the factory

---

[3] *Fangzhi zhanxun* (Shanghai), 5 May 1967, p. 1, CCRM 4:0949. "CCRM" refers to the collection of unofficial newspapers and handbills from the Cultural Revolution published by the Center for Chinese Research Materials, Washington, D.C., 1975. The number before the colon is the volume number; the number after is the page number.

militia (if one existed), grassroots union officers and ordinary Party members—that is, the trusted clients of the Party apparatus—formed these organizations.[4] These mass organizations, later called by their opponents "conservative" (*baoshou*) or "royalist" (*baohuang*) because of their close association with the Party organization and its leadership, typically led campaigns in which individuals similar to those targeted by the work teams would be captured, put through struggle sessions, and sometimes beaten and imprisoned.

Factionalism emerged in a factory when individuals other than these trusted clients of the Party organization sought to participate in the movement, especially when these people presented criticisms of factory leaders or made demands for the redress of grievances. The earliest "rebels" of this kind were in most cases severely suppressed, either by the work teams or the factory leadership or by attacks from royalist mass organizations. In some cases these independent critics were promptly fired or had their wages reduced.[5] In other cases, the incipient rebels would themselves be made targets for persecution, seized by the work team or a royalist group, subjected to struggle sessions and beatings that brought some close to death.[6] When groups of

---

[4] My Hong Kong interviewees were virtually unanimous on this point; the main lines of variation appear to be whether lower-ranking factory officials also joined in significant numbers in the early stages and whether the organization was formed at the direct instigation of the factory leadership or grew up more spontaneously, sometimes even after leading Party officials were forced to step down. Informants nos. 1, 2, 3, 4, 6, 12, 15, 20, 25, 34, 45, 55, 57, 62, 64, 68. The association of these royalist factions with youth league and Party members, model workers, and members of factory militias is suggested in documentary sources as well. See, e.g., *Geming gongren bao* (Beijing), January 1967, pp. 3–4, CCRM 9:2501–2; *Wenge tongxun* (Guangzhou), 9 October 1967, pp. 5–6, CCRM 14:4610.

[5] For example, in the Xi'an Municipal Construction Brigade, where almost all the employees are contract workers, 38 rebels were summarily fired (*Shoudu hongweibing* [Beijing], 10 January 1967, p. 3, CCRM 11:3495); in one Guangdong factory 21 rebel workers in a workforce of 108 found their requests for medical expenses and sick leave denied and their wages cut; after a number of months, 17 were fired (*Xinxing gongren* [Xinxing county, Guangdong], 16 February 1968, pp. 3–4, CCRM 5:1134). At the Beijing Internal Combustion Engine Plant the wages of rebel workers were cut (*Dongfang hong* [Beijing], 19 April 1967, p. 3, CCRM 13:4152). In another Beijing factory, apprentices who put up wall posters criticizing the Party leadership were sent to perform labor in a remote village (*Geming gongren bao* [Beijing], 12 January 1967, p. 2, CCRM 9:2497).

[6] For example, one outspoken critic of the Party secretary was elected to a committee to conduct the Cultural Revolution in one factory, prompting the Party secretary to mobilize loyal workers to detain him as a "bad class element" and subject him to a violent struggle session, tying him up and holding him for 24 hours

independent critics began to form and hold rallies and meetings or to invite students or others from outside to assist them in their struggle, they were often disrupted by the royalist organizations, and violence typically ensued.[7] By the orthodox logic of Party organizations throughout the country, unsanctioned criticisms from outside the Party's own network of royalists against the Party itself was by definition an attack against socialism, a counterrevolutionary act to be punished severely. The severity of the repression against these critics was magnified by the fact that

without food (*Xuanjiao zhanbao* [Beijing], 12 April 1967, p. 1, CCRM 6:1480); in another factory, an early wall-poster critic of Party leaders was subjected to several struggle sessions, beaten, and tortured to the point where his feet required several operations and he was unable to walk (*Hongse zhigong* [Beijing], 17 January 1967, p. 4, CCRM 7:1870); struggle sessions were organized against workers who were members of the rebel organization (*Dongfang hong* [Beijing], 19 April 1967, p. 3, CCRM 13:4152); a sanitation worker in Beijing put up a wall poster and was put under surveillance, then seized, beaten, and tortured until he was close to death, when he was sent unconscious to the public security bureau, which dumped him onto a truck full of corpses (other victims of the Cultural Revolution) being taken to the crematorium; after being discovered alive there he was put into prison for three months until the tide turned (*Hongse zaofan bao* [Beijing], 12 January 1967, p. 3, CCRM 7:1994); the royalist faction in the Beijing Machine Tools Plant attacked workers who attended a rally to denounce the Party leaders and seized, struggled, interrogated, and tortured a number of them (*Hongse zaofan bao* [Beijing], 26 December 1966, p. 3, CCRM 7:1992); rebel workers in the Beijing transportation system had their houses searched and were detained, struggled, tortured, tied up, and imprisoned (*Xuanjiao zhanbao* [Beijing], 27 April 1967, p. 4, CCRM 6:1485); the Party secretary at Beijing Electric Wire attacked those who criticized him in posters as counterrevolutionaries and rightists (*Hongse zhigong* [Beijing], 2 March 1967, pp. 2, 4, CCRM 7:1876); rebels in a Tianjin horse cart cooperative who held a June 1966 struggle session against their Party secretary quickly found themselves detained and struggled as counterrevolutionaries (*Jinggang shan* [Tianjin], 22 March 1967, pp. 3–5, CCRM 3:0585–87).

[7] For example, rebel workers in one Xi'an factory were attacked and beaten by a violent group of royalist red guards, the "Red Terror Team," called in by factory Party officials (*Shoudu hongweibing* [Beijing], 10 January 1967, p. 3, CCRM 11:3495); rebels in a Guangdong factory were beaten up by workers loyal to the Party leadership (*Xinxing gongren* [Xinxing county, Guangdong], 16 February 1968, pp. 3–4, CCRM 5:1135–36); a royalist organization formed at one Beijing factory by the head of the factory militia disrupted rebel meetings, beating and injuring more than a dozen severely (*Geming gongren bao* [Beijing], 20 January 1967, p. 4, CCRM 9:2502; and *Hongse zaofan bao* 12 January 1967, p. 3, CCRM 7:1994); similar attacks were reported from other Beijing factories (*Hongse zaofan bao* [Beijing], 12 January 1967, p. 2, CCRM 7:1993; and *Dongfang hong* [Beijing], 19 April 1967, p. 3, CCRM 13:4152); one in Nanchang resulted in more than seventy rebel casualties that were serious enough to require hospitalization (*Hongweibing* [Beijing], 19 January 1967, p. 3, CCRM 8:2291).

these officials' positions were threatened—both by signs from above that there were to be purges of unknown magnitude within the Party and by the critics from below who sought to name key members of grassroots Party organizations as hidden enemies of the revolution. As it became clear later in 1966 that Mao's faction indeed sanctioned such attacks, factory leaderships rapidly became vulnerable to attack from emerging independent organizations of "rebels."

The Rebellion against Party Networks

The earliest rebels in factories came from more diverse and less easily identifiable backgrounds than the members of the first royalist organizations.[8] The identity of early rebels appears to have varied according to recent political events in the factory and the composition of its labor force. Prominent among the first rebels were those who harbored fresh grievances that stemmed from the conduct of the first stages of the movement—the victims of the work teams, factory Party leaderships, or the royalist organizations.[9] These could be people who were up to this time part of the Party leadership itself or trusted clients of the Party organization, people who found themselves subjected to exaggerated or false charges, sometimes the result of preexisting personal animosities and rivalries within the power structure.[10] They could also be members of the Party or the youth league who had made the mistake of voicing direct public criticism of the malfeasance or persecutions of factory officials and who were punished as a result. They more commonly were ordinary workers or staff who had never been involved actively in Party-sponsored activities but who

---

[8] This portrait of the early rebels is drawn from interviews with the following informants: nos. 1, 3, 4, 6, 12, 15, 20, 25, 27, 34, 45, 55, 62, 68.

[9] Informant no. 4 was a staff cadre attacked at the outset of the Cultural Revolution for his overseas Chinese background; he rebelled against his former persecutors when the political tide turned.

[10] Accounts of this are available in *Hongse zhigong* (Beijing), 2 March 1967, pp. 2, 4, CCRM 7:1876, which recounts that the deputy chief of staff of the Party Committee of the Beijing Electric Wire factory was beaten and persecuted at the hands of the work team and became mentally unstable for a period before emerging later as a vocal rebel. See also *Hongse zaofan bao* (Beijing), 8 March 1967, p. 2, CCRM 7:2003, in which a cadre at Beijing Crane who shortly before had been demoted because of personal animosities between himself and bureau officials joined the rebel faction early and provided useful testimony to the "reactionary" natures of these officials.

had found themselves subject to arbitrary attack in the early stages, or ordinary workers who had a history of conflict with their supervisors or Party branch secretaries and had been punished as a result.

In addition to this diverse array of individuals who had a history of conflict with or victimization by factory authorities, informants commonly mentioned certain demographic or occupational categories as being notable sources of recruitment for early rebel factions. Young workers, those who had never been involved in and were typically disdainful of Party-sponsored activities and who tend to form antiauthoritarian subcultures in factories, were one such source. Also mentioned frequently were apprentice workers, recent hires who earned nominal salaries close to subsistence levels. Temporary and contract workers, who were excluded from factory politics, subjected to harsher labor discipline, and assigned to undesirable jobs, and who received wages and benefits inferior to those of permanent employees, were also prominently mentioned as members of the early rebel organizations (I will return to this group below).

As individuals with these diverse backgrounds began to piece together organizations and formulate accusations and attacks against top factory officials—sometimes with the assistance of radical students who entered the factories to stimulate such rebellion against revisionists within the Party—the "rebel" movement was born and the "conservative" label attached to factions formed from among the Party's trusted clients. The Cultural Revolution entered a chaotic new stage of escalating factional conflict between conservative and rebel factions in factories, one in which typically a variety of smaller "fighting groups" with different political agendas gradually formed alliances.[11] Rebels ignored the kinds of people typically victimized in the earlier stage of the movement and formulated direct criticisms of top factory officials. Suppression of the mass movement (and opposition to Mao and the Cultural Revolution), persecution of individual rebels, corruption and special privilege, and indifference to workers' material demands were all charges typically lodged against the heads of the power structure as a struggle to "seize power" began in earnest.

---

[11] This process, described by a number of informants, is also described in Wu Lianqing, "Shangchai enhou ji," in *Shinian qiyuan lu,* pp. 119–25 (Beijing: Qunzhong chubanshe, 1986); and *Xuanjiao zhanbao* (Beijing), 27 April 1967, p. 4, CCRM 6:1485.

The Paralysis and Destruction of Factory Party Organizations

As rebel factions gained strength, they put factory officials through public struggle sessions; made demands for material support for their faction; held prisoners in offices and storerooms; and in some cases beat, tortured, and even killed top officials and their supporters in the course of interrogation sessions. The violence was especially severe in those factories where officials had earlier sponsored brutal attacks against early rebels.[12] Many rebel groups, as part of their assault against previous networks of power, also made direct attacks upon model workers and activists whom they saw as the tools of the "reactionaries."[13]

National directives from the Maoist faction made clear that Party leaders were to be attacked, and original royalists realized that such leaders could no longer protect them from people who were not trusted members of Party networks. The Party organizations themselves clearly were being called into question, and anyone was licensed to make criticisms. Royalist organizations nonetheless persevered, even after the top Party leaders of the factory were under attack or had already stood aside. They often shifted their political orientations in subtle ways, turning to attack leading factory cadres as well—although not the same ones the rebels attacked. Factional conflict within a factory commonly evolved into a contest between factions to "drag out" of office and humiliate different sets of factory officials—each faction seeking to protect "good" officials that the other faction sought to attack as "reactionary." Factional divisions began to blur as former royalist

---

[12] As one might imagine, revenge was often an important motivation for these attacks. For example, a model worker who had been accused of leading severe beatings of critics of the Party secretary of the Sanitation Department of Chongwen district, one of whom was left for dead (see the case mentioned in note 6 above and an account by another victim in *Hongse zaofan bao* [Beijing], 12 January 1967, p. 2–3, CCRM 7:1993–4), found the tables turned on him near the end of 1966. The rebel faction captured him and subjected him to repeated struggle sessions and tortures. He became ill and went insane as a result of his treatment, eventually dying of his injuries eight years later (*Renmin ribao*, 6 July 1978, p. 4).

[13] For example, *Gongren ribao* (Beijing), 9 October 1978, p. 2, which recounts a citywide model worker in Tianjin who was struggled, beaten, and crippled by rebels in his factory and then divorced by his wife. These kinds of events took place on a wide scale; in Tianjin, almost all the model workers in one part of the city were criticized or attacked in some way, just under half subjected to "severe persecution"—which indicates the kind of treatment described above. Treated especially harshly, as also indicated above, were those who had won citywide recognition as model workers (*Gongren ribao* [Beijing], 10 November 1978, p. 1).

organizations sought to frame themselves as rebels and as both kinds of factions began to forward occupational demands that appealed to a worker membership that each was trying to build up in a quest to "seize power." The membership figures of factions shifted widely with their political fortunes; when one faction clearly gained the upper hand or was able to seize power, its membership levels rose as members of the opposing faction defected.[14] Through time, the memberships and professed aims of factions began to look increasingly similar, with only subtle differences in their declared aims and rhetoric.[15] Moreover, when factions in factories sought outside alliances to strengthen them in their local struggles, it was not unusual for a "conservative" group in the factory to forge an alliance with a "rebel" alliance citywide, or vice versa, and there was often in any event more than one rebel alliance in a city at some point in the movement.[16] Their

---

[14] See, e.g., *Geming gongren bao* (Beijing), 12 January 1967, p. 2, CCRM 9:2497, in which the membership of a rebel faction is said to triple after they seize power in a factory. Informants commonly reported such increases.

[15] Informants consistently described a process whereby factional memberships and aims became blurred in the struggle to seize power after it was apparent that the old officials could no longer stand; informant no. 3 stated that workers were initially split between two factions but eventually all joined the rebels; no. 15 said that after the factory officials fell, the conservatives turned into critics of the leadership as well and concentrated upon leaders with historical problems or questionable class backgrounds; no. 25 said that the two factions split over whether the Party secretary or the director should be removed from office; no. 27 said that the factions were mainly divided over which cadres to attack; no. 45 admitted that as time went by it was difficult to tell any difference between the factions; no. 55 said that after the (conservative) Scarlet Guard alliance was defeated in Shanghai, almost all their members eventually joined rebel groups; no. 62 said that the two factions became more similar through time, both attacking cadres (but different ones), both putting targeted officials through struggle sessions, and both vying for army support in the end. Documentary sources from the period also refer to the changing orientations and aims of former royalist factions and to the tendency of factions on both sides of the original "conservative-rebel" divide to forward demands for improved worker pay and benefits. See, e.g., *Geming gongren bao* (Beijing), January 1967, p. 3, CCRM 9:2501; *Hongse zaofan bao* (Beijing), 12 January 1967, p. 2, CCRM 7:1993; handbill, title partially obscured (Tianjin Municipal Chemical Industry Repair Plant), 12 September 1966, pp. 1–4, CCRM 19:6390–93; *Xianfeng* (Beijing), 23 February 1967, p. 2, CCRM 5:1094; *Xuanjiao zhanbao* (Beijing), 27 April 1967, p. 4, CCRM 6:1485. Subsequent accounts by Chinese writers refer to the same phenomenon: see, e.g., Wu Lianqing, "Shangchai enhou ji," in *Shinian qiyuan lu*, pp. 119–125 (Beijing: Qunzhong chubanshe, 1986); and Liu Guokai, *A Brief Analysis of the Cultural Revolution*, ed. Anita Chan (Armonk, N.Y.: M. E. Sharpe, 1987).

[16] Informant no. 62 noted, after describing this phenomenon, "Factional alignments citywide were strange. One faction in the factory would join up with Red Flag [Guangzhou's "rebel" alliance], but in another factory, a group with the same

main differences at this point in the evolution of conflict were their former ties with, or antagonism toward, factory leaders and the mutual animosities that accumulated with every confrontation.

Once rebel organizations gained a foothold in a factory, increasingly common by the late fall of 1966 and early winter 1966–67, factory Party organizations became completely paralyzed, with officials either under direct attack, performing manual labor under mass supervision or voluntarily, or staying at home to avoid involvement. The issue was no longer whether rebels were licensed to attack the Party or whether the Party organization would be protected by its clients from attack. The issue was now which of the evolving factions within the factory would be able to seize power and suppress its opponents. As several months of rivalry, struggle, and physical skirmishes built up reserves of animosity among factions, the fighting became more violent (kidnaping and torture, armed battles, murder and assassination), often leading factory groups to seek help from outside in broader alliances with other organized groups locally.[17]

---

viewpoint might be aligned with the East Wind [the "conservative" alliance]. There was no real relationship between one's beliefs and pledging loyalty to one or another citywide organization. It was a very strange kind of factionalism." The same tendency is described in the detailed history of factionalism at the Shanghai Diesel Engine Plant, in which the factory's "conservative" faction, upon hearing that the "rebel" Workers' General Headquarters had seized power in Shanghai, rushed to send a delegation to affiliate with it, beating the factory's "rebel" faction to the punch and setting off chronic factional strife through much of 1967—unusual for Shanghai. See Chen Xianfa, *Minzu lei: Hongdong zhongwai de 'basi' shijian* (Shanghai: Tongji daxue chubanshe, 1988). Liu Guokai's *Brief Analysis of the Cultural Revolution* describes the same phenomenon.

[17] Such battles grew increasingly common during 1967 and took a variety of forms. One common type of event was a violent skirmish between factions within a factory, for example the one at a Beijing factory over control of the loudspeaker and telephone systems that left two workers dead and seven seriously wounded (*Xianfeng* [Beijing], 23 February 1967, p. 2, CCRM 5:1094). A similar small skirmish at the Shanghai Diesel Engine Plant on August 3, 1967, led the next day to a retaliatory raid by the allies of the victims of the first attack in which thousands of workers surrounded and attacked the plant, leaving 983 injured and 121 permanently crippled, after which 683 were captured and imprisoned (Wu Lianqing, "Shangchai enhou ji," pp. 119–125; and Andrew G. Walder, *Chang Ch'un-ch'iao and Shanghai's January Revolution*, Michigan Papers in Chinese Studies, no. 32 [Ann Arbor: Center for Chinese Studies, University of Michigan, 1978], p. 75). The deadliest encounters occurred after workers left their plants to join in activities with factional allies. Workers on their way to a citywide rebel demonstration in Guangzhou in July 1967 were attacked by an opposing red guard faction; after a violent street battle twenty-seven workers were kidnaped by the attackers, taken into the Sun Yat-sen Memorial Hall, tortured, and summarily executed; the disfigured

Absenteeism rose, production slowed or halted, and in many factories, for a period, no one was clearly in charge.[18]

The Mobilization for Labor Demands

It was precisely at this point, as factory officials found themselves under escalating attack from rebels and began to step down
from their posts, and as former royalist factions, with no more
Party leadership to defend, began to reformulate their messages
and aims, that groups of workers throughout the country began to
forward demands of a kind commonly associated with labor
movements. This tendency was exhibited not only by the marginal members of the labor force whose public demands for redress
of grievances have formed a central theme in existing interpretations of the rebel movement.[19] Similar demands were made by factions that had originated as royalists, factions that often contained
veteran workers and members of the factory trade union structures, some of whom would have been involved in the
Communist-led labor movement less than two decades before.[20] In
addition, workers who were initially uninvolved in the skirmish-
ing between factory power networks and their opponents now
seized the opportunity to besiege tottering factory officials with
demands for better treatment and pay.

---

corpses were found in the basement the next day (*Dongfanghong, Jida hongqi*
[Guangzhou], 2 August 1967, p. 2, CCRM 13:4206). In some areas, especially
western China, street skirmishes took place between factions armed with military
weapons; in May 1967 a "people's war" declared in Chengdu by one citywide factional alliance against another led to one battle in which more than three thousand
injuries were claimed and close to thirty killed (*Bingtuan zhanbao* [Chengdu] 30
May 1967, pp. 1–2, CCRM 11:3361).

[18] Documentary sources from the period detail the effect of factional conflict
upon production, in some cases because the losing faction takes sick leave in large
numbers after their defeat (*Hongse zhigong* [Beijing] 2 March 1967, p. 1, CCRM
7:1875) or because one faction takes to the streets in protest (*Jinggang shan* [Beijing]
23 January 1967, p. 4, CCRM 3:0362; *Hongwei zhanbao* [Shanghai], 15 January 1967,
p. 3, CCRM 8:2195; *Jinggang shan* [Beijing] 23 January 1967, p. 4, CCRM 3:0362;
Hongse zaofan bao [Shanghai] 12 January 1967, p. 3, CCRM 7:1994). They also
confirm that workshop leadership structures were being replaced completely in
some factories by members of the winning rebel faction (e.g., *Jinggang shan* [Beijing]
23 January 1967, p. 4, CCRM 3:0362).

[19] See, e.g., Hong Yung Lee, *The Politics of the Chinese Cultural Revolution* (Berkeley: University of California Press, 1978); and Walder, *Shanghai's January Revolution.*

[20] See Elizabeth Perry, *Shanghai on Strike: The Politics of Chinese Labor* (Stanford,
Calif.: Stanford University Press, 1993).

The most prominent marginal subgroup in the labor force to mobilize during this period was the temporary and contract workers, who were not granted the job security, benefits, and pay of permanent members of the labor force.[21] Early in the rebel movement, these workers either formed small workplace or district-level factions of their own or allied themselves with the rebels and demanded an end to arbitrary firings and improvement in their benefits and pay.[22] In some cases, contract workers fired in the past returned to former workplaces demanding jobs.[23] Such groups were for a time prominent members of citywide rebel coalitions.[24] In Beijing, groups claiming to be national organizations of temporary and contract workers demanded an end to the system and immediate hiring as permanent workers; attacked, sacked, and shut down the neighborhood service stations that supplied temporary workers to factories; held demonstrations at central government offices; and occupied the offices of the All-China Federation Trade Unions and the Ministry of Labor for more than a week, fighting with rebel groups that had already seized power there and looting the buildings of equipment and supplies.[25]

A wide array of other marginal members of the labor force also pushed actively for better treatment, usually as part of emerging rebel coalitions. Apprentices demanded immediate promotion to Grade 1 worker and retroactive pay.[26] Workers from Shanghai who had been sent to undesirable interior regions to work in factories relocated for national defense purposes returned to Shanghai to demand reassignment.[27] Thousands of pedicab workers in Beijing, thrown out of work early in the Cultural Revolution when radical students denounced their trade as a remnant of imperialism, mobilized to reinstate their jobs and gain compensation for their pedicabs, which had been seized from them and sold.[28] One

[21] Andrew G. Walder, *Communist Neo-Traditionalism: Work and Authority in Chinese Industry* (Berkeley: University of California Press, 1986), chap. 2.

[22] See, e.g., *Laogong zhanbao* (Guangzhou), 3 February 1968, p. 1, CCRM 10:2919; *Shoudu hongweibing* (Beijing), 10 January 1967, p. 3, CCRM 11:3495.

[23] *Hongse zaofan bao* (Beijing), 25 January 1967, p. 4, CCRM 7:1996.

[24] See, e.g., Walder, *Shanghai's January Revolution*, pp. 43–46.

[25] *Zhidian jiangshan* (Beijing), 9 March 1967, pp. 2–3, CCRM 2:0266; *Jinggang shan* (Beijing), 3 March 1967, p. 8, CCRM 3:0382.

[26] *Hongse zaofan bao* (Beijing), 25 January 1967, p. 4, CCRM 7:1996.

[27] See *Dongfanghong bao* (Beijing), 23 January 1967, p. 4, CCRM 13:4218; and the sources cited in Walder, *Shanghai's January Revolution*, pp. 44–45.

[28] *Sanlunche zhanbao* (Guangzhou), 20 December 1967, pp. 2–4, CCRM 11:3396–98; *Dongfang hong* (Beijing), 27 January 1967, p. 4, CCRM 13:4102.

group of artists fired in 1958 formed a rebel organization in Shanghai, demanded jobs and back pay, and for a brief period played a highly visible role in the citywide rebellion.[29] Construction workers, graduates of vocational schools, and demobilized soldiers all demanded pay raises in the course of their participation in rebel organizations.[30]

Such demands were hardly limited to the marginal or to rebel groups. Organizations that had begun as royalists often shifted to wage demands after the toppling of the leaders of their workplaces. Factions aligned with Shanghai's Scarlet Guards demanded higher pay and better housing for workers.[31] Similar factions in large Beijing factories demanded wage raises and bonuses and denounced the current wage system as unfair to labor.[32] Still other demands were made by workers with no apparent factional affiliation. Workers denounced disciplinary fines and demanded their abolition, occupied public housing, and demanded job transfers;[33] groups of veteran workers even demanded retroactive cancellation of pay cuts dating to the early 1950s, when their workplaces were nationalized and put under more spartan state pay scales.[34]

By the end of 1966, besieged by both factional attacks and interest-group demands, on the verge or under threat of being pulled from their offices and subjected to struggle sessions, factory officials (or those who survived after the initial wave of attacks) began to cave in to such demands nationwide.[35] Factories declared

[29] *Geming lou* (Shanghai), 10 March 1967, pp 2–3, CCRM 9:2508–9.

[30] *Dongfang hong* (Beijing), 27 January 1967, p. 4, CCRM 13:4102; *Hongse zhigong* (Beijing), 17 January 1967, p. 2, CCRM 7:1868.

[31] *Huoche tou* (Beijing), 14 January 1967, p. 2, CCRM 8:2353.

[32] *Hongse zhigong* (Beijing), 17 January 1967, p. 3, CCRM 7:1869.

[33] *Jingji pipan* (Beijing), 5 June 1967, p. 4, CCRM 3:0338. *Xin beida* (Beijing), 18 January 1967, pp. 2–3, CCRM 5:1267; *Zaofan* (Shanghai), 15 January 1967, pp. 1–2, CCRM 12:3958. *Hongse zaofan bao* (Shanghai), 12 January 1967, pp. 2, 4, CCRM 7:2008–9.

[34] *Hongse zaofan bao* (Shanghai), 12 January 1967, p. 3, CCRM 7:2009.

[35] Informant no. 55, a manager in a large Shanghai factory, reported that "there were all kinds of different rebel organizations—temporary and contract workers also—all looking for benefits and material gains, like people who didn't get raises during the last readjustment." He was locked up in his office by rebels who demanded large wage raises and funds for travel to Beijing and was told he would not be released until he signed the requisite forms. He did so, protesting that this was not legal and that the bank would not honor them, but because rebels had taken over the banks as well, the payments were made. Compare this account with the official campaign against "economism" described below, in which it was asserted that government officials and managers like the informant conspired to lure

wage readjustments and appointed rebels to committees to carry them out.[36] Back pay and special bonuses were handed out in large amounts.[37] Apprentices were promoted, contract workers were given permanent jobs and food subsidies, and workers fired previously were rehired.[38] The balances in the bank accounts of enterprises and government agencies began to drop rapidly as besieged officials met these rising demands, and the recipients of these funds jammed the department stores of large cities in buying sprees.[39]

Countermobilization against Labor Demands

At the very beginning of 1967 the shifting coalition of Maoist officials who steered the direction of the Cultural Revolution took decisive action against this growing tendency toward interest-group activity and sought to reign in the kind of factional fighting that had paralyzed production and transportation in many parts of the country. The immediate result was a strenuous propaganda campaign against "economism," a label taken from Lenin's early denunciation of trade union consciousness and reformist labor movements.[40] As manipulated in the media and in official communiqués and as echoed in the red guard press, "economism" was an amorphous term extended to any kind of mass action that disrupted production. It was extended, of course, to the kinds of interest-group demands described above. It also covered any transfer of public property to rebel organizations that were contending for power and demanding cash or material support for

---

workers into demanding material rewards by offering them money.

[36] *Dongfanghong bao* (Beijing), 23 January 1967, p. 4, CCRM 13:4218. Informant no. 34, among the first in his group to rebel against factory leaders, reported that one of their first demands was that wages be readjusted for all. The workers had expected a readjustment that never materialized, and they were not satisfied with the Party secretary's explanation that this was a central policy beyond his control. Wage readjustments were the way in which nationwide pay raises were granted upon the discretion of the central government, usually every two or three years. One would normally have been due in 1965 or 1966; the last previous one, in 1963, affected only a portion of the workforce.

[37] *Dongfang hong* (Beijing), 27 January 1967, p. 4, CCRM 13:4102; *Hongse zhigong* (Beijing), 17 January 1967, p. 3, CCRM 7:1869.

[38] *Hongse zaofan bao* (Beijing), 25 January 1967, p. 4, CCRM 7:1996; *Hongse zhigong* (Beijing), 17 January 1967, p. 3, CCRM 7:1869.

[39] *Dongfang hong* (Beijing), 27 January 1967, p. 4, CCRM 13:4102.

[40] See, e.g., *Hongwei zhanbao* (Shanghai), 15 January 1967, p. 4, CCRM 8:2196.

their activities and to any protest activity that removed large numbers of workers from their posts during their shift.[41]

Ever mindful of their factional aims, the national officials who sought to steer the Cultural Revolution developed a propaganda line that blamed all disruptions of production on the scheming of revisionist leaders who sought to protect themselves from attack by "diverting the true aims of the Cultural Revolution." When formerly royalist or unaligned groups were absent from work or made demands for pay or other benefits, they were said to collude with revisionist power holders in an effort to protect them. When rebel or marginal groups, in the course of attacking these officials, made similar material demands, they were said to have been "tricked" or "provoked" by the leaders they were attacking to make these demands. Every instance in which factory or other officials gave in to demands was seen as an effort to divert the "spearhead of struggle" away from themselves toward irrelevant material issues. True to the political mindset of those who pushed the Cultural Revolution forward, all of these actions were portrayed as part of a nationwide conspiracy of reactionary officials to preserve their power and oppose the Cultural Revolution. Workers were ordered in no uncertain terms to stop succumbing to, or conspiring with, the plots of revisionists and to return to work immediately. This was the only mark of a true rebel—to stay on the job and "promote production and revolution."[42]

This propaganda offensive was accompanied by a series of official directives that ordered workers back to their posts; declared a moratorium on all work-related demands; required the return of all funds paid out; canceled all promotions, raises, and new hires made in the face of worker demands; curtailed the sales of expensive consumer goods and the hours of other retail outlets; demanded an end to illegal occupations of public housing; and froze funds in bank accounts.[43] Workers who failed to return to

---

[41] See, e.g., *Dongfanghong bao* (Beijing), 23 January 1967, p. 4, CCRM 13:4218; *Xin beiqi* (Beijing), 9 March 1967, p. 3, CCRM 5:1266; *Zaofan* (Shanghai), 15 January 1967, pp. 1–2, CCRM 12:3958.

[42] *Hongse zhigong* (Beijing), 17 January 1967, p. 2–3, CCRM 7:1868–9; *Hongwei bao* (Shenyang), 28 January 1967, p. 1, CCRM 8:2254; *Hongse zaofan bao* (Shanghai), 12 January 1967, p. 3, CCRM 7:2008; *Huoche tou* (Beijing), 14 January 1967, p. 4, CCRM 8:2354. See also Walder, *Shanghai's January Revolution*, pp. 49–63.

[43] See, e.g., *Zaofan* (Shanghai), 15 January 1967, pp. 1–2, CCRM 12:3958; handbill, "Jinji tongling" (Beijing), 17 January 1967, CCRM 19:6027; *Tiyu zhanxian* (Beijing), 27 February 1967, p. 3, CCRM 12:3694.

work and who continued to make material demands were threatened with arrest, and public security bureaus were publicly ordered to be prepared for action.[44] To publicize these directives, mass rallies and discussion meetings were held in many parts of the country, the ones in Beijing attended by top officials in the Maoist faction.[45]

Although these directives appear to have broken the back of the "wave of economism," a number of worker groups who knew very well that they had not been lured into error by revisionists persisted in their demands. Most prominent were national and regional organizations of temporary and contract workers, some of whom denounced these directives and the officials who authored them and who continued their collective protests. Maoist officials responded with the public release of directives naming a long list of specific organizations as "reactionary" and filled with "bad elements" and ordering their immediate disbanding and the arrest of their members.[46] Despite their suppression, organizations of temporary and contract workers persisted in these along with other demands in some parts of the country into 1968, requiring additional propaganda, directives, and arrests.[47]

The End of the Game: Power Seizure and Repression

The campaign against "economism" marked the beginning of a period in which the Maoist faction in Beijing sought to consolidate new regional leaderships loyal to them and then in turn to

---

[44] See, e.g., *Zaofan* (Shanghai), 15 January 1967, pp. 1–2, CCRM 12:3958.

[45] See, e.g., *Hongse zaofan bao* (Shanghai), 20 January 1967, p. 2, CCRM 7:2013; *Huoche tou* (Beijing), 14 January 1967, pp. 1–2, CCRM 8:2353, which reproduces a speech by Zhou Enlai at such a rally, where other central leaders were in attendance; and *Dongfang hong* (Beijing), 22 January 1967, pp. 1, 4, CCRM 13:4045, 4048, which reports on a speech by Chen Boda.

[46] See *Zhidian jiangshan* (Beijing), 9 March 1967, pp. 2–3, CCRM 2:0266; and *Jinggang shan* (Beijing), 3 March 1967, p. 8, CCRM 3:0382, which outlaw as "counterrevolutionary" the "National League for the Rebellion of Red Laborers" (Quanguo Hongse Laodongzhe Zongtuan), a group of temporary and contract workers active in Beijing; and *Tiyu zhanxian* (Beijing), 27 February 1967, p. 3, CCRM 12:3694, which attacks a long list of groups of temporary and contract workers, sent-down youth, army reclamation brigades, and state farm workers as organizations filled with "bad elements" that sought to "sabotage the Cultural Revolution."

[47] See, e.g., *Gongren pinglun* (Guangzhou) June 1968, pp. 3, 4, CCRM 9:2799–2800; *Guangtie zongsi* (Guangzhou), February 1968, p. 1, CCRM 9:2713; *Xin beida* (Beijing), 18 January 1967, pp. 2–3, CCRM 5:1267.

suppress factional violence and all mass organizations of whatever claimed orientation. If "economism" was a deviation from the proper course, then "power seizure" in the name of Chairman Mao's headquarters was the correct one. This correct course required all factions to unite under the leadership of new power holders certified by the Maoist faction in Beijing. Once these local leaderships were consolidated and approved, they moved quickly, usually with the support of the army, to suppress all popular organizations in factories and schools.

The leadership structures of almost all factories appear to have been smashed, and along with them the network of loyal activists cultivated over the prior decade or more. A number of cadres had been killed or had committed suicide in the earlier struggles; others had been tortured and remained imprisoned in makeshift cells called "cow sheds" (*niupeng*) in which victims were routinely locked up for interrogation and beatings.[48] The luckier ones had quietly "stood aside," staying at home or performing manual labor in the shops or cleaning factory toilets by day and sleeping in the factory "under masses' supervision" by night. In most factories it appears that the entire leadership structure down to the shop and work-group level was disbanded, with control being exercised by one or more factions that replaced former leaders with their own. Sometimes a single faction simply took over a factory; in other factories, different factions controlled different offices and work-shops.[49]

There are two broad patterns through which Party authority was reasserted and networks of royalists rebuilt. The first appears to have been common only in Shanghai, where a civilian Maoist leadership seized power in mid-January 1967, received unambiguous support from Chairman Mao himself, and set about with the use of the public security forces and military primarily as a backup to incorporate a large rebel alliance into a new structure of

---

[48] Informant no. 1 reported that the cadres in his factory had been beaten bloody in struggle sessions, locked in cow sheds for long periods, and in some cases murdered. Informant no. 15 reported similarly violent struggle sessions and a number of suicides. My impression from interviews is that this degree of cruelty did not occur in all factories, despite that fact that struggle sessions appear to have occurred everywhere. On the other hand, violence of this kind was not unusual.

[49] This account of the effect of the first stages of the Cultural Revolution on the authority structures of factories and of the subsequent process of rebuilding is based, unless otherwise noted, on the accounts provided by the following informants: nos. 2, 4, 5, 6, 19, 27, 28, 34, 45, 62, 64, 70.

power. The city's new Revolutionary Committee was set up with the support of a factional alliance called the Workers' General Headquarters. This factional alliance became in effect a mass organization under the control of the Party faction that supported the restoration of order and production and the smashing of "economism," and its leaders were incorporated into new power structures headed by revolutionary committees being newly set up within factories.[50] Workers in this "official" rebel alliance had defeated the other major ("conservative") alliance in the city, which melted away, but it had to defend the new power structure against rebel workers and students who opposed its rapid about-face into guardian of production and public order (a role for which its members had only weeks before criticized the "conservative" faction). Opposition eventually was broken up with the decisive assistance of the bureau of public security and military forces, and the city was spared the violent factional fighting that continued to rock much of China for many months thereafter. Unless factional discord continued within a factory, as it did in the widely publicized case of the Shanghai Diesel Engine Plant, members of the victorious factions took over positions of authority within newly established revolutionary committees and leadership structures, alongside selected managers and Party secretaries who were rehabilitated and permitted to retain their posts.

Far more common in the rest of China was a pattern in which small forces of military officers were dispatched to factories to set up new "great alliances" and eventually revolutionary committees. Military Control Commissions were established at the municipal level, and Military Control Committees were set up at each level of the hierarchy, down through industrial bureaus and, if the factory was large enough, within the factory itself. The military teams moved into factories, established themselves in the offices, and began investigating the factory's political situation. Different factions understood that the officers were empowered to designate a faction as "revolutionary" or "reactionary," and they also understood that the officers would select the members of a new revolutionary committee. For this reason factions rarely opposed the

---

[50] The leader of the citywide federation, Wang Hongwen, was a security department cadre, Party member, and former soldier who worked in the No. 17 Cotton Textile Mill. He is the kind of rebel who was motivated to rebel because of conflicts with the Party secretary of his workplace. He was eventually rewarded for his service with promotion to the top national leadership.

soldiers, but instead tried to cultivate them. Often heads of factions were invited to attend a "Mao Thought study session" (Mao Zedong sixiang xuexi ban), but found this to be a euphemism for detention and interrogation in the form of mutual criticism and confession sessions in which they were to inform on the others and confess the crimes they had committed in the course of the movement. The factional organizations headed by these leaders were at the same time disbanded. In virtually all cases I have heard of, the military officers decided which factional leaders would receive punishments and which would receive positions of leadership. Sometimes the officers favored one faction over another, but they appear often to have tried to provide representation of all sides on a new committee, as long as the included factory cadres were deemed reliable. Until 1970 or 1971, the revolutionary committee was often headed by one of the officers and had other military representatives, but sometimes all officers withdrew from the factory after the new leadership committee was set up and directed its activities from the Military Control Committee of the bureau.

Whether the new factory revolutionary committees were set up in the Shanghai fashion or by army officers, there was little relationship between the political origins of a worker faction and its eventual designation as "conservative" or "rebel." By the time this process began in a factory the original royalist group had either disappeared or had transformed itself into a rebel group that also targeted factory officials for attack. Groups that were considered "royalist" within the factory often aligned themselves with "rebel" factions citywide, and vice versa. In Shanghai, once the Workers' General Headquarters was designated the official "rebel" faction, factions within factories throughout the city raced to its offices to either establish or consolidate an affiliation with them and be declared the true rebel faction—and thereby seize power.[51] Moreover, whatever the political history of a workers' faction, whatever faction the army officers designated as the "revolutionary rebels" in a factory would thereafter be treated as such, and if the opposing faction refused to acknowledge this arrangement, it would be labeled a conservative faction for opposing Chairman Mao and the Cultural Revolution.[52] It is fruitless to attempt any generalization

---

[51] Informants nos. 45 and 62; and Chen Xianfa, *Minzu lei.*

[52] This was apparently very common in Guangzhou, where the army tended to support as revolutionary the factions that had begun as "conservatives" and set about to persecute members of the former "rebel" factions. This was explained to

about what kind of faction won these struggles. The divisions began over attempts to defend, or attack, the Party's networks of power at the factory level. These networks no longer existed, but they were being built anew by a national Party faction composed predominantly of officials from the propaganda, security, and military apparatuses. Whoever demonstrated loyalty to the agents of this new national and local leadership was designated as revolutionary; all others, whoever they may have been, were labeled reactionary and dealt with severely.

Persecution and Terror: "Proletarian Dictatorship" Reborn

As 1967 turned into 1968, China's military and security apparatus, in cooperation with civilian Maoist officials, turned their attention fully to the consolidation of the new order. Local bureaus of public security, working in concert with the military control committees that supervised the new factory revolutionary committees, ushered in a period of repression and terror that was as severe as anything seen since 1949 and that has to this day gone largely unchronicled. Out of this period of repression new structures of authority emerged—ones purged of every conceivable type of suspected class enemy, from those with "historical problems" to leaders of mass factions during the Cultural Revolution.

This repression, which lasted from 1968 through 1971, arrived in the form of three separate persecution campaigns. The largest and best documented of these purges was the "cleansing of the class ranks" (*qingli jieji duiwu*), which occurred first and lasted longest.[53] Similar in orientation, though smaller, were the

---

me at some length by informant no. 64, and it is also explained in detail by Liu Guokai in *Brief Analysis of the Cultural Revolution*. See also the complaint lodged by a rebel faction in the Guangzhou Railway Bureau, which charges that the army installed the former royalist faction and most of the leading cadres earlier targeted by the rebel faction on the new leadership committee (*Guangtie zongsi* [Guangzhou], 15 July 1967, p. 4, CCRM 9:2703).

[53] The movement was launched to clean out "the class enemies who have sneaked into the ranks of the revolutionaries." The first document circulated was dated May 25, 1968, and was titled "Circular Transmitting Chairman Mao's Comment on 'The Experience of the Military Control Committee of the Beijing Xinhua Printing Plant in Mobilizing the Masses to Wage Struggle against the Enemy'." *Renmin ribao*, 1 October 1968, p. 2; *Zhonggong nianbao* 1971, p. 7-1.

"anti–May 16 elements" (*fan wuyaoliu fenzi*) and "one strike, three oppose" (*yida sanfan*) campaigns.[54]

Official directives sent out to military control committees throughout the nation specified a very long and vague list of potential suspects, giving local officials broad discretion in persecuting citizens under them. One directive circulated in the unofficial press specified the targets of the "cleansing of the class ranks" as follows: capitalist roaders, traitors, secret agents, counterrevolutionaries, other bad elements—with "special attention" to be paid to the "leading members" of the new revolutionary committees; also to be "cleaned out" were people who were said to have "sneaked into mass organizations"—landlords, rich peasants, counterrevolutionaries, bad elements, rightists, former occupants of labor camps who had not mended their ways, backbones of counterrevolutionary parties and organizations before 1949, members of counterrevolutionary religious groups, Nationalist officers and secret agents, criminals, and family members of these reactionaries; capitalist roaders, cadres purged during the "Four Cleans" campaign of 1965, and reactionary academic authorities.[55] This list of suspects is noteworthy in two respects: it provides no guidance on how to recognize such individuals, and it excludes virtually no one. Thus historical and class enemies of the Party, the Party's own veteran cadres, and the leaders of mass organizations were all put explicitly on the list.

In the first stage of a factory campaign, the existing leadership group first settled upon a list of suspects and then for each

---

[54] The "May 16 Group" was said to be a national network that radiated out from the "May 16 Red Guard Corps of the Capital," a Beijing rebel faction that resisted the imposition of martial law and was thereby officially labeled a "counterrevolutionary organization manipulated by a small handful of bad leaders." The case was also connected to a purge of "ultra-leftists" within the Maoist faction among the top Party leadership—though tracing this thread is beyond the scope of this paper. The significance of this "conspiracy" is that the charge of membership in it could be—and was—leveled against any local faction that resisted the imposition of military control in any way. See *Renmin ribao*, 3 September 1967. The "one strike, three oppose" campaign began in 1970. "One strike" was short for "strike at the handful of counterrevolutionaries who sabotage socialist revolution and construction in a vain attempt to restore capitalism," and the "three oppose" short for "oppose corruption and theft, oppose speculation and profiteering, oppose extravagance and waste." See *Renmin ribao*, 9, 10 October 1970; 1 January 1971.

[55] See *Guangzhou hongdaihui* (Guangzhou), 22 June 1968, p. 2, CCRM 9:2604; and also the shorter directive in *Wenge tongxun* (Guangzhou), June 1968, pp. 4–5, 16, CCRM 14:4634–35, 4640.

suspect established a "special investigation group" (*zhuan'an zu*, literally "special case group") drawn from among members of the new leadership committee and trusted political activists. The committees worked in a way characteristic of Party purge campaigns. Incriminating materials were collected, primarily by soliciting accusations from acquaintances in the workplace, also by scouring the individual's political dossier, which was kept by the factory's personnel department. A charge of conspiracy or disloyalty was made and, in the style characteristic of Communist purges going back to the days of Stalin's great terror, a confession extracted from the suspect through threats (e.g., the suspect would be executed if he or she refused to confess or his or her spouse or other relatives would be interrogated and tortured), sleep deprivation, beatings, and even torture. Special investigation groups held interrogation sessions late into the night, and many factories had special rooms set aside for interrogation and torture. Because the campaign was designed to uncover conspiracies, targets were required not only to confess, but to name names. Not surprisingly, the extraction of confessions and implications of others through threats and torture led not uncommonly to escalating bouts of victimization in which large numbers of people were persecuted for participation in wholly imaginary conspiracies.

Hit especially hard during this period, in factories or other industrial sites that had been established before 1949, were older staff and workers who had some past association with any organization affiliated with the Nationalist regime. The largest casualty lists for this campaign are usually found in these older plants, where large suspected networks of Nationalist spies were uncovered through violent public struggle sessions and the brutal extraction of confession under torture.[56] These were extreme cases,

---

[56] For example, in the Qinchuan Machine Tools Plant in Shanxi, 280 employees, some 22 percent of the total, were investigated as "Nationalist remnants." Of these, 110 were brutally beaten—five to death—and five others were permanently crippled. Three entirely fictional spy organizations were uncovered, and sixty-nine workers were attacked. One of those tortured and crippled was an old Party member who had many years before denied the membership application of the person heading the campaign in the factory. The "advanced experience" of this factory in catching enemies was given wide publicity, and three hundred thousand people came from around the country to learn about it (*Shaanxi ribao* [Xi'an], 16 December 1978, p. 1). At the Tongchuan Coal Mine, an "Anti-Communist Salvation Army" was uncovered, as older workers with "historical problems" were seized, accused, and tortured until they confessed, until more than three hundred were attacked, with fifty subjected to struggle sessions; five attempted unsuccessfully to commit suicide, six were crippled, and six killed (*Shanxi ribao* [Taiyuan] 15 De-

but at least some people with bad class backgrounds or suspicious historical associations were targeted in almost every factory during the period. And almost inevitably there were some who either defied factory authorities or who through a slip of the tongue or a pen found themselves accused of counterrevolution and subjected to struggle sessions, torture, and summary execution.[57]

Many former factory rebels, especially the leaders of factions, also found themselves targeted in these campaigns, both those included on the new leadership committees and (especially) those

---

cember 1978, p. 1). In the Yumen Oilfields, a former Nationalist enterprise, a former Nationalist Party member who later joined the Communist Party was tortured, eventually confessing that he was a spy and naming others. This led to an escalating process of torture, confession, and implication whereby 247 actual "spies" were caught and subjected to struggle sessions and brutal tortures. In the end, seventeen were murdered, eight of them workers, "hundreds crippled, and thousands terrorized" (Song Keli, "Shiyou he zuozheng," in *Chunfeng hua yu ji*, vol. 1, pp. 340–47 [Beijing: Qingzhong chubanshe, 1981]). In the Datong Coal Mining Bureau, 3,600 workers and cadres were accused of membership in a Nationalist spy organization; 980 were detained, interrogated, and subjected to struggle sessions, and sixty were killed or crippled (*Shanxi ribao* [Taiyuan] 15 December 1978, p. 1). In the Hong'an Machine Tools Plant, 547 were accused as Nationalist spies, including 40 percent of the workers in one workshop; the accused were brutally tortured, and seventy-four were crippled, thirteen went insane, nineteen attempted suicide, and twenty-one died as a result (*Shaanxi ribao* [Xi'an] 19 September 1978, p. 1). Similar cases were also reported at the older portions of the Capital Iron and Steel Company (*Beijing ribao*, 6 July 1978, p. 1), at a military armaments plant in Shenyang (*Gongren ribao* [Beijing], 10 November 1978, p. 1), and at the Shanghai Railway Bureau.

[57] For example, a worker in a Hebei factory who defended Liu Shaoqi (the highest-ranking official purged during the Cultural Revolution and the chief "capitalist roader") and refused to recant was arrested and shot twenty-two days later ("Zhengqi ge," in *Chunfeng hua yu ji*, vol. 2, pp. 102–109 [Beijing: Qunzhong chubanshe, 1981]); a factory accountant was arrested for putting up a wall poster defending Liu Shaoqi in 1968 and was eventually executed in 1970 (*Renmin ribao* [Beijing], 4 June 1980, p. 3); an old worker in the Shanghai Railway Bureau was attacked and accused of being a former Nationalist because he had tried to defend someone accused of being a former Nationalist during a struggle session (*Gongren zaofan bao* [Shanghai], 19 December 1968, p. 3, CCRM 9:2835); a worker in Anhui inadvertently wrote "down with Mao" and was brutally struggled and sentenced to jail as a counterrevolutionary (*Gongren ribao* [Beijing] 27 November 1979, p. 3); and (during the *yida sanfan* campaign) a technician in a chemical fertilizer plant inadvertently wrote over the name of Chairman Mao and was accused of counterrevolution and jailed, and an older brother of someone suspected of writing a counterrevolutionary slogan in a factory was interrogated around the clock and deprived of sleep and water; he was eventually provoked into striking his interrogators, after which he was badly beaten, his leg broken, and he was put into prison for two years (*Renmin ribao* [Beijing], 23 August 1978, p. 2).

from the factions who felt left out of the new leadership committees and who resisted the new committees, however passively.
Informants commonly mentioned that one or another of these
campaigns victimized former leaders of mass factions—whether or
not they were included in the new power arrangements—who had
earlier attacked power holders violently, who had murdered people in the course of their activities, or who had resisted the army
as it moved in to set up new leadership committees. Workers
who had risen into positions of authority because of their factional
activities commonly found themselves removed from their positions and attacked for having a suspicious past or questionable
class background or for taking privileges that cadres who had earlier held such positions enjoyed. The "anti–May 16 elements" and
"one strike, three anti" campaigns seem especially to have focused
on the heads of former factions who were increasingly deemed
untrustworthy and unsuitable for the new Party hierarchies being
established in this remarkably tense atmosphere of extreme security consciousness. These former worker-leaders sometimes found
themselves (once again) invited to "study classes" (*xuexi ban*) that
turned out to be involuntary thought-reform sessions in which
they were to confess their errors and crimes; sometimes they were
themselves put in cow sheds and subjected to struggle sessions
and interrogations; sometimes they were sent down to the countryside, put in prison, or even turned over to the security forces
for public executions.[58]

This political assault effectively eradicated organized activity
by worker factions, especially the kinds of movements earlier
denounced as "economism." The tools of terror were turned to the
restoration of labor discipline. Workers were threatened with
accusation as counterrevolutionaries if they did not report to
work; requests for unpaid overtime were phrased as "loyalty to
Mao work"—a clear threat in the reigning political atmosphere.
Industrial accidents and fires might touch off a hunt for counterrevolutionary saboteurs.[59] Factory political life was infused with

---

[58] Informants nos. 6, 28, 31, 34, 51, 57, 62, 64, and 68 are the sources for this
description of the effect of the campaigns on former leaders of worker factions.
No. 64 reported that ten people were locked up and interrogated in his factory for
telling other workers that the army had decided to end the Cultural Revolution
and that they opposed the killings that they were committing in the course of doing so.

[59] As it did in a Shenyang textile mill (*Liaoning ribao* [Shenyang], 19 October
1978, p. 1).

empty and at times bizarre ritual. Workers in many factories found themselves compelled to bow toward a portrait of Chairman Mao in the morning and "ask for instructions," pulling out and reading an appropriate passage from Mao's "little red book"; at the end of the shift they bowed again to the portrait and "gave a report"—all in loud, cadenced, stereotyped chanting. In this period workers were also compelled periodically to show their undying loyalty to the Chairman (and not coincidentally, to his representatives in the factory) by performing the "loyalty dance" (*zhongzi wu*), usually clumsy steps resembling calesthenics done to the tune of a patriotic national song. In this frightening and sometimes bizarre atmosphere of repression, terror, and purge, new factory power structures were forged out of those who survived as loyal servants of the Chairman and his newly certified and true representatives.

Chinese Labor and the State: The Cultural Revolution's Legacy

Although it is easy to agree that history matters, it is less easy to agree on what precisely this means. In this paper, political networks within factories—the residue of seventeen years of Communist efforts to reorganize factory labor relations after 1949—are seen to have decisively shaped patterns of cleavage and conflict within Chinese factories. Decisively, but not exclusively—we have seen that both "rebel" and "conservative" factions showed a tendency toward demands and collective action more commonly associated with labor movements in China before 1949 and elsewhere in the world, and others have noted the ways in which pre-1949 divisions in the labor force could be mirrored in the factional activity of the period. Although the Party's networks in factories did not eliminate divisions rooted in China's occupational structure, whether before or after 1949, they nonetheless generated a violent and vindictive form of political factionalism. The initial divisions within the labor force emerged directly from the distinction between those loyal to factory leaders and who sought, often violently, to defend them, and those who had been victimized by the Party in the past or otherwise marginalized in the power structure and status hierarchy the Party sponsored in the workplace.

The grievances and animosities generated in the first wave of attack and defense along this cleavage continued to dominate factional fighting even after the leaders of the factory's Party networks had long since been dragged out of their offices by rebels.

Indeed, the politics of accusation, kidnaping, torture, extraction of confession, and murder, all too typical of the period, were generated not only by the local structures of power, but by a political mentality that China's radical Maoists had inherited directly from Stalin.[60] Were it not for the existence of the Party's political networks within factories, it is unlikely that the Party's political conceptions could have shaped mass political activities to the degree that they did.

The Cultural Revolution itself occupies a pivotal place in the history of the Chinese state's relation to its working class. The legacies of this period continued to shape patterns of conflict and protest long after the imposition of military control and the cleansing of the class ranks. These draconian efforts to restore order and rebuild a stable network of loyal workers, however, were only partially and temporarily successful. The death and claimed conspiracy of Lin Biao led to the rapid withdrawal of Military Control Committees from factories in 1971 and to inevitable conflict in factories over the political settlement the committees imposed. Moreover, subsequent jockeying at the center and in the provinces between civilian Maoists and a more moderate faction of leaders returning to power after Cultural Revolution purges led to similar factionalism between factory officials who had survived the movement and retained their posts and new leaders who had risen to positions of power during the period. Isolated local rebellions by former factional leaders provided the opportunity for labor protest that, like the wave of "economism" during the Cultural Revolution, often found radical rhetoric mixed with labor demands (the same ones that had been ignored and suppressed since 1966). The result in the mid-1970s was chronic labor protest and a series of general strikes in major industrial cities, still only partially documented. At the same time, the rebels of 1966–67 who were suppressed and often brutally persecuted from 1968 to 1971 began

---

[60] That this kind of politics was generated by the workforce divisions created by Party organizations is suggested also by the observation that the groups who appear to have engaged in collective protest more common to labor movements were those subgroups within the labor force that were marginal to the factories and labor forces organized by the Party. Temporary and contract workers, sent-down youth, state farm workers, and other marginal groups forwarded occupational demands and engaged in demonstrations, petitions, and occupations of buildings, sometimes violent. But I have so far found little evidence that they were deeply involved in the kidnaping and torture of officials or in factional competition inside factories.

to form a dissident subculture that found its expression in pro-democracy protests that emerged in China between the "Li Yizhe" protests in Guangzhou during 1973 and 1974 through the "democracy wall" movements of 1978 and 1979. Indeed, it is to this brutal period that subsequent historians of Chinese communism are likely to trace the roots of its demise.

APPENDIX: List of Informants Cited in the Text

Interviews conducted at the Universities Service Centre, Hong Kong, November 1979 to August 1980

Number	Background and Experience
1	Draftsman in a Beijing construction company; during 1964–66 a construction worker. Member of rebel workers' faction.
2	Engineer who worked as manual laborer in a Beijing chemical plant.
3	Technician in a Shanghai machine-building plant, fitter in workshop, 1966–68. Member of original work team during the movement on the eve of the Cultural Revolution; later joined worker faction that aligned itself with the rebels citywide.
4	Staff member in a Kunming planning bureau, later a worker in an auto repair plant (1968–72).
5	Manager in a Canton textile mill, later fitter in a workshop (1967–70).
6	Technician in a Canton chemical fertilizer plant.
8	Electrician in a Beijing machine-building plant.
12	Technician and shift supervisor in a Hangzhou textile mill; 1967–69, production worker.
15	Technician in a Fushun heavy machinery plant; worker in shop, 1967–69.
19	Technician in a Beijing lumber mill; worker in shop 1968–69.
20	Technician in a Beijing construction design institute.
25	Technician in a Canton machine tools research institute.

27	Painter in a Beijing construction company.
28	Office staff in a Tianjin textile mill; production worker beginning 1967.
31	Worker in a Tianjin machine-building plant.
34	Worker in a Canton machine-building plant.
45	Technician and repair worker in a Shanghai glass works.
51	Worker in a Fuzhou electrical machinery plant.
55	Manager in a Shanghai steel mill; production worker, 1967–69.
57	Worker in a Beijing auto parts plant.
62	Technician and repair worker in a Canton chemical fertilizer plant.
64	Repair worker in a Canton auto repair plant. Active in rebel faction, later chosen vice-head of revolutionary committee and head of a special investigation group.
68	Technician in a Shanghai auto assembly plant.
70	Manager in a Hunan machine-building plant.

SEVEN

Chinese Sex Workers in the Reform Period

GAIL HERSHATTER

Over the past fourteen years, at first occasionally and then with increasing frequency, foreign reporters, tourists, and businessmen in China have returned with reports that prostitution has reappeared in Chinese cities. Since the mid-1980s, official Chinese broadcasts and publications have also intermittently discussed prostitution, usually in the course of a campaign to eliminate it. To date none of these campaigns has been successful, and it seems likely that prostitution will continue to be an important source of income for a variety of sex workers, pimps, hotel staffs, massage and beauty parlor owners, roadside stall operators, and the police—to name only some of the groups who are involved with the developing sex trades.

This essay explores the appearance of female prostitution in 1980s and 1990s urban China, after three decades of apparent absence. It makes a preliminary attempt to describe how prostitution is organized and to whose financial benefit. As prostitution has once again become a feature of Chinese society, it has become embroiled—as it was before 1949—in a larger public discussion about what kind of modernity China should want and what kind of sex and gender relations should characterize that modernity. Accordingly, it is important to ask not only how and where sexual services are sold, but also what meanings are attributed to such transactions by sellers, buyers, government regulators, and social critics in contemporary China. How has the state categorized and sought to regulate reform-era prostitution? What do other significant groups—emergent social scientists, Women's Federa-

My thanks to David Roberts for research assistance and to Emily Honig and Wang Zheng for accompanying me on my fieldwork trip to the Hongqiao Hotel.

tion cadres, women's studies scholars, journalists, fiction and nonfiction writers—have to say about prostitution? What do we know about why women are becoming sex workers, and through what categories do they understand their own experience? Would the categorization of prostitution as sex work, and therefore as a sector of the labor market, make any sense to them? In short, how is prostitution formulated in late-twentieth-century China? And because, unsurprisingly, state formulations dominate the public discussion, what is the effect of those formulations on how the wider society understands prostitution?

The concept of "formulation" requires some explanation here. In his innovative study *Doing Things with Words in Chinese Politics*, Michael Schoenhals argues that "formalized language and formalized speech acts help constitute the structure of power within China's political system." In addition to registering publications and controlling photocopy equipment, he says, the state "exercises direct control over political discourse" by controlling the formulation of problems.[1] A formulation (*tifa*) is a fixed way of saying something; Party leaders maintain that deviation from the correct scientific way of framing a problem can lead to confusion among the masses.[2] Although Schoenhals sees the importance of formulations diminishing in the reform era, I am not sure that the state has discarded them so thoroughly or that we should abandon them so quickly as a means of understanding the complex nexus of language, regulation, and social flux in contemporary China. Here, with apologies to Schoenhals, I want to expand his use of the term "formulation" to include not only the precise choice of words and phrases, but also somewhat broader acts of classification.

If we look at recent attempts by the Chinese state to create formulations about prostitution, we see a series of shifts in the late 1980s and 1990s. As the numbers of women selling sexual services grew, state authorities first formulated the problem as one of vice, linked to a wider spread of bourgeois liberalization. By the early 1990s the vice formulation had been joined by formulations that classified prostitution as a violation of women's rights or as a

---

[1] Michael Schoenhals, *Doing Things with Words in Chinese Politics: Five Studies*, China Research Monograph, no. 41 (Berkeley: Institute of East Asian Studies, University of California, 1992), chap. 1; quoted passages are from pp. 1–2.

[2] For instance, in August 1965 it was considered correct to say that socialist society contained classes (*you jieji de shehui*) but not that it was a class society (*jieji shehui*). Ibid., p. 7.

crime. Because in the 1990s the state no longer has a monopoly on formulations, we can also examine the inclusion of prostitution in larger academic and popular conversations about sexuality and commerce.

Paying attention to the way a problem is formulated is not merely a matter of linguistic politesse. Particularly in a situation where the state is both naming and regulating a phenomenon, the way prostitution is formulated (as bourgeois vice, as feudal violation of rights) has immediate policy implications and palpable effects on the daily lives of those classified as prostitutes. In this sense, regulatory language does not merely describe a preexisting phenomenon called "prostitution"; it also constitutes that phenomenon and, having created it, immediately moves to alter it.

It is not only in China that classificatory strategies are significant. The English term "prostitution" itself has acquired multiple connotations, most of them having to do with vice, fallen virtue, and the loss of physical and ethical integrity. Deciding that the term is irredeemable, many advocates of prostitutes' rights in the United States and Europe have adopted the term "sex work," which calls attention to the labor involved in transactions involving sexual services. I use the term "prostitution" in this essay not out of any fondness for its Victorian resonances but because it is a closer approximation than "sex work" of the way sex-for-money transactions are named in Chinese discourse.

How prostitution is named affects how it will be discussed, in turn shaping interventions by the state and others. Significantly, prostitution in reform-era China has rarely been formulated as a labor market question. Among other consequences, this means that an entire range of approaches to and understandings of prostitution have not been invoked. A formulation does not only name; it silences other possibilities. The final section of the essay will examine the implications of that silencing.

Life in the Sex Trades: A Sketch

The most striking feature of prostitution in late-twentieth-century China is the proliferation of venues, prices, and migration patterns. In slightly more than a decade, complex and segmented markets for sexual services have emerged in Chinese cities and towns, drawing out-of-province women as well as local ones into sex work.

As early as 1982, an unpublished Women's Federation investigation in Xian (not one of the early-developing coastal areas) found prostitutes from rural areas working out of small hotels with a local clientele. Many were married women who had been sent by their husbands; in some cases the husbands acted as pimps. Others had fled unhappy family situations. Still others worked in clothing repair at the railroad station and moonlighted as prostitutes. These women were not called prostitutes (*jinü*) because they did not specialize in the sale of sexual services. Rather, they were classified as "women who sell sex" (*maiyin funü*), a term that emphasized an action rather than an ontological or occupational status.[3]

By 1987, fewer of these women could be found in Xian; they appear to have moved to county seats and smaller towns. In the city a new type of prostitution had emerged, one that was also found in the coastal cities and special economic zones. High-priced prostitutes (still called *maiyin funü*), working mainly out of hotels, sought out a foreign clientele.[4] A 1989 police investigation in a guesthouse in Humen, Guangdong, gives some sense of how hotel prostitutes worked. Police found about thirty prostitutes staying in the guesthouse as permanent guests. They were referred to as "northern girls"; they came from Hunan, Guangxi, Sichuan, Shanghai, Shenyang, Heilongjiang, Hubei, and Guizhou (but not from Guangdong; apparently prostitutes generally worked outside their own provinces). Most were about twenty years old. They followed guests to their rooms and propositioned them directly or else called the rooms. Some had been brought there under the control of pimps, who also stayed in the guesthouse. Some hired bodyguards. They earned a hundred yuan per encounter, five hundred for an entire night. Their earnings supported pimps and bodyguards, as well as payoffs to hotel attendants and security personnel. One woman told an undercover investigator that the attendant on duty received a ten-yuan tip for each session. Attendants regularly colluded with prostitutes, letting them know when guests were in their rooms. The women also asserted that the hotel manager wanted the prostitutes there because more guests would stay at the hotel if prostitutes were available. They said that the manager sent appropriate presents to the public security bureau, which rarely checked the place.

---

[3] Interview with Gao Xiaoxian, Xian, 1 July 1993.
[4] Interview with Du Li, Xian, 1 July 1993.

Clients were Hong Kong and Macao tourists, as well as managers and marketing people from various companies, cadres, and workers.[5]

In Shanghai's Hongqiao Hotel in 1993, high-priced prostitutes frequented the disco and bar on the thirtieth floor. Unlike other customers at the disco, they did not pay the cover charge of eighty-five yuan (seventy-five on weekdays) upon entry; some had permanent free-entry status as honored guests; others deposited some form of identification and received a tag indicating that they would pay when they left. They danced with other patrons of the disco, some of them foreigners from Hong Kong and other Asian nations, others rich local men. Some accompanied guests into one of the dozen or so karaoke booths in the back, which could be rented by the hour. (These were private but not concealed from view; all had windows opening on the hallway.) Prostitutes were not completely distinguishable from other women in the bar, unless one watched them over a period of time. After dancing with a man, a prostitute would move with him away from the deafening music of the dance floor and toward a tiny lounge near the karaoke booths. Some sat and conversed with their potential customers in several languages; others stood silently next to men, apparently engaged in protracted negotiation over prices. The absence of flirtatious or overtly sexual behavior was noticeable; many of the women exhibited all the animation of statues, except when they clustered in groups to talk to one another or joked with the attendant in the women's room. They also appeared to be on friendly terms with the waitresses in the bar area, who were dressed in military camouflage outfits and shorts. Some of the prostitutes wore beepers; others crowded the small bank of phones at one end of the lounge, apparently dialing rooms inside the hotel in quick succession. A man from Hong Kong who was accompanying two visiting Korean businessmen explained that the women charged eighty-five yuan (the cost of the cover charge) to dance and converse with a man. Unlike the situation elsewhere in Japan and Korea, the amount of time that the man had purchased was not standardized, and angry customers often found that women abruptly left them in midchat. A woman could conduct

---

[5] "NPC Examines Prostitution, Countermeasures" (text). Hong Kong *Jiushi niandai* in Chinese (1 October 1991), no. 216, pp. 11–13. Translation by the Foreign Broadcast Information Service (as are all subsequent FBIS citations). *FBIS Daily Report—China*, 9 October 1991 (PrEx 7.10: FBIS-CHI-91-196), pp. 27–28.

several of these conversations in an evening and make substantial money without ever leaving the disco or agreeing to an act of sexual intercourse. To have sexual relations with a prostitute, a man had to offer enough money to exceed what she could make at the disco.[6]

Meanwhile, at the lower end of the hierarchy of prostitution, young women, some only fourteen years old, worked in roadside hostels that catered to truck drivers and traveling businessmen and officials. In Zhejiang the local *Legal Daily* found thirty-four prostitutes working in a single eastern district; it noted that only three of them had received any secondary schooling.[7]

Although numbers are particularly unreliable where illegal activities are concerned, government statistics on arrests can give some indication of the growth of prostitution. According to the Ministry of Public Security, from 1981 to 1991 authorities detained 580,000 prostitutes and "whoremongers" (pimps?). (The number of repeat offenders included in this statistic is not clear.)[8] In 1989 alone, 110,000 prostitutes and customers were processed by police, nine times the 1982 figure; by 1990, the number had increased to 146,000.[9] In two months of 1991 alone, 29,315 prostitutes and their customers (not disaggregated) were detained. By 1991, about 56,000 prostitutes had passed through 103 reeducation centers nationwide.[10]

State Formulations: Resurgent Prostitution

Virtually everyone who commented on late-twentieth-century prostitution referred back to China's past, usually to invoke the bad old days of semicolonial weakness and vice or to make comparisons with the good old days of the 1950s when the state

---

[6] Personal observation, Shanghai, 26 June 1993.

[7] "Official Journal Cited on Cases of Prostitution" (text). Hong Kong Agence France-Presse in English (16 January 1989 at 0935 GMT). In *FBIS Daily Report—China*, 17 January 1989 (PrEx 7.10: FBIS-CHI-89-010), pp. 34–35.

[8] "Security Ministry Cracks Down on Prostitution" (text). Beijing Xinhua in English (6 September 1991, 0847 GMT). In *FBIS Daily Report—China*, 10 September 1991 (PrEx 7.10: FBIS-CHI-91-175), p. 31.

[9] "Gu Linfang on Drugs, Vice Sweeps" (text). Hong Kong *Tzu ching*, 14 (5 November 1991), pp. 10–12. In *FBIS Daily Report—China*, 25 November 1991 (PrEx 7.10: FBIS-CHI-91-227), p. 29.

[10] "Security Ministry Cracks Down on Prostitution" (text). Beijing Xinhua in English (6 September 1991, 0847 GMT). In *FBIS Daily Report—China*, 10 September 1991 (PrEx 7.10: FBIS-CHI-91-175), p. 31.

successfully closed brothels. The first commentators to invoke these historical comparisons were foreign reporters in 1980s China. Ever alert for discrepancies between what the government said about socialist society and what could be observed in daily social life, reporters noted that prostitutes were increasingly visible in hotels and coffee shops patronized by foreigners. Their articles— with titles like "What the Revolution in China Wiped Out, Reform Brought Back," "Prostitution Is Back, and Peking Isn't Happy," "Prostitution Returns, Chinese Officials Say," "Newest Economics Revives the Oldest Profession," and "Prostitution Thriving Again in China"—invariably classified prostitution as a resurgent phenomenon.[11] Embedded in much of the foreign writing on China was an assumption that prostitution is a "natural" feature of society that will always exist, absent tireless enforcement of state restrictions. Alternatively, foreign writers characterized it as an inevitable product of a market economy.

As some of these headlines suggest, Chinese officials shared this characterization of prostitution as something that had disappeared, then reappeared. State propaganda had long touted the elimination of prostitution in the early 1950s as one of New China's victories over imperialism, and its resurgence is portrayed as a cost of letting the West back in. State attitudes have varied over the last decade on the question of whether that cost is acceptable, and even now officials can be heard to grumble (though not in print) that prostitution is an inevitable part of society and that the state should tax it rather than waste time and resources in futile attempts at suppression.

On the surface, this shared assumption that prostitution was here, then gone, then here seems like the most undeniable sort of common sense. Like most commonsense understandings, however, this one prevents certain questions from being asked. For instance, is there anything historically specific about the emergence of prostitution at this time, anything that is not a mere replication of prostitution in pre-Communist China? Is there anything locally specific about the emergence of prostitution in this

---

[11] "What the Revolution in China Wiped Out, Reform Brought Back" (Adi Ignatius and Julia Leung, *Wall Street Journal*, 15 November 1989); "Prostitution Is Back, and Peking Isn't Happy" (John F. Burns, *New York Times*, 6 October 1985); "Prostitution Returns, Chinese Officials Say" (Daniel Southerland, *Washington Post*, 7 October 1985, p. A20); "Newest Economics Revives the Oldest Profession" (Edward Gargan, *New York Times*, 17 September 1988, p. 4); "Prostitution Thriving Again in China" (Lena Sun, *Washington Post*, 12 March 1992).

place, something that is not an exact replication of the situation in southeast Asia, Latin America, or the United States? Some of these questions are addressed by nonstate commentators, but they are generally ignored in state documents. Instead, state authorities have characterized prostitution either as a vice, in which case it should be addressed by antivice campaigns, or as a crime against both women and social order, in which case it should be addressed by new and better laws.

State Regulation: Prostitution as Vice

After trial runs in various localities, in mid-November 1989 the central government announced a concerted campaign against what it labeled the "Six Vices": prostitution (being a prostitute or patronizing one), pornography, trafficking in women and children, using and dealing in narcotics, gambling, and profiting from superstition.[12] The campaign, or *yundong*, is a method much favored by the late Mao Zedong. Rather than relying primarily on the daily operations of institutions like the courts and the police, it mobilizes appropriate government and Party organizations and in turn has them mobilize the populace to achieve a particular end. (The Cultural Revolution, discussed by Andrew Walder in chapter six, was the largest and most radical campaign in PRC history.) It is perhaps not coincidental that this quintessentially Maoist method was revived to combat prostitution in the autumn following the June 1989 crackdown on the popular movement. Perhaps the government hoped to return to a simpler time, when the degree of national consensus was such that the population could be mobilized to achieve some common social goal. Perhaps this use of a mobilization campaign was part of a larger move to reassert mechanisms of mutual surveillance that had fallen into partial disarray during the reform decade (as the leadership found out to its dismay when it tried to run a full-scale purge after June 4). In any case, the language and methods of the campaign would have been familiar to any resident of Mao's China.[13]

---

[12] Chang Hong, "Security Minister Condemns 'Six Social Vices'" (text). Beijing *China Daily* in English (14 November 1989), p. 1. In *FBIS Daily Report—China*, 16 November 1989 (PrEx 7.10: FBIS-CHI-89-220), p. 17; "Wang Fang Announces Prostitution Crackdown" (text). Beijing Xinhua in English (13 November 1989). In *FBIS Daily Report—China*, 21 November 1989 (PrEx 7.10: FBIS-CHI-89-223), pp. 25–26.

[13] In fact, the *South China Morning Post* commented, "Analysts say the way the

The State Council initiated the campaign via a telephone conference with provincial authorities. Wang Fang, minister of public security, charged that the Six Vices had "seriously polluted our society, disturbed public order, and undermined the physical and mental health of vast numbers of people, especially the young people." The State Council called for all levels of government to "provide support in terms of funds, shelters, medical personnel, medicines, and equipment which are needed for sheltering and educating prostitutes, their patrons, and drug addicts, for taking forceful measures to help drug addicts, and for examining and treating venereal diseases."[14]

As the campaign got under way, political commentators stressed that eliminating the Six Vices was key to combating the pernicious effects of foreign influence on the Party and the people. A *People's Daily* commentary linked the return of the "Six Evils" to a decline in the strength of Party leadership:

> [D]ue to the influence of the ideological trend of bourgeois liberalization, the revolutionary will of some Communist Party members has been waning. They did not dare criticize or resist disgusting social phenomena and did not dare carry out struggles against bad people and bad things. This is what those people who are trying to subvert and sabotage our country would like to see. It is also a vicious means used by people with ulterior motives to corrode our Party, cadres, and socialist system.[15]

Even more directly accusatory was the comment by Shanghai's Public Security Bureau director, who said, "Wiping out the six vices is an important measure for intensifying socialist spiritual construction and a grave struggle against the inroads and infiltration of decadent capitalist ideology and the concept of peaceful evolution."[16]

'Six Evils' campaign was implemented is reminiscent of the mass movements launched by the late Chairman Mao Tsetung to 'purify the spirit' of the people." Willy Wo-lap Lam, "Beijing Roots Out 'Unorthodox Party Members'" (text). Hong Kong *South China Morning Post* in English (27 November 1989, p. 9). In *FBIS Daily Report—China*, 22 November 1989 (PrEx 7.10: FBIS-CHI-89-228), p. 45.

[14] "State Council Calls for Eliminating 'Six Evils'" (text). Beijing Domestic Service in Mandarin (13 November 1989, 1030 GMT). In *FBIS Daily Report—China*, 22 November 1989 (PrEx 7.10: FBIS-CHI-89-224).

[15] "Commentator's Article Condemns 'Six Vices'" (text). Beijing *Renmin ribao* in Chinese (15 November 1989), p. 1. In *FBIS Daily Report—China*, 30 November 1989 (PrEx 7.10: FBIS-CHI-89-229), p. 21.

[16] "Shanghai Prepares Campaign Against Six Vices" (text). Shanghai City Service in Mandarin (9 November 1989, 1000 GMT). In *FBIS Daily Report—China*, 7 December 1989 (PrEx 7.10: FBIS-CHI-89-234), pp. 41–42.

Prostitution was thus firmly classified as one vice among many, all but one (feudal superstition) attributable to foreign capitalist/ bourgeois/revolution-eroding influences. It is perhaps not coincidental that a *People's Daily* columnist ran a story during this period alleging that student leader Wuer Kaixi had visited prostitutes and then bragged about it.[17] In short, prostitution was yoked to a post–June 4 discourse of Maoist redemption from capitalist perdition via a mass campaign.

Almost simultaneously with the central government's announcement of the Six Vices campaign, provincial governments began to publicize their own operations. Jiangxi took up the campaign with particular enthusiasm. There the provincial Party committee and the provincial government declared a four-month campaign against the vices and urged offenders to surrender voluntarily to public security organs.[18] Hearkening back to venerable Maoist concepts, the province's deputy Party secretary emphasized the importance of the mass line and called for "arous[ing] the masses to wage total war against the six social evils."[19] Unlike the Jiangxi authorities, the Shanghai Public Security Bureau decided to disaggregate the vices, concentrating on prostitution and pornography before January 1 and moving on to gambling and superstition as the Lunar New Year festival approached.[20] Guangdong overfulfilled its quota by declaring a campaign against seven vices, rather than six.[21] Some provinces held press conferences to publicize the campaign; still others established special offices to supervise its progress.[22] Even the

---

[17] "*Renmin Ribao* Answers Reader's Criticism" (text). Beijing *Renmin ribao* in Chinese (31 December 1989), p. 3. In *FBIS Daily Report—China*, 8 January 1990 (PrEx 7.10: FBIS-CHI-90-005), p. 18.

[18] "Jiangxi Begins Operation Against Six 'Scourges'" (text). Beijing Xinhua Domestic Service in Chinese (13 November 1989, 1130 GMT). In *FBIS Daily Report—China*, 21 November 1989 (PrEx 7.10: FBIS-CHI-89-223), p. 45.

[19] "Jiangxi Meeting Discussing 'Social Evils'" (text). Nanchang Jiangxi Provincial Service in Mandarin (11 November 1989, 1100 GMT). In *FBIS Daily Report—China*, 29 November 1989 (PrEx 7.10: FBIS-CHI-89-228), pp. 35–36.

[20] "Shanghai's Prostitution, Drug Campaign Outlined" (text). Beijing Xinhua in English (15 November 1989, 0914 GMT). In *FBIS Daily Report—China*, 22 November 1989 (PrEx 7.10: FBIS-CHI-89-224), p. 58.

[21] The seventh vice was underworld activities. "Guangdong Sentences 31 Criminals to Death" (excerpt). Guangzhou Guangdong Provincial Service in Mandarin (11 January 1990, 1000 GMT). In *FBIS Daily Report—China*, 12 January 1989 (PrEx 7.10: FBIS-CHI-90-009), p. 38.

[22] "Hunan Advances Against 'Six Vices'" (text). Changsha Hunan Provincial Service in Mandarin (19 November 1989; 2300 GMT). In *FBIS Daily Report—China*, 30 November 1989 (PrEx 7.10: FBIS-CHI-89-229), p. 54; "Shaanxi Mobilizes Against

army was mobilized to take part; the deputy director of the Guangzhou Military Region announced an effort to prohibit prostitution at guesthouses and hostels for army units, a tacit admission that sex workers were active in army-run enterprises.[23] Within several weeks, most cities and provinces had declared success in arresting hundreds, even thousands, of criminals. Because the vices were discussed as a group, it was often unclear exactly how many of the arrests were related to prostitution.[24] In many areas, particularly inland, arrests for gambling and other offenses apparently far outnumbered those for prostitution.[25] Two months after it began, the campaign virtually disappeared from the

---

'Six Vices'" (text). Xian Shaanxi Provincial Service in Mandarin (19 November 1989, 0030 GMT). In *FBIS Daily Report—China*, 30 November 1989 (PrEx 7.10: FBIS-CHI-89-229), pp. 69–70.

[23] "Guangdong Military Official Condemns Prostitution" (text). Guangzhou Guangdong Provincial Service in Mandarin (18 November 1989, 0040 GMT). In *FBIS Daily Report—China*, 30 November 1989 (PrEx 7.10: FBIS-CHI-89-229), p. 46.

[24] See, among others, "Jiangxi County Cracks Down on 'Six Vices'" (text). Nanchang Jiangxi Provincial Service in Mandarin (20 November 1989, 1100 GMT). In *FBIS Daily Report—China*, 30 November 1989 (PrEx 7.10: FBIS-CHI-89-229), p. 43; "Fujian Launches Campaign Against 'Six Vices'" (text). Fujian Provincial Service in Mandarin (19 November 1989, 1100 GMT). In *FBIS Daily Report—China*, 1 December 1989 (PrEx 7.10: FBIS-CHI-89-230), p. 30; "Tianjin 'Victories' Against 'Six Vices' Reported" (text). Tianjin City Service in Mandarin (21 November 1989, 1000 GMT). In *FBIS Daily Report—China*, 1 December 1989 (PrEx 7.10: FBIS-CHI-89-230), p. 42; "Heilongjiang Clamps Down on 'Six Vices'" (text). Harbin Heilongjiang Provincial Service in Mandarin (22 November 1989, 2200 GMT). In *FBIS Daily Report—China*, 30 November 1989 (PrEx 7.10: FBIS-CHI-89-229), p. 62; "Beijing Mayor Calls for Crackdown on Six Vices" (text). Beijing Xinhua in English (23 November 1989, 0851 GMT). In *FBIS Daily Report—China*, 13 December 1989 (PrEx 7.10: FBIS-CHI-89-238), p. 61; "Nationwide Crackdown on Six Vices Yields Results" (text). Beijing Television Service in Mandarin (7 December 1989, 1100 GMT). In *FBIS Daily Report—China*, 15 December 1989 (PrEx 7.10: FBIS-CHI-89-240), p. 28; "Anhui Governor Calls for Eliminating Six Vices" (text). Anhui Provincial Service in Mandarin (11 December 1989, 1100 GMT). In *FBIS Daily Report—China*, 20 December 1989 (PrEx 7.10: FBIS-CHI-89-243), pp. 28–29; "Hainan Launches Operation Against Six Vices" (text). Haikou Hainan Provincial Service in Mandarin (15 December 1989, 2300 GMT). In *FBIS Daily Report—China*, 20 December 1989 (PrEx 7.10: FBIS-CHI-89-243), p. 33.

[25] In Ningxia, for instance, 1,300 gamblers were arrested, as were 148 prostitutes and their clients. Many of the prostitutes were said to be "castaways from the neighboring provinces of Shaanxi and Gansu." Among the inns that lost their licenses for permitting prostitution was the guesthouse of the Yinchuan Canning Factory. "Ningxia Cracks Down on Six Vices" (text). Yinchuan *Ningxia ribao* in Chinese (12 December 1989), p. 1. In *FBIS Daily Report—China*, 10 January 1990 (PrEx 7.10: FBIS-CHI-90-007), pp. 64–65.

Chinese press, to be replaced less than a year later by government pronouncements indicating that prostitution continued to grow along with other vices and serious crimes and that none of these problems was amenable to quick solutions.[26]

Reports on the Six Vices campaign vacillated between representing women as victims (of traffickers) and victimizers (of social order), but in general the campaign focused less on prostitutes per se than on prostitution as one among many symptoms of social decay. The categorization of prostitution as a vice in this campaign meant that authorities approached it as an evil habit that could be eliminated by a combination of education and coercion. The possibility that prostitution's financial rewards for women might be substantial enough to compete favorably with other occupations was nowhere discussed.

State Regulation: Prostitution as Crime

Government bureaus responded to the appearance of prostitution in the early 1980s with a patchwork of proclamations and local regulations. On June 10, 1981, the Ministry of Public Security issued a "Circular on Resolutely Stopping Prostitution"; it was followed by similar documents almost every year for the next decade.[27] Local authorities, particularly in coastal areas where prostitution was most visible, responded to the problem with their own bans, often grouping prostitution with gambling and other activities. In 1985, a member of the Shenzhen city committee stated to a reporter that opening casinos or brothels in Shenzhen did "not conform with the principle of our socialist system" and indicated that casinos and brothels would be banned.[28] In June

---

[26] See, for examples, "Guangdong Faces 'Grim' Law, Order Situation" (text). Hong Kong *Ta kung pao* in Chinese (7 September 1990), p. 2. In *FBIS Daily Report—China*, 18 September 1990 (PrEx 7.10: FBIS-CHI-90-181), p. 43; "Qiao Shi Promises Continuing Crackdown on Crime" (text). Beijing Xinhua in English (22 October 1990, 0835 GMT). In *FBIS Daily Report—China*, 23 October 1990 (PrEx 7.10: FBIS-CHI-90-205), p. 23.

[27] "Situation Concerning the Investigation and Banning of Prostitution and Prostitute Patronization," submitted to twentieth session of seventh National People's Congress standing committee, printed June 18, 1991, cited in "Document Studies Situation" (text). Hong Kong *Jiushi niandai* in Chinese (1 October 1991), no. 216, pp. 19–21. In *FBIS Daily Report—China*, 9 October 1991 (PrEx 7.10: FBIS-CHI-91-196), pp. 28–30.

[28] "Casinos, Brothels Prohibited in Shenzhen" (text). Hong Kong *Xinwan bao* in Chinese (27 June 1985), p. 1. In *FBIS Daily Report—China*, 11 July 1985 (PrEx 7.10:

1987, the Guangdong Provincial People's Congress promulgated a provincial regulation banning prostitution. While singling out for criminal punishment "those luring, allowing, and forcing women to engage in prostitution," it was much less strict with pimps and prostitutes. Pimps could be detained for fifteen days or sentenced to reform through labor (presumably for repeat offenders); they could also be fined five thousand yuan. Prostitutes were to be detained fifteen days, fined five thousand yuan or sentenced to reform through labor, and "ordered to write a statement of repentance." Examination and treatment for sexually transmitted diseases was compulsory, with detainees to pay their own medical costs.[29] In November 1988, Hainan province passed a virtually identical regulation. Significantly, one of the articles on the new rules noted that five thousand yuan was less than two month's salary for a masseuse.[30]

During 1990 and 1991, government authorities turned increasingly to the question of abductions of women and children. Although articles on the subject made it clear that most abducted women were sold as wives rather than prostitutes, in some highly publicized cases traffickers who had forced women into prostitution were executed;[31] in others, top authorities directly linked prostitution to crackdowns on abduction.[32] This particular formulation of prostitution, which characterized women primarily as victims of traffickers and pimps, eventually found expression in the 1992 Law Protecting Women's Rights and Interests. Chapter 6 of that law, "Rights of the Person," includes the following articles:

> Article 36. It is prohibited to abduct and sell or kidnap women. It is prohibited to buy abducted or kidnaped women....
> Article 37. Both working as a prostitute or [sic] visiting prostitutes are prohibited. It is prohibited to organize, coerce, lure, keep, or

FBIS-CHI-85–133), pp. W11–12.

29 "Guangdong Regulation Bans Prostitution" (text). Guangzhou *Nanfang ribao* in Chinese (20 June 1987), p. 1. Translation by the Joint Publications Research Service. In JPRS-CAR-87-038 (25 August 1987), pp. 93–94.

30 Fak Cheuk-wan, "Dealing with 'Vice Capital' Label" (text). Hong Kong *Hongkong Standard* in English (15 November 1988), p. 7. In *FBIS Daily Report—China*, 17 November 1988 (PrEx 7.10: FBIS-CHI-88-222), pp. 60–61.

31 See, for instance, "Beijing Court Orders Execution of Repeat Offender" (text). *Beijing ribao* (18 November 1990), p. 1. In *FBIS Daily Report—China*, 20 December 1990 (PrEx 7.10: FBIS-CHI-90-245), pp. 69–70.

32 "Qiao Shi, Others at Meeting on Sale of Women" (text). Beijing Television Service in Mandarin (18 December 1990, 1100 GMT). In *FBIS Daily Report—China*, 19 December 1990 (PrEx 7.10: FBIS-CHI-90-244), p. 13.

introduce women to work as prostitutes, or hire or keep women to engage in obscene activities with others.[33]

In one strand of national legal thinking, then, prostitution appears primarily as a violation of the rights of the woman-as-person; the ban on "working as a prostitute" sits awkwardly within this framework but is not elaborated here or elsewhere in the law.

By late 1990, however, a competing legal formulation of prostitution had emerged: that it was a crime, and that existing provisions for punishing prostitutes themselves, as well as traffickers and pimps, should be provided by criminal law rather than local regulations or administrative decrees. The most elaborated statement of this position was put forward by Chen Yehong in the *Huazhong shifan daxue xuebao.* Chen concurred with the dominant state formulation of prostitution as a recurrent "evil social phenomenon," "influenced by decadent ideas and lifestyles of the Western bourgeoisie," but went on to argue that it had to be dealt with through legislation rather than periodic campaigns. Although the current criminal code did specify prison terms for coercing or luring women into prostitution, Chen argued that it was not possible "to curtail prostitution by punishing related activities." The penalties meted out to prostitutes themselves were governed, not by the criminal code, but by public security regulations that

> stipulated that one convicted of prostitution may be detained for no more than 15 days, or given a warning, or ordered to sign a declaration of repentance, or be sentenced to rehabilitation through labor... and may be fined up to 5000 yuan. It is this writer's opinion that, for the prostitutes who willingly wallow in degeneration, a few days' confinement and criticism and education are of little consequence.... As for a fine of less than 5000 yuan, it is nothing. As a young prostitute by the name of Wang said, "I can make back tomorrow every penny they fine me today."[34]

Chen went on to argue that luring women into prostitution was an external factor, while "the prostitutes' own will" was the "basis that determines the nature of their conduct." To aim legal penalties exclusively at pimps and madams, Chen insisted, was "putting the cart before the horse."

---

[33] "Law Protecting Women's Rights, Interests." Beijing Xinhua Domestic Service in Chinese (7 April 1992, 0414 GMT). In *FBIS Daily Report—China,* 14 April 1992 (PrEx 7.10: FBIS-CHI-92-072-S), pp. 17–21. Quotations from p. 19.

[34] Chen Yehong, "On Prostitution and the Application of Criminal Law" (text). Wuhan *Huazhong shifan daxue xuebao,* 6 (1 December 1990), pp. 35–40. Translated in JPRS-CAR-91-005, pp. 65–70.

Prostitution, in Chen's argument, was not a victimless crime; nor was the prostitute herself the victim. The victims were "China's socialist social morals and the people's physical and mental health," or more abstractly "the normal order of social administration." Crimes against social administration were already punishable under chapter 6 of the criminal law. Prostitution, Chen suggested, should be officially added to that catalogue of crimes.

Chen argued for a precise definition of prostitution, involving five elements:

1. The prostitute had sexual intercourse, and did not merely abscond with a customer's money (which would be fraud).
2. The prostitute sold her own body and not someone else's (which would be procuring or keeping women for prostitution).
3. The prostitute sold her body of her own free will (otherwise the legal liability would lie with the person who coerced her).
4. The prostitute took an active role in soliciting customers.
5. The prostitute was in business for money or other goods, not for other reasons.

All of these conditions could be read as the description of a woman in business for herself, performing certain acts of her own free will, actively planning her next business move, and trying to maximize her income (not unlike the petty capitalist women discussed in chapter 5 by Hill Gates). Yet although this formulation comes closer than others to portraying prostitution as work, Chen departs dramatically from a labor framework when he characterizes the prostitutes' motivation as criminal:

> The prostitutes know that their conduct will disrupt the order of social administration and corrupt society's morals, but because they love leisure and hate work and are greedy for material goods, and in order to obtain money, they enter into prostitution deliberately. . . . [T]he motive behind the crime of prostitution is sheer laziness, greed, and pursuit of an extravagant and degenerate lifestyle.

This characterization of prostitute desires echoes the state-sponsored denunciations of petty capitalists during the Cultural Revolution. (See the chapters by Hill Gates and Andrew Walder herein.) Here, commercial gain of any type is seen as immoral; "work," as a category, disappears from the formulation.

In September 1991, the National People's Congress enacted a ban on prostitution and visiting prostitutes that responded to many of Chen's criticisms of existing law. The new law increased the penalties for organizing, assisting, or coercing others into acts of prostitution. It brought both prostitution and hiring prostitutes ("whoring") under the regulations governing offenses against public order (with the penalties Chen had decried as inadequate— fifteen days, five thousand yuan, repentance, etc.), but added that the people convicted could be sentenced to "centralized mandatory corrective legal and moral education as well as productive labor...for a period between six months and two years." Repeat offenders were to be sent for labor education and fined. Medical examinations for sexually transmitted diseases, and treatment for them, were made compulsory. Prostitutes or customers who knew they were infected with sexually transmitted diseases but had commercial sexual contact anyway could be imprisoned for up to five years and fined up to five thousand yuan. The new law also stipulated stiff fines for hotel and entertainment facilities that permitted prostitution on their premises.[35]

The promulgation of this law served notice that prostitutes were to be held responsible for their own acts, not automatically regarded as minor offenders or victims of others. Prostitution began slowly to move into the category of "crime." The law did little, however, to change the way state authorities dealt with prostitutes: announcement of periodic crackdowns and campaigns (Guangdong and Shandong were particularly active in 1992), followed by announcement of numbers arrested, followed by sober official assessments that the struggle to eliminate prostitution would be a long one.

Social Commentary: Analyzing Prostitution's Causes

Just as prostitutes have appeared during the reform period, so have a host of professionals who study them: sociologists, legal scholars, researchers for the Women's Federation, journalists, and creators of reportage literature. Although China's press and journals remain subject to state censorship, the severity of control has abated enough to make audible a variety of voices on prostitution. They are not unified, but as a group they depart in several respects from the analytical framework enunciated by state authorities. They tend to attribute more agency to individual prostitutes,

---

[35] "Decision on Prostitution" (text). Beijing Xinhua Domestic Service in Chinese (4 September 1991, GMT 2020). In *FBIS Daily Report—China*, 5 September 1991 (PrEx 7.10: FBIS-CHI-91-172), pp. 28–30.

to concern themselves more with the question of motivation, and to take seriously the economic lure of prostitution for many women. Like state authorities, however, they do not classify prostitution primarily as a labor market question.

Most of these commentators base their studies to some degree on investigations they have conducted among prostitutes, usually ones who have been detained by state authorities for education and treatment. Contemporary prostitutes seldom speak directly in the written record (if we except the scattered quotations gathered by Western reporters like the ones cited above, who occasionally spend an evening in a bar or dance hall interviewing prostitutes). Therefore, the work of these commentators provides the most extensive account we have of how prostitutes view their own situations. What we hear of prostitutes' voices here is hardly transparent speech, collected as it is from incarcerated women by investigators whom they have little reason to trust. It is, however, what we have to work with, and perhaps it can suggest something of the formulations through which prostitutes make meaning of their lives.[36]

In a 1990 article entitled "Deep in the Heart of a Prostitute," sociologist Ning Dong analyzed the attitudes of prostitutes in reformatories in the cities of Chengdu and Deyang.[37] Ning first described the enormous variety of ages, educational levels, physical attractiveness, and fees charged among the 139 women she studied. Without directly noting that this was a highly differentiated and segmented labor market, Ning stressed that virtually any woman could become a prostitute, provided that she wanted to do so. Ning thus attributed a degree of choice to the women. The question that interested Ning was why women became prostitutes. Noting that many of them were about seventeen years old, Ning attributed their choices partly to inexperience, which made it possible for them to "drift easily onto the wrong paths." Ning also noted that all but one had had previous sexual encounters with men, adding that "[s]ince sexual relations are so casual, it is not at all that difficult to wander onto the road of prostitution."[38]

---

[36] For a discussion of the problem of "hearing" the "voices" of prostitutes, see Gail Hershatter, "The Subaltern Talks Back: Reflections on Subaltern Theory and Chinese History," *Positions: East Asia Cultures Critique* 1, no. 1 (Spring 1993), pp. 103–130.

[37] Ning Dong, "Deep in the Heart of a Prostitute," *Shehui* 5 (20 May 1990), pp. 12–14. Excerpts translated in JPRS-CAR-90-055 (26 July 1990), pp. 88–90.

[38] Ibid., p. 89.

Another motivation, in Ning's view, was that "they have bad habits of being fond of eating and averse to work and being afraid of difficulties and fatigue." "[E]ven if they have a job," Ning continued, "they do not go to work. In the daytime they sit in the tea houses or go to restaurants; in the evenings they go to the dance halls, living a life of wanton extravagance." If Ning's formulation posited laziness and love of luxury, however, her examples also showed that women made shrewd economic assessments of their moneymaking possibilities. One woman rejected work in a brick factory (too hard) and as a babysitter in favor of earning twenty to thirty yuan per trick. A second abandoned a physically easy (but probably modest-paying) job as a telegrapher for the much more remunerative work of sleeping with men for fifty yuan per encounter. She described this as "easy money, much better than regular work." Ning hypothesized that in their careers as prostitutes, women had seen men at their worst: "As far as they are concerned, the entire world is nothing but a den of lechers, and the men lie in wait for them all the time and everywhere, and try every possible way—by lies, by force, or buying with money, or any sly trick—and exert every effort to possess them."[39] Under these circumstances, the women figured, why not make money themselves?

In contrast to the state's frequent characterization of women as victims (and therefore presumably amenable to rescue and rehabilitation), Ning stressed that they were deeply set in their ways. Here Ning's explanations were psychological rather than economic. She commented that these prostitutes were distinguished by their lack of shame, as illustrated by the following scene she witnessed in a detention center: "The women had just sat down to study when one woman stood up and started walking out. When an instructor asked her what she was doing, she said shamelessly, in a loud voice, 'my ... itches.' And all the prostitutes in the room broke out in loud laughter." Ning concluded that whatever "positive results" the women gained from labor and classes in the detention centers was being undone by their informal bull sessions, where they "talked about the shamelessness of their customers, talked about the hypocrisy of men, exchanged their feelings about prostitution, and summed up the lessons they learned from being caught." In her view, women were so deeply marked by prostitution that it was unlikely they would leave it.[40]

---

[39] Ibid., pp. 89, 90.
[40] Ibid., p. 89; ellipsis in original.

Unspoken in her analysis, but evident in her examples, was the economic calculation made by women who became prostitutes.

A subsequent article by Zhang Yiquan in the same sociological journal obliquely disputed two of the standard state formulations on prostitution: that it was "back" and that its resurgence could be traced to Western influence. Zhang saw one major difference between pre-1949 prostitution and the reform era situation: whereas earlier prostitutes had been "forced into the profession," "[t]oday, most prostitutes take up the profession voluntarily."[41] Zhang initially attributed the change to two factors: changing sexual attitudes, which lessened the value of female chastity, and the desire of prostitutes to make money. Zhang's complete analysis, however, was more complex, even contradictory. On the one hand, Chinese society was experiencing a "removal of sexual prohibitions," and this change allowed "people's primitive sexual desire" to emerge. Paradoxically, these "primitive" sexual desires were shaped by such modern factors as "'newfangled' theories, movies, televisions, magazines, and other media that teach them about sex," as well as "modern technology that helped improve birth control drugs and methods." The result was the appearance of "ravenous carnal desire" in which "[w]omen who have overcome the psychological shadow cast by the social consequences can go after sexual pleasures without fear or worry." On the other hand, women were still affected by a traditional double standard in morality, in which men had sexual privilege and could seek out prostitutes, but "one careless step [could] land a woman on the road of no return, and one wrong move [could] ruin her whole life." Both men and women were also affected by what Zhang called continuing flaws in the Chinese marriage system, where an estimated 60 percent of all marriages were based on economic considerations rather than love. Zhang argued that sexual satisfaction was impossible in loveless marriages and that sexually frustrated men would seek out prostitutes.[42] In short, the psychological

---

[41] Zhang Yiquan, "The Social Background of Prostitution," *Shehui* 68 (20 October 1990), pp. 38–40, translated in JPRS-CAR-91-005 (31 January 1991), pp. 62–65; quotation on p. 62. For a far more vehement statement of the distinction between pre- and post-1949 prostitutes, see Chen Yehong, "On Prostitution," p. 68. My own research indicates that pre-1949 prostitutes were by no means all coerced into the work. See Gail Hershatter, "Sex Work and Social Order: Prostitutes, Their Families, and the State in Twentieth-Century Shanghai," in *Family Process and Political Process in Modern Chinese History*, Zhongyang yanjiuyuan jindai shi yanjiusuo, ed. (Taipei: Academia Sinica, 1992), 2:1083–1124.

[42] Zhang Yiquan, "Social Background," pp. 62, 63, 64.

factors predisposing men and women to exchange money for sex were not all attributable to foreign influence.

Zhang also devoted considerable attention to economic motivations for prostitution. Increased mobility had provided both the demand and the "cultural environment" for prostitution. Although overall living standards had improved during the reform period, Zhang noted, some regions were getting rich more quickly than others. Women were not forced into prostitution by absolute poverty, as they had been before 1949. Rather, they were attracted to prostitution as a way out of *relative* poverty. Here Zhang stopped just short of a labor market formulation of prostitution:

> People resort to different means to escape this kind of relative poverty. Some work hard physically and some rely on science and technology. But some women who love ease and hate work and are anxious to get rich may, under certain conditions, turn to prostitution to achieve their goal.[43]

For Zhang, prostitution was neither vice nor crime; it was a strategy women adopted to achieve certain economic and psychological ends. Nevertheless, women who chose this work appeared to Zhang to have a character flaw; rather than relying on physical or mental labor, they chose to sell their bodies. In this formulation, work and the sale of sexual services were mutually exclusive.

Prostitution and the Market for Female Labor

In all of this public discussion about prostitution, virtually no one characterizes it as work or as a phenomenon shaped in part by labor market conditions, even though much of the evidence presented in the course of the discussion could lend itself to that type of analysis. When Hainan's capital Haikou was emerging as a "vice capital," for instance, one Hong Kong reporter noted that the massive influx of people to the newly created Special Economic Zone had created a serious unemployment problem. The population of Haikou had gone from 310,000 to 400,000 after the zone was established, with thirty to forty thousand people traveling between Hainan and the mainland each day. Most worked as vendors, earning about 150 yuan per month, but dancing girls (who, the article strongly implied, sold sexual services)

---

[43] Ibid., pp. 63, 64, 65; quotation on p. 63.

could earn a monthly salary of 4,000 yuan—twenty times what they could earn on the mainland. The article did not indicate whether this "salary" included income from sexual encounters with clients. Clearly, sex work was more lucrative than any other option available to women and paid better than many types of work open to men as well.[44]

Yet when the Party secretary of Hainan province, Xu Shijie, took up the same topic four months later, he classified prostitution with gambling as one of the "ugly social phenomena" brought about by the large influx of people, lack of police controls, and "decadent lifestyles [which] have made inroads into the province." He mentioned unemployment as a general problem predisposing people toward crime, but not as a factor inducing women in particular to work as prostitutes. Still less did he acknowledge that prostitution was a particularly lucrative line of work for women. His proposed solution matched the problem as he had defined it: "Crack down on serious criminal activities, and exercise firmness in getting rid of various ugly phenomena.... Check the blind inflow of population and tighten control over outside people coming into the province."[45] Similarly, a growing literature has noted the rise in transient population in China's major cities (1.8 million in Shanghai, or more than a quarter of the city's population; 17.6 percent of the Beijing population; 20 percent of the Hangzhou population).[46] Women make up roughly a third of all transients, and transients as a group tend to be young.[47] Many prostitutes are part of this transient population: lower-class prostitutes tend to be immigrants from the countryside; high-class prostitutes frequently work in a city other than their home town. Lower-echelon Guangzhou sex workers, for instance, come from Guangxi, Hunan, and Jiangxi, but high-priced prostitutes are from Shanghai and other Jiangnan cities.[48] (In high-class Shanghai hotels, however, the

---

[44] Fak Cheuk-wan, "Unemployment Problem Increasing" (text). Hong Kong *Hongkong Standard* in English (16 November 1988), p. 6. In *FBIS Daily Report—China*, 17 November 1988 (PrEx 7.10: FBIS-CHI-88-222), pp. 62–63.

[45] "Hainan Secretary on Social Order 'Pressure'" (text). Beijing *Zhongguo xinwen she* in Chinese (27 March 1989, 0845 GMT). In *FBIS Daily Report—China*, 29 March 1989 (PrEx 7.10: FBIS-CHI-89-059), pp. 57–58.

[46] "Analysis of Criminal Activities in Urban Areas" (text). Shanghai *Shehui* in Chinese, 5 (20 May 1988), pp. 12–16. Translated in JPRS-CAR-88-047 (19 August 1988), pp. 44–48. Statistics from p. 44.

[47] See the Chinese studies cited by Dorothy Solinger, *China's Transients and the State: A Form of Civil Society?* (Hong Kong: Hong Kong Institute of Asia-Pacific Studies, 1991), p. 11, nn. 60–63.

[48] "Guangdong Launches Campaign Against Prostitution" (text). Hong Kong *Ta*

prostitutes are Shanghai natives. For more on how native place structures labor markets in Shanghai and elsewhere, see Emily Honig's chapter herein.) Transients move about China principally to find better-paying work, and they often send remittances home. Yet Chinese writings on transients make virtually no mention of prostitution or its relative desirability as a work option for female transients.[49]

Why do China's state authorities and social scientists by and large find a labor market framework uncongenial? Good historical method cautions against hypothesizing about something that does not happen, but perhaps some observations are in order about something that does.

Regulatory discourse in the 1990s centers on the task, in a rapidly changing reform economy, of returning women to stable work and family situations. As work opportunities for women in fact become less stable, the state calls increasingly for stability, particularly through the reconfiguration of new, happy, "modern" families. (For a discussion of the centrality of family in the Korean context, see Hagen Koo's chapter herein.) In this way, the state argues, China can both modernize and resist the disruptions engendered by "bourgeois liberalization." In each of these cases modernity is seen as simultaneously displacing women (who are both victimized and set loose) and requiring that they be resituated (both protected and contained) with the help of strong state authority. At stake is the very control of what modernity looks like and means, as well as what "women" are and should be. In this formulation, prostitution appears as an interruption of stable work and family, rather than as a form of work that may, in fact, be helping to support many Chinese families.

Party and government leaders, as we have seen, are committed to an analytical framework organized around prostitution as vice and crime that flourishes whenever foreign influence is permitted. In the 1950s, their forebears devised an approach that identified prostitution with foreign vice and weak domestic government control, then removed the foreigners, strengthened the government, and eliminated prostitution.[50] In the 1980s and 1990s, Party and

---

kung pao in Chinese (17 June 1992), p. 4. In FBIS Daily Report—China, 19 June 1992 (PrEx 7.10: FBIS-CHI-92–119).

[49] See the sources cited by Solinger, China's Transients, and Dorothy Solinger, "The Floating Population in the Cities: Chances for Assimilation?" (paper presented at the Conference on Urban China, Woodrow Wilson Center, 1–4 May 1992).

[50] On this process, see Gail Hershatter, "Regulating Sex in Shanghai: The Reform of Prostitution in 1920 and 1951," in Shanghai Sojourners, ed. Frederic Wakeman, Jr.,

government policy welcomes foreigners and advocates reduced government control over many areas of Chinese life. The only element of their original approach that remains is the categorization of prostitution itself as vice—an approach that commits them to endless rounds of cleanup campaigns followed by periods of benign neglect and local payoffs. Within this framework, prostitutes are either duped, depraved, or greedy—alternately victims and perpetrators of vice. As long as even a piece of the earlier "vice" framework remains in place, however, it will not be possible to see them as workers or to formulate policies that might make other types of labor for women more available and lucrative.

For China's new social scientists, who have done so much to enliven investigation of Chinese social life during the reform period, the issue is more complex. Unlike state authorities, they are not wedded to a disintegrating analytical framework (although they do have a love affair of sorts with Western social science theory, which may or may not continue to serve their purposes). For many of them, "crime" appears to be a particularly attractive topic of investigation, partly because the opportunities for new and better criminal activities make crime an expanding field, partly because open discussion of social problems has for so long been restricted that their research is truly pioneering work. Labor, on the other hand, is an old and shopworn topic, exhaustively (even numbingly) discussed throughout the prereform period.

Likewise, social scientists who have turned their attention to gender, often with an eye to combating growing gender inequalities, have an ambivalent attitude toward research on women's labor. On the one hand, they are extremely concerned about women's increasing exclusion from better-paying and high-prestige jobs, and many of them regard with dismay the decision of some women to leave paid employment and return home (the controversy around Tianjin's Daqiu Village is the most hotly debated example of this trend). This concern has generated a substantial literature on the question of women's employment.[51] On the other hand, many of these scholars are in active retreat from a Maoist analytical framework that took employment as the sole

---

and Wen-hsin Yeh, China Research Monograph, no. 40 (Berkeley: Institute of East Asian Studies, University of California, 1992), pp. 145–185.

[51] See, for example, Liu Bohong, "Guanyu nüxing jiuye wenti zongshu" [A summary of the women's employment question], in *Zhongguo funü lilun yanjiu shinian* [Ten years of research on Chinese women's theory], ed. Xiong Yumei, Liu Xiaocong, and Qu Wen (Beijing: Zhongguo funü chubanshe, 1992), pp. 310–357.

criterion of women's liberation. As sociologist Chen Yiyun put it
in a 1989 forum on theories about women,

> During the early years of liberation, because of an inadequate edu-
> cational foundation, emphasis was placed on employment of
> women. This not only surpassed the level of development of the
> productive forces, but also surpassed the awareness and capability
> of women themselves.[52]

Li Qiang of People's University, who made the most vehement
statement on the insufficiency of an approach that stressed jobs for
women, ended by advocating the Daqiu approach:

> In China, where the level of civilization has not reached a certain
> level, women are often considered liberated when a large number of
> women are employed and they play the role of men. Actually, this
> is another form of wrecking women. There are not many women
> who are doing intellectual work at a high level. Most women are
> still engaged in hard manual labor. This is precisely the reason
> why Chinese women look much older than their counterparts in
> developed countries. Therefore, we propose that ordinary women
> working in various trades have the right to go home to take care of
> their children when they are needed to raise them.[53]

Many of the theorists at this forum went on to argue that the key
to women's liberation was education, not employment.[54] Li Ming
of the Ministry of Civil Affairs put it most succinctly: "If the 'May
4th' period was mainly for the liberation of 'feet' and the early
years of the People's Republic of China were mainly for the liberation of 'hands,' then the women's liberation today is aimed at the
liberation of 'brains.'"[55]

This dissatisfaction with a framework that analyzes women's
status exclusively through the matrix of employment has helped
produce numerous new formulations for looking at gender inequality: ones that focus on female psychology, marriage, sexuality, and crime as well as on education. At the same time, however, the new intellectual stances on "the woman question" make

---

[52] "Reform and Opening Up to the Outside World and a New Train of Thought
on the Women's Liberation Movement—Notes on the Symposium on Theories
Concerning Women" (text). Beijing *Qiushi* in Chinese, 5 (1 March 1989), pp. 42–45.
Translated in JPRS-CAR-89-049 (19 May 1989), 36–40; quotation from pp. 39–40.

[53] Ibid., p. 38.

[54] Among those expressing this argument were Chen Yiyun, Dai Qing, and Jin
Nan. Ibid., pp. 38–40.

[55] Ibid., p. 37.

it highly unlikely that prostitution will be assimilated to a formulation that classifies it as labor.

Nevertheless, while these scholars do not regard prostitution itself as labor, being much more likely to see it as a sign of women's unequal status and resultant victimization, some of them believe that only new labor training policies will help curb the spread of prostitution. Chen Yiyun, for instance, notes that prostitutes in detention spend time in useless make-work projects rather than being taught a skill that would allow them to make a decent living upon release without returning to prostitution.[56] (Training programs, of course, are expensive, and it is unlikely that local governments will willingly do anything to increase the cost of running detention centers.) The nascent social work profession may yet come to see prostitution, if not as a form of work, then at least as an income-generating activity that looks more attractive than other available options.

It bears restating here that this essay does not make the argument that prostitution is "really" labor and that all Chinese commentators are operating under the cloud of false consciousness. I find it more fruitful, and certainly less imperialistic, to look at the formulations people choose as well as the ones they foreclose and ask why these choices are being made. Furthermore, if I were to design my own personal favorite formulation of prostitution, it would pay as much attention to questions of sexuality (male and female), disease, marriage markets, abduction, and Chinese constructions of "modernity" as it would to labor. Nevertheless, the women in the disco on the thirtieth floor of Shanghai's Hongqiao Hotel, as they coolly approach customers and later negotiate prices, exhibit the kind of concentration and seriousness that I, for one, associate with work. And if sexologist Pan Suiming is correct, prostitutes report that their occupation involves much of the drudgery, even alienation, often associated with work. Pan comments,

> Individual interviews with prostitutes ... found that the majority of them describe their experience as "tiresome," "indifferent," "no alternative," "have to tolerate".... There is [a] popular joke today: "The prostitute says to her customer, move your head, I am watching TV."[57]

---

[56] Chen Yiyun, personal conversation, Beijing, 6 July 1993.

[57] Pan Suiming, "Decipher the Myth of Prostitution" (text). Shanghai *Shehui* in

More than any other Chinese scholar, Pan comes closest to a labor market analysis of prostitution, again through a joke:

> A family of three were talking about prostitution. The husband said, "One act of a prostitute in xx city is worth three years of my salary!" The wife immediately responded, "Then, never visit a prostitute." The daughter unexpectedly said, "I should do this work."[58]

Chinese, 87 (20 April 1992), pp. 25–26. Translated in JPRS-CAR-92-044 (24 June 1992), pp. 55–56; quotation from p. 55.

[58] Ibid., p. 55.

EIGHT

Regional Identity, Labor, and Ethnicity in Contemporary China

EMILY HONIG

Compared to the prominence of ethnic identities, divisions, and antagonisms as issues in U.S. labor history, ethnicity is almost completely absent in studies of labor in China. This absence may be partly due to the seeming racial homogeneity of the population (some 90 percent of which is Han) and the concomitant notion that ethnic identities are rooted in racial or national distinctions. Thus, only groups officially designated as "national minorities" in China—such as Koreans, Uighurs, Kazaks, and Miao—and their relations with the dominant Han people are considered arenas for the exploration of ethnicity. And few studies of such "minorities" have attended to the intersection of their ethnic identity and work experience.

Yet as anthropologists have begun to insist on the socially constructed dimensions of ethnicity, we can begin to identify and analyze potential ethnic divisions among people who share racial and national identities. Recent anthropological scholarship argues that cultural differences invoked as ethnic markers are not limited to physical or primordial characteristics. Ethnicity does not involve inherent traits brought by people from one place to another, but instead involves a process of creating and articulating boundaries between groups of people in specific local and historical contexts.[1] Such an analysis has recently been explored in the

---

[1] See, for example, Karen Blu, *The Lumbee Problem: The Making of an American Indian People* (New York: Cambridge University Press, 1980); James Clifford, *The Predicament of Culture: Twentieth-Century Ethnography, Literature, and Art* (Cambridge: Harvard University Press, 1988); John Comaroff, "Of Totemism and Ethnicity: Consciousness, Practice and the Signs of Inequality," *Ethnos* 52, 3/4 (1987): 301–23; Brackette F. Williams, "A Class Act: Anthropology and the Race to Nation across Ethnic Terrain," *Annual Review of Anthropology* 18 (1989): 401–44; and Sylvia Junko

context of U.S. history, as scholars have analyzed the regionally defined ethnic identities of people such as the "Oakies" in California and the Appalachian "hillbillies" who migrated to northern cities.[2] It can also be applied to China, allowing an examination of ethnic identities and divisions among the Han Chinese population and an analysis of the implications of those identities and divisions for working-class history.

Although scholars of Chinese history and society have long recognized the centrality of native-place identity to Chinese conceptions of self and community, few have linked it to an analysis of ethnicity. G. William Skinner, in his analysis of urban systems in Qing China, proposed that patterns of economic specialization by native place be understood as an "ethnic division of labor" and that enclaves of regional traders in Chinese cities, such as Ningbo merchants in Beijing or Canton, Shanxi merchants in Fuzhou, or Anhui merchants in Chongqing, represented "ethnic minorities." This analysis has been applied in several case studies, although in somewhat limited ways. Both David Ownby and Stevan Harrell, for example, describe divisions between migrants to Taiwan from different localities in southeast China in the late Qing as ethnic. Hill Gates analyzes the process through which relationships between mainlanders and native Taiwanese became ethnic in the decades following World War II. Finally, C. Fred Blake, analyzing the social structure of a market town in the New Territories outside Hong Kong, describes ethnic identities defined largely by native place.[3]

In *Creating Chinese Ethnicity: Subei People in Shanghai, 1850–1980* I attempted a more detailed analysis of the potentially ethnic

Yanagisako, *Transforming the Past: Tradition and Kinship among Japanese Americans* (Stanford, Calif.: Stanford University Press, 1985).

[2] James Gregory, *American Exodus: The Dust Bowl Migration and Okie Culture in California* (New York: Oxford University Press, 1989).

[3] G. William Skinner, "Introduction: Urban Social Structure in Ch'ing China," in *The City in Late Imperial China*, ed. G. William Skinner (Stanford, Calif.: Stanford University Press, 1977), p. 544. David Ownby, "The Ethnic Feud in Qing Taiwan: What Is This Violence Business Anyway? An Interpretation of the 1782 Zhang-Quan *Xiedou*," *Late Imperial China* 11, 1 (June 1990): 75–98. Stevan Harrell, "From *Xiedou* to *Yijin*: The Decline of Ethnicity in Northern Taiwan, 1885–1995," *Late Imperial China* 11, 1 (June 1990): 99–127. Hill Gates, "Ethnicity and Social Class," in *The Anthropology of Taiwanese Society*, ed. Emily Martin Ahern and Hill Gates (Stanford, Calif.: Stanford University Press, 1981), pp. 241–81. C. Fred Blake, *Ethnic Groups and Social Change in a Chinese Market Town* (Honolulu: University Press of Hawai'i, 1981).

dimensions and implications of native-place identity in China, focusing on immigrants from northern Jiangsu (the so-called Subei or Jiangbei people) in Shanghai from the mid-nineteenth century through 1980.[4] In that case, it seemed appropriate to describe native-place identity as ethnic for several reasons. First, native place was the basis on which social and economic hierarchies in Shanghai were structured, so that Subei people dominated the ranks of unskilled laborers—rickshaw pullers, dockworkers, construction workers, night soil haulers and garbage collectors, barbers, and bathhouse attendants. The Shanghai elite, composed mostly of people from Jiangnan, despised Subei people for their poverty, and from the early twentieth century, calling someone a "Subei swine" meant that the person, even if not actually from Subei, was poor, ignorant, dirty, and unsophisticated. In other words, the place Subei became a metaphor for class. Subei origins became the basis on which labor markets were structured, individuals hired or fired.

A second reason for considering Subei identity as ethnic is that it represented not the embodiment of some objective, inherent traits, but rather the construction of a social category that enabled one group of people to declare its superiority over another in a specific historical context. For Subei was not a "real" place with clearly defined boundaries. Nor did Subei people have a sense of peoplehood, shared heritage, common language, or even shared geographic origins before migrating to Jiangnan and Shanghai. Areas of northern Jiangsu were labeled "Subei" only after migrants from that region flocked to the wealthier southern cities such as Shanghai, where the name "Subei folk" was invoked to distinguish them from Jiangnan natives, with whom they shared a racial (Han) and provincial (Jiangsu) identity. Jiangnan, whatever its internal differences, became the embodiment of wealth and urbane sophistication, while Subei, whatever its variety, became the embodiment of poverty and rural backwardness. In a process not altogether different from that of "Latinos" (immigrants from a vast variety of Latin American countries and cultures) in the United States, the experience of all northern Jiangsu immigrants in Shanghai was homogenized into a single "Subei" identity: the various local dialects were conflated into one "Subei dialect," and the different local operas categorized as "Subei opera." In other words, the idea of a homogeneous Subei identity or that Subei

---

[4] (New Haven: Yale University Press, 1992).

people constituted a coherent category emerged from Shanghai's development as an immigrant city. Neither the place-name "Subei" nor the social category "Subei people" had previously existed.

This is the sense in which Subei was a historical and social construction. Only by understanding Subei people as constituting an ethnic group, analogous to African Americans or Chicanos in the United States, do these structures of inequality and processes of social construction bound to native place emerge.

Creating Chinese Ethnicity raises, but does not really address, the applicability of this argument beyond the case of northern Jiangsu migrants to Shanghai. Chinese urban history is replete with instances of labor markets divided by native-place cliques: William Rowe observes the importance of hometown bonds for securing jobs in nineteenth-century Hankou. In a study of modern Beijing, David Strand describes factions among workers based on native place. Likewise, Gail Hershatter identifies links between local origins and employment in Republican-period Tianjin. And in her study of Chongqing during World War II, Lee McIsaac finds a working class sharply divided along native-place lines, with immigrants from eastern China performing skilled jobs, while Chongqing natives dominated the unskilled sector.[5] Are all of these to be considered ethnic? Under what circumstances does labor migration create native-place identities that assume ethnic meanings?

These questions gain particular significance in the context of contemporary China, where, since the late 1970s, for the first time since the revolution of 1949, vast numbers of peasants have been leaving their rural homes to seek work in cities. By looking at contemporary labor migration, this essay will explore the relationship among native-place identity, structures of social and economic hierarchy, and ethnic solidarities and divisions in China.[6] If one accepts the proposition that ethnicity among

---

[5] William Rowe, *Hankow: Commerce and Society in a Chinese City, 1796–1889* (Stanford, Calif.: Stanford University Press, 1984). David Strand, *Rickshaw Beijing: City People and Politics in the 1920s* (Berkeley: University of California Press, 1989). Gail Hershatter, *The Workers of Tianjin* (Stanford, Calif.: Stanford University Press, 1987). Lee McIsaac, "Urban Life in Wartime China: Workers in Chongqing, 1928–1945" (dissertation in progress, Yale University); for a discussion of similar divisions among workers in wartime Kunming, see Kuo-Heng Shih, *China Enters the Machine Age: A Study of Labor in Chinese War Industry* (Cambridge: Harvard University Press, 1944), pp. 4, 8–11, 99.

[6] The following is not meant to be a complete analysis of migrant workers in

China's Han population is tied to local origins and native-place identity, it then becomes crucial to consider when or how native place assumes ethnic meanings. The point is not simply to determine the applicability of the term "ethnic," the meaning of which is highly contested in the anthropological literature. At stake is the construction of social categories, identities, solidarities, and divisions that structure the workforce in a particular locality.

Contemporary Migration and Urban Labor Markets

In the decade following the assumption of power by the Chinese Communist Party in 1949, the government undertook extensive efforts to curb the flow of rural migrants to urban areas. The household registration system, promulgated in 1958, made it nearly impossible for peasants to move their residence to cities. The post-Mao economic reforms, however, particularly the dissolution of the commune system, made the surplus of rural labor so extreme that the government began to sanction the temporary movement of peasants to cities.[7] A 1991 report estimated that some eighty million rural laborers could not be absorbed by employment in agriculture and rural industry and therefore had no choice but to seek work in urban areas.[8]

Thus, in the 1980s and 1990s, for the first time since 1949, massive numbers of peasants have left their rural homes to work in cities.[9] By 1988, migrants represented nearly one-fourth of the population of China's cities with populations over 1,000,000. This was an enormous increase over previous decades. In Chengdu during the 1950s, for example, only about 40,000–50,000 migrants lived and worked in the city; in the 1960s, the number of migrants had increased to 80,000–120,000, and in the 1970s was up to

contemporary China, but rather a discussion of preliminary data in terms of ethnicity. It draws heavily on research that has been conducted by Dorothy Solinger.

[7] For a more detailed account of CCP policies on migration, see Dorothy J. Solinger, *China's Transients and the State: A Form of Civil Society?* (Hong Kong: Hong Kong Institute of Asia-Pacific Studies, 1991), pp. 7–9.

[8] Ge Xiangjian and Zhu Weiying, "Xiyou chanbande mingongchao" (The joys and sorrows of the tide of laborers), in *Baozhaxing xinwen* (Explosive news), ed. Zhang Chijian, Xie Jinhu, and Jiang Yaopo (Gaige chubanshe, 1991), p. 96.

[9] For an overview of migration patterns in post-1949 China, see Sidney Goldstein and Alice Goldstein, *Population Mobility in the People's Republic of China*, Papers of the East-West Population Institute, no. 95 (Honolulu: East-West Population Institute, East-West Center, 1985).

200,000. By 1984, the number had jumped to 270,000; in 1987 it was up to 530,000.[10] Normally, only about 200,000 outsiders would go to Shanghai each year; the number rapidly escalated during the 1980s, reaching about 2,000,000 in 1988.[11] And in Guangzhou, the number of migrants increased from 235,000 in 1979 to 1,700,000 in 1988.[12]

More than vast numbers distinguished this recent wave of migration from those of previous post-1949 decades. The reasons for movement from rural to urban areas were also different from those of the past, when most migrants went to cities to visit relatives, seek medical assistance, or go to school. By the late 1980s, in contrast, the majority were going to cities in search of work.[13] Urban labor markets are therefore structured by the influx of migrant labor in a way that may represent continuities with China's pre-Liberation past but that is unprecedented in post-1949 Chinese history. The prominence of issues related to this massive population movement is reflected in Chinese social science literature, which regularly reports the results of surveys concerning migrants, or "floaters" (*mangliu*) as they are commonly called.

Even a cursory glance at these data suggests several aspects of the role of migrant labor in urban centers that may be (but is not necessarily) related to the formation of native-place-based ethnic identities. The first concerns the status of migrant workers in the labor market and the ways in which urban labor markets have become divided along "native"/"immigrant" lines, with "natives" dominating the skilled sector and "immigrants" the unskilled sector. According to a survey of migrants in China's seven largest cities published in 1991, 30.31 percent worked at construction jobs, 22.12 percent made a living as market peddlers, 6.08 percent did repair work, and 18.54 percent had household service jobs (mostly as *baomu*, or maids). The survey also notes the concentration of migrant labor in textiles, chemical industries (where workers are

<hr/>

[10] Li Mengbai and Hu Xin, *Liudong renkou dui dachengshi fazhan de yingxiang ji duice* (The influence of the floating population on the development of large cities and measures to deal with it) (Beijing: Jingji ribao chubanshe, 1991), p. 217.

[11] Chai Junyong, "Liudong renkou: Chengshi guanli de i da kunrao" (The floating population: a major challenge for city management), *Shehui* 10 (1990): 8.

[12] Li Mengbai and Hu Xin, *Liudong renkou*, p. 192.

[13] For example, in 1988, some 67.5 percent of Shanghai's migrants came to work in factories or service occupations or to engage in business; 22.9 percent came to visit relatives, see a doctor, marry, or travel; 4.4 percent came for education or professional meetings; 5.2 percent for other reasons. Ibid., p. 152; also see p. 265.

exposed to toxic substances), and sanitation (sweeping streets, cleaning public bathrooms, collecting garbage and night soil). In Wuhan, for example, 84 percent of the city's sanitation workers are "floaters."[14]

More than skill divides the labor market of urban dwellers and rural migrants. The terms of employment are different as well, with large numbers of migrants being hired as contract workers, temporary workers, or members of construction brigades. Moreover, the jobs they do are "hard, heavy, and dangerous," as the authors of one survey observed.[15] They often perform physically arduous factory jobs where they are exposed to toxic substances or jobs that are both arduous and dangerous. A textile machinery factory in Zhengzhou, for example, unable to recruit urban workers, hired rural laborers to do jobs that required a great deal of physical strength and that exposed workers to toxic fumes. It proudly declared that by employing the migrants for short periods of time, cases of muscle strain and silicosis, common occupational hazards in that factory, were successfully avoided.[16]

Identifying the general sectors of the labor market dominated by migrant workers is not always adequate, for often one finds that within particular occupations migrants congregate in the lowest-status, least lucrative, and most physically demanding jobs. For example, a number of peasants from the northern Jiangsu village of Dazonghu (near Yancheng) have sought factory work in the Jiangnan cities of Suzhou and Wuxi. Most, it turns out (including three hundred women), have been employed as day laborers loading and unloading freight; the more desirable jobs were performed by local residents.[17]

One of the major reasons migrant labor has come to dominate the unskilled and service sector is that under the economic reforms, young urban residents have increasingly sought employment in the foreign-dominated sector of the labor market. In Hangzhou, for instance, as the tourist industry has expanded, many urban youth have secured jobs in hotels, restaurants, and

---

[14] Ibid., pp. 9, 11, 16, 174.

[15] Ibid., pp. 9, 11, 16.

[16] Ibid., p. 35.

[17] Kazutsugu Oshima, "The Present Condition of Inter-Regional Movements of the Labor Force in Rural Jiangsu Province, China," *The Developing Economies* 28, 2 (June 1990): 206. It is worth noting that day laborers in Suzhou or Wuxi, if employed all year, can earn 5,000 yuan, as opposed to the roughly 1,000 yuan they would earn at similar jobs in Yancheng city.

travel agencies, leaving the traditional silk embroidery, textiles, machinery, and construction industries unable to recruit labor within the city.[18] The result is that by 1989, some 20 percent (230,000) of the city's workforce was composed of migrant labor. One state-run factory in Hangzhou, unable to find urbanites willing to work, has since 1985 been recruiting rural workers, hiring them on fifteen-year contracts. "Most of them do heavy and dirty jobs that urban youth are not willing to do, and work in units operating a three-shift system," the authors of one survey observed.[19] In Shanghai as well, migrants are described as doing the heavy, labor-intensive jobs that urban residents disdain.[20] There, urban youth prefer to work in foreign or jointly owned enterprises, hotels, or restaurants. State-owned enterprises or those catering to tourists are their second choice. They are completely uninterested in textiles, dock work, or sanitation. "We'd rather be beaten to death than do that," they reportedly declare. Even if not literally true, a significant number of urban youth would rather be unemployed than accept low-status, physically arduous jobs doing factory work, construction, or sanitation. These occupations are therefore almost completely dominated by rural recruits.[21] The same situation prevailed in other cities as well, including Zhengzhou and Shijiazhuang, where textile factories were unable to attract urban workers and therefore turned to rural migrants.[22]

Although it is relatively easy to document a general division between the kinds of jobs done by urban residents and those performed by migrant workers, it is somewhat difficult to demonstrate the existence of divisions of labor *among* migrants based on more specific local origins. This difficulty is partly a result of the available data, which tend at best to identify the provincial origins of workers in various cities. Only occasionally are more specialized occupational niches identified. For instance, of the more than fifty thousand women working as maids in Beijing in 1987, the majority came from Wuwei xian in Anhui.[23] A 1990 survey of

---

[18] Li Mengbai and Hu Xin, *Liudong renkou*, p. 33.

[19] Ding Jianhua, "Nongmin hetonggong de qidai" (Waiting period for peasant contract workers), *Shehui* 11 (1989): 17–18.

[20] Li Mengbai and Hu Xin, *Liudong renkou*, p. 157.

[21] Ge Xiangjian and Zhu Weiying, "Xiyou chanbande mingongchao," p. 99; also see Li Mengbai and Hu Xin, *Liudong renkou*, p. 33.

[22] Li Mengbai and Hu Xin, *Liudong renkou*, p. 33.

[23] Ibid., pp. 41–42.

migrant labor in Chengdu reveals that most workers doing repair services are from Wenjiang county; most engaged in the recovery and resale of waste materials are from Peng county; most who work restuffing cotton quilts are from Ba county; most beggars, from Shuangliu county; and most bean-curd makers, from villages in Zhejiang.[24] In Shanghai, it is commonly believed that most maids are from Anhui and most construction workers from Sichuan.[25] In a survey of Jiangnan towns and villages, Kazutsugu Oshima found that the large number of workers from Sichuan were all from the same three counties (and from certain villages within those counties), largely because they secured jobs through personal connections.[26] Finally, in the market town of Nanxi, in Canton's Pearl River Delta, anthropologist Helen Siu found that the "shoe-repair women" who lined the main street year round all came from a particular county of Zhejiang and that itinerant jugglers hailed from Hunan.[27]

Although these data are suggestive of work "cliques" based on local origin, a much more detailed analysis of the origins of migrant workers in specific urban areas would be necessary to analyze the meaning of native-place identities and categories and their potentially ethnic dimensions (see below).

Residential patterns, too, reveal both a general division between "urbanites" and migrants as well as, sometimes, the concentration of migrants from particular regions in certain neighborhoods. Observers have identified a distinct "Zhejiang village" and "Xinjiang village" in the Beijing suburbs; a survey of Taiyuan reveals that most migrants from Zhejiang live together, forming a "Zhejiang village"; and in Shanghai, Subei migrants are reported to concentrate in particular areas of the city's outskirts.[28] Political scientist Dorothy Solinger, who has been conducting research on China's "floating population," reports the emergence of "local-colored 'villages,'" such as Zhejiang or Jiangsu "villages," within

---

[24] Pan Li, "Nongcun liudong renkou de diyuan juji xiaoyin he diyuan liansuo xiaoying" (The effect of the geographic concentration of the rural floating population and its geographic chain reaction), *Shehui* 6 (1991): 24.

[25] Personal conversations.

[26] Oshima, "Inter-Regional Movements," p. 212.

[27] Helen Siu, "The Politics of Migration in a Market Town," in *Chinese Society on the Eve of Tiananmen: The Impact of Reform*, ed. Deborah Davis and Ezra Vogel (Cambridge: Council on East Asian Studies, Harvard University, 1990), p. 63.

[28] Li Mengbai and Hu Xin, *Liudong renkou*, p. 141; Pan Li, "Nongcun liudong renkou," p. 14; Solinger, *China's Transients*, p. 13.

cities. According to some sources, she observes, "Each of these communities is governed by its own special 'coethnic' chiefs, who mediate the negotiations between their confreres and the local authorities."[29]

Occupational and residential divisions between urban residents and migrants are accompanied by attitudes of disdain and hostility. (Migrants are most easily identified by language, as they often speak dialects different from those spoken by urban residents. In some cases dialects are mutually incomprehensible, as Oshima found among Henan and Sichuan migrants to Jiangnan cities such as Wuxi.) Urbanites commonly look down on rural newcomers to the city, viewing with contempt the "tasteless garb of the bumpkin, or the peasant's sun-darkened skin, and as one urban woman depicted it, his or her 'flavor of muddiness.'" In Shanghai, the expression that "outsiders are backwards" has become commonplace. Helen Siu observed that migrants were easily identified by their "weather-beaten complexions" and less-than-fashionable clothes. A woman interviewed by Solinger in Tianjin asserted that "we wouldn't accept them as regular urban people.... People look down on them as peasants.... Tianjin people don't want to marry outsiders."[30]

These attitudes toward migrants are in part a prejudice against "outsiders," but they also reflect a contempt of urban dwellers toward peasants, as the vast majority of migrants to large cities are increasingly from rural areas, as opposed to townships. Migrants also tend to be less well educated than their urban counterparts, adding to the urbanites' sense of superiority and contempt.[31]

Much as Subei people in Republican-period Shanghai were disdained for their shack settlements on the periphery of the International Settlement, the dilapidated dwellings of migrants in

---

[29] Solinger,"The Floating Population in the Cities" (paper prepared for conference "City Living, City Lives: The Potential for Community and Autonomy in Post-Mao China," Woodrow Wilson International Center for Scholars, Washington, D.C., May 1–4, 1992), p. 12. The term "coethnic" is a very loose translation of *bang* (the word used in the original Chinese source), more literally translated as "clique."

[30] Oshima, "Inter-Regional Movements," p. 218. Solinger, "Floating Population," p. 11. Rong Chu, "Dushi 'mangliu' mianmian quan" (A glance at the urban floating population), *Shehui* 1 (1990): 8. Siu, "Politics of Migration," p. 63. Solinger, "Floating Population," p. 20.

[31] Li Mengbai and Hu Xin, *Liudong renkou*, pp. 10–11, 14.

contemporary cities are considered a blight on the urban landscape. Some migrants, lacking money and having no relatives or friends in the city, sleep in public latrines, at garbage dumps or bus or train stations, on the stairways of dormitories, or along the docks. They become unwitting targets for criminal elements (or, as one writer put it, they provide "opportunities" and an "activity space" for criminals). Such was the case of an eighteen-year-old girl who had gone from her home village to Changsha, where, sleeping on the side of a road by the river, she provided an "evil person" the opportunity to rape her and steal her clothes and the 10 yuan she had.[32]

The disdain for outsiders is fueled by (and fuels) the conviction that many urban problems are due to the influx of migrant workers. As in late-nineteenth- and early-twentieth-century Shanghai, when Subei people were blamed for high crime rates in contemporary Chinese cities, the "floating population" is deemed largely responsible for escalating crime and disorder. Almost every study of crime in contemporary urban China cites migration and the increasing number of "outsiders" among the urban population as a major cause. Specific "crimes," such as prostitution, are attributed to the influx of migrants.[33]

Studies of migrants themselves, too, dwell on the problem of criminality, and some, with titles such as "An Analysis of the Characteristics of Robbers Who Come to Shanghai from the Outside," are entirely devoted to them.[34] In Beijing, for instance, surveys emphasize that migrants engage in gambling, rent apartments where men and women illicitly cohabit, and operate brothels. "They decrease the moral fiber of society," the authors concluded.[35] In an unnamed southwestern city, the majority of prostitutes as well as their "clients" are said to be outsiders.[36] Helen Siu found that town residents in the Pearl River Delta felt besieged by

---

[32] Huang Bicheng, Liutong, and Peng Shaoxi, "Laizi Changshashi laowu shichang de baogao" (Report from the labor market of Changsha), *Shehui* 3 (1988): 16.

[33] See, for example, Xu Dafang, "Fajun gongan jiguan zai shehui zhian zonghe zhilizhong de zhoyong" (Promote the function of public security agencies in imposing social order), *Shehui* 7 (1991): 33; and Zhang Yichuan, "Maiyin xianxiang de shehui beijing" (The social background of the phenomenon of prostitution), *Shehui* 10 (1990): 40.

[34] Sha Song, "Waidi laihu renyuan taoqiao fanzui de tedian fenxi" (An analysis of the characteristics of robbers who come to Shanghai from the outside), *Shehui* 10 (1990): 10–12.

[35] Li Mengbai and Hu Xin, *Liudong renkou*, p. 141.

[36] Ibid., p. 51.

the increased crime and disorder that they associated with the influx of migrant labor.[37]

Such observations are usually accompanied by alarming statistics linking migrants and criminality. In Guangzhou, for example, migrants represented only 2.2 percent of the criminals brought before the Public Security Bureau in 1979, whereas by 1988 the number had skyrocketed to 57.9 percent. In Shanghai, it rose from 6.8 percent in 1983 to 31.4 percent in 1989 and had reached 39.3 percent by 1991.[38] There, the author of one survey noted, some 40 percent of criminals who received death sentences for their crimes in 1990 were "outsiders," as were 80 percent of individuals arrested for drug dealing, trafficking of young women, and smuggling.[39] Another survey's author pointed out that 80 percent of the people arrested for selling counterfeit boat tickets were "outsiders," as were fifteen of the seventeen individuals convicted of robbing taxi drivers.[40] "Lots of outsiders band together with friends or people from their same hometown to organize crime, and then they are even more dangerous," the same author warned;

> for example, most who engage in stealing are in the Xinjiang clique (*bang*), most who trick people on the streets are in the Guiyang or Liuzhou clique, most thieves belong to the Subei or Anhui clique, and most robbers to the Dongbei clique. There are also those who resell boat tickets at high prices, who belong to the Wenzhou clique.[41]

Violations of the government-sponsored family planning policy, begging, overcrowding of public transportation, and even price increases are also linked to the influx of outsiders. As one survey observed, "[Urban residents] often resentfully cry, 'Everything is spoiled by outsiders.'"[42]

Whether outsiders are actually responsible for soaring crime rates or instead are being scapegoated is difficult to determine. At least one account—Anita Chan, Richard Madsen, and Jonathan Unger's study of Chen village—suggests the possibility that the immigrant population is indeed scapegoated. "The Chens

---

[37] Siu, "Politics of Migration," p. 77.

[38] Li Mengbai and Hu Xin, *Liudong renkou*, p. 48. Also see Zhao Rongliang, "Renkou kongzhi yu liucuan fanzui" (Population control and the crime of fleeing), *Shehui* 10 (1992): 34.

[39] Zhao Rongliang, "Renkou kongzhi," p. 34.

[40] Chai Junyong, "Liudong renkou," pp. 8–9.

[41] Ibid., p. 8.

[42] Li Mengbai and Hu Xin, *Liudong renkou*, pp. 58–59.

gossiped among themselves that most of the newcomers were untrustworthy," they observed,

> that one could never entirely be sure who they were and where they came from, that they were likely dangerous. The Chens reasoned that if they were in the outsiders' shoes—still impoverished and living next door to idle occupants of villas such as their own—*they* would feel resentful, and so they imputed such hostility—and vengeful acts—to the newcomers.... Within Chen Village, the rising crime rate was generally laid at the door of the immigrants within the village—even though the thieves who were caught usually turned out to be young local men.[43]

Migration and Native-Place Ethnicity

Does the association of migrants with specific jobs and neighborhoods and the prejudice against them evidence the construction of a kind of native-place ethnic identity? Solinger, the only scholar to have addressed this question, answers with a clear affirmative. In "The Floating Population in the Cities," wherein she asserts that ethnicity among Han Chinese is based on local origin and accompanying linguistic difference, she identifies ethnicity as one of five traits characterizing the floating population. In *China's Transients and the State* she draws on G. William Skinner's contention that "because natives of the same locality tended to specialize in the same craft or to trade in the same local products, an 'ethnic division of labor' by place of birth was characteristic of migrant enclaves."[44] Ditto for contemporary China, implies Solinger: a division of labor based on local origins is an "ethnic division of labor," and migrant communities therefore constitute ethnicity. Left unanalyzed, however, is the meaning of ethnicity in this context, perhaps because Solinger's primary concern in these essays is to address the possibilities for migrant assimilation and the extent to which migrant populations represent civil society. What does ethnicity mean in the context of contemporary labor migration?

Inasmuch as ethnicity, as noted above, involves the construction of social categories and divisions, a first question concerns the specific content of such categories in contemporary China.

---

[43] Anita Chan, Richard Madsen, and Jonathan Unger, *Chen Village under Mao and Deng*, 2d ed. (Berkeley: University of California Press, 1992), p. 303.

[44] Solinger, "Floating Population," pp. 10–13; idem, *China's Transients*, p. 6.

Solinger assumes that they are based on specific local origins. For example, she contends that "as in old Hankow, the unskilled labor market in today's Chinese cities is sectioned off by localized labor gangs, each with its own boss and turf, and brawls over economic opportunity are serious or frequent enough to be treated in the literature."[45] Yet one would want to have concrete evidence of the "localized" nature of the labor gangs. How they actually identify themselves is equally crucial: do they define themselves by shared regional, provincial, or county origins? In addition, it is important to know how they are categorized by urban residents. The history of Subei people in Shanghai clearly demonstrates that the ways in which Jiangnan people labeled Subei people differed, often dramatically, from the self-identification of immigrants from northern Jiangsu.

Obviously, no single answer to these questions exists, and each locale can be expected to witness the creation of its own specific social categories. At this point, the data concerning locally defined categories are too scanty to demonstrate the emergence of native-place identities or ethnicities. If anything is clear from the surveys, it is the emergence of a more general, but very profound, division between urban residents and migrants. This "insider"/ "outsider" identity and division, rather than any more specific local identity, stands out in all the expressions of prejudice cited above. It is reiterated in the statement by two writers from the Shanghai City Party Committee School, who describe the "outsiders" as not only different from but inferior to urban residents. "When the outside laborers inhabit a region," they claim,

> it is very likely to be a dirty place.... They lack a concept of public morality.... There are some who come to Shanghai with the thought of getting rich by foul means.... So behavior that harms the prevailing social customs occurs time and time again.... The city residents are dissatisfied because they disturb normal life and livelihood.[46]

Not all characterizations of peasant outsiders are negative. For instance, in enumerating the "positive traits" brought by peasants to the city, survey authors commonly praise their adeptness at hard labor. They are "strong," "accustomed to hard work," and "generally have a good attitude toward work," a survey of migrant workers in Beijing points out.[47] These characterizations

---

[45] Solinger, "Floating Population," p. 24.
[46] Cited in Solinger, *China's Transients*, p. 15.
[47] Li Mengbai and Hu Xin, *Liudong renkou*, p. 134.

possibly represent a process of articulating "markers" between peasants and city dwellers, markers that get created in the urban context and then read backward as traits peasants inherently possess.

The question is whether we are witnessing something more than a renewed (or reformulated) city dweller versus peasant divide. If the significant category in most cities (both from the perspective of migrants themselves and from that of urban residents) turns out to be "peasant immigrant" (or "country bumpkin"), does that represent an ethnic identity? (An analogy in the United States would be to consider all immigrant workers as constituting a coherent ethnic group.)

Part of the answer involves the extent to which there is job discrimination or competition between the urban dwellers and rural migrants. In Republican-period Shanghai, for example, immigrants from Jiangnan and Canton, threatened by the prospect of Subei people claiming their jobs, actively fought to prevent Subei people from obtaining apprenticeships for skilled positions and went to great lengths to elaborate distinctions between themselves and Subei natives.[48] Moreover, large numbers of factory managers, themselves of Jiangnan origins, preferred to hire Jiangnan natives, a practice that resulted in discrimination against Subei people in certain sectors of the labor market. In contemporary Chinese cities, however, there is no evidence that factory managers are replacing urban residents with cheaper labor from the countryside. Instead, as noted above, most surveys point out that factory managers, frustrated in their attempts to recruit urban workers, have almost reluctantly turned to hiring rural migrants to do jobs that urban residents now shun. It is possible that the surveys have overstated the extent to which young urban workers are leaving labor-intensive jobs for "classier" jobs in the foreign-dominated sector. Although they might desire those jobs, it may be that only certain categories of urban residents are able to secure them. One might then actually find competition between those urban residents who depend on unskilled jobs and the rural migrants who are increasingly taking them. This would change the meaning of the division between urban resident and rural migrant. The point is to identify how lines of difference are categorized as such conflicts occur.

---

[48] Honig, *Creating Chinese Ethnicity*, p. 76.

There are, as we have seen, scattered instances of more localized native-place "cliques," that is, people from specific local origins occupying particular niches in an urban labor market or gathering together in particular urban neighborhoods. If researchers
paid particular attention to this issue, more elaborate native-place
divisions among migrants might become visible. Only in the Pearl
River Delta of Guangdong have several anthropologists and
sociologists focused on this issue, and their preliminary findings
suggest that in that region, at least, native-place identities are
assuming increasing importance. For example, in her study of
female workers in an electronics plant in Shenzhen (where
roughly 50 percent of the workers came from outside Guangdong
province), Ching-Kwan Lee found that native-place networks
played a crucial role in workers' lives. Women from the same
locality (and who shared a common dialect) helped each other get
jobs, taught each other work skills, assisted each other when sick,
and established loan funds to provide each other financial support. Josephine Smart found similar patterns among workers
employed at factories established by Hong Kong investors in the
Pearl River Delta. With few locals willing to take jobs in these
factories, most workers came from Hunan, Sichuan, Anhui, Henan,
and Jiangxi. Those from the same area (defined, Smart found,
sometimes by province and sometimes by more specific prefec-
tures or villages) tended to live together and to congregate in the
same workshops of particular factories. They assisted one another
in most of the same ways as workers in Shenzhen, also helping
with each other's laundry. Hunan natives commonly shared chili
peppers brought from home to "spice up" the bland Cantonese
food and make it more palatable to their tastes. Smart found occasional instances of conflict between workers of different origins,
such as one between Hunan and Anhui locals, although the causes
were not always clear. Nor was it clear whether social and
economic status varied according to the workers' native place, so
that workers from some regions enjoyed higher status or better-
paying jobs than others.[49]

---

[49] Ching-Kwan Lee, "Familial Hegemony and Localistic Despotism: Gender and
Shopfloor Cultures in South China's Industrial Capitalism" (paper prepared for
conference of the North American Chinese Sociologists' Association, Miami Beach,
August 11–12, 1993); Josephine Smart, "The Impact of Foreign Direct Investment
on Gender Relations in the Pearl River Delta, PRC" (paper prepared for annual
conference of the North American Chinese Sociologists' Association, Miami Beach,
August 11–12, 1993). Some of the data cited here is not included in the latter paper itself but is based on a personal conversation with the author.

Do these instances of native-place "cliques," more than the general urban dweller and peasant migrant categories, represent ethnicity? Again, no uniform answer exists, and we would need to know much more about how migrants and local residents identify themselves and each other, what kinds of formal and informal organizations among them have been established, and what forms migrant culture has assumed in urban areas.

Local history is also crucial to the construction of ethnic categories, for contemporary labor migration does not take place in a historical vacuum. So, for example, when people from northern Jiangsu seek work in Shanghai today, they are reinforcing and reconstituting an ethnic animus with deep historical roots. The influx of large numbers of Sichuanese, in contrast, is a relatively new phenomenon, and whether or not one can identify a Sichuan ethnicity in Shanghai remains to be seen. This situation serves as a reminder that one cannot expect every instance of migration to a particular city to have identical meanings and implications.

One should not conclude that ethnicity can emerge only in localities where social and economic hierarchies were, historically, structured along native-place lines, where prejudices and antagonisms were focused on peoples of specific local origins. The creation of ethnic categories, however, does involve a historical process. Evidence of social or economic divisions based on local origins in contemporary Chinese cities may call attention to patterns that in fact have a long, yet previously unexplored, history. Or it may mark the beginning of a process of the creation of new ethnic categories.

Indeed, one of the difficulties in assessing the social categories associated with contemporary migration concerns its relatively short duration. This process is, after all, only a little more than a decade old. Moreover, most migration does not seem to have resulted in permanent, or even long-term, urban residence, even though rural migrants have spent increasingly longer periods of time in cities. In Beijing, for instance, most migrants before 1982 spent only several days at a time in the city, whereas by the late 1980s the majority stayed more than three months. In Shanghai, Guangzhou, and Wuhan, more than half were staying more than six months by the late 1980s. Nevertheless, the number of migrants who have lived in any city for more than five years remains extremely small, either because they only recently left their rural homes or because they tend to migrate seasonally.[50] In

---

[50] Li Mengbai and Hu Xin, *Liudong renkou*, pp. 7, 129–30, 155, 168, 193. Even

other words, much more time may be required to see the emergence of native-place ethnicity.

Conclusion

As the case of Subei people in Shanghai illustrates, ethnicity is not a trait that people are born with or carry with them, but rather involves a process created in the context of particular social relationships and in particular historical contexts. It is those processes and social relationships that need to be examined in regard to migrant workers in contemporary Chinese cities. A consideration of ethnicity among these workers will help reveal the points of contention and conflict that may require the articulation of a sense of difference. The point is not simply to determine whether or not it represents ethnicity, but rather to identify the social categories created that inform and fuel structures of inequality.

These issues extend beyond China to other parts of East Asia as well, where oftentimes a presumed racial homogeneity may obscure issues of ethnicity, particularly in regard to the working class. Attention to regionally defined ethnic identities in Japan, Korea, and Taiwan might well shed light on certain structures of inequality and bases of worker solidarity. Certainly scattered evidence suggests the possibility of native-place ethnicities forged in the context of labor migration. In Meiji-period Japan, for example, migrants to Tokyo from Tohoku, identified as "different" from urban natives by dint of dialect, were looked down on and denied access to the most lucrative jobs.[51] Likewise, a worker in a nineteenth-century silk filature recorded in her diary divisions among women based on local origins. In her factory, workers from the poorer rural district of Shinshu were looked down on, and calling someone a person from Shinshu implied that she was backward and ill mannered.[52] The broader meaning of these prejudices is difficult to discern, and a much more extended analysis of the nature and scope of regionalism in the Japanese labor market would be necessary to begin even a preliminary analysis of its potentially ethnic dimensions.

Solinger acknowledges that neighborhoods that appear to be defined by local origins of migrants are constantly in flux, as numerous migrants move in accordance with shifts in the jobs they can secure. Solinger, *China's Transients*, p. 14.

[51] This is based on informal comments by Andrew Gordon.

[52] Wada Ei, *Tomioka nikki* (Tomioka diary) (Tokyo, 1978), p. 59.

Ditto for Korea. At least one study of the contemporary Seoul labor force documents divisions of labor and structures of inequality based on local origin. It contrasts the experience of migrants from Yongnam, who concentrated in white-collar jobs in Seoul, with migrants from Honam, who were more likely to secure service and production jobs. The author, Eui-Young Yu, attributes the low status of Honam migrants to historic patterns of discrimination, but he does not analyze its origins, causes, or cultural elaborations. He nevertheless concludes that "regionalism is one of the most powerful and hitherto underestimated social mechanisms in Korea—and dictates the lives of millions of workers. Nevertheless, policy makers and intellectuals have been less than forthright about confronting the issue of region-based discrimination."[53]

These studies suggest the need to examine, throughout East Asia, the relationship between regional identity, labor, and ethnicity. Regionalism and native-place identity, as Eui-Young Yu argues, need to be taken more seriously as structuring labor markets and working classes. They also need to be analyzed in less literal but more symbolic and complex ways, attending to the meanings attached to certain regional identities and the processes through which those meanings are created and transformed. Considering these identities through the lens of ethnicity helps highlight those processes of social construction. It also may reveal forms of ethnicity in East Asia that are very different from ethnic identities in other cultural contexts. The relative silence on the issue of ethnicity in scholarly literature on East Asian labor does not mean it is nonexistent, but rather that its basis may need to be reconsidered. Almost all divisions of labor are accompanied by a cultural elaboration of difference, and, hopefully, further studies of East Asian labor will seek to identify their historical and contemporary markings and meanings.

---

[53] Eui-Young Yu, "Regionalism in the South Korean Job Market: An Analysis of Regional-Origin Inequality among Migrants in Seoul," *Pacific Affairs* 63, 1 (Spring 1990): 38.

Index

INSTITUTE OF EAST ASIAN STUDIES PUBLICATIONS SERIES

CHINA RESEARCH MONOGRAPHS (CRM)

33. Yue Daiyun. *Intellectuals in Chinese Fiction*, 1988
34. Constance Squires Meaney. *Stability and the Industrial Elite in China and the Soviet Union*, 1988
35. Yitzhak Shichor. *East Wind over Arabia: Origins and Implications of the Sino-Saudi Missile Deal*, 1989
36. Suzanne Pepper. *China's Education Reform in the 1980s: Policies, Issues, and Historical Perspectives*, 1990
sp. Phyllis Wang and Donald A. Gibbs, eds. *Readers' Guide to China's Literary Gazette, 1949–1979*, 1990
38. James C. Shih. *Chinese Rural Society in Transition: A Case Study of the Lake Tai Area, 1368–1800*, 1992
39. Anne Gilks. *The Breakdown of the Sino-Vietnamese Alliance, 1970–1979*, 1992
sp. Theodore Han and John Li. *Tiananmen Square Spring 1989: A Chronology of the Chinese Democracy Movement*, 1992
40. Frederic Wakeman, Jr., and Wen-hsin Yeh, eds. *Shanghai Sojourners*, 1992
41. Michael Schoenhals. *Doing Things with Words in Chinese Politics: Five Studies*, 1992
sp. Kaidi Zhan. *The Strategies of Politeness in the Chinese Language*, 1992
42. Barry C. Keenan. *Imperial China's Last Classical Academies: Social Change in the Lower Yangzi, 1864–1911*, 1994
43. Ole Bruun. *Business and Bureaucracy in a Chinese City: An Ethnography of Private Business Households in Contemporary China*, 1993
44. Wei Li. *The Chinese Staff System: A Mechanism for Bureaucratic Control and Integration*, 1994
45. Ye Wa and Joseph W. Esherick. *Chinese Archives: An Introductory Guide*, 1996
46. Melissa Brown, ed. *Negotiating Ethnicities in China and Taiwan*, 1996
47. David Zweig and Chen Changgui. *China's Brain Drain to the United States: Views of Overseas Chinese Students and Scholars in the 1990s*, 1995
48. Elizabeth J. Perry, ed. *Putting Class in Its Place: Worker Identities in East Asia*, 1996

KOREA RESEARCH MONOGRAPHS (KRM)

9. Helen Hardacre. *The Religion of Japan's Korean Minority: The Preservation of Ethnic Identity*, 1985
10. Fred C. Bohm and Robert R. Swartout, Jr., eds. *Naval Surgeon in Yi Korea: The Journal of George W. Woods*, 1984
13. Vipan Chandra. *Imperialism, Resistance, and Reform in Late Nineteenth-Century Korea: Enlightenment and the Independence Club*, 1988
14. Seok Choong Song. *Explorations in Korean Syntax and Semantics*, 1988
15. Robert A. Scalapino and Dalchoong Kim, eds. *Asian Communism: Continuity and Transition*, 1988
16. Chong-Sik Lee and Se-Hee Yoo, eds. *North Korea in Transition*, 1991
17. Nicholas Eberstadt and Judith Banister. *The Population of North Korea*, 1992
18. Hong Yung Lee and Chung Chongwook, eds. *Korean Options in a Changing International Order*, 1993
19. Tae Hwan Ok and Hong Yung Lee, eds. *Prospects for Change in North Korea*, 1994
20. Chai-sik Chung. *A Korean Confucian Encounter with the Modern World: Yi Hang-no and the West*, 1995